GOLD experience

2ND EDITION

TEACHER'S RESOURCE BOOK

A2+

Pre-Preliminary for Schools

Pearson Education Limited
KAO TWO,
KAO Park
Hockham Way,
Harlow, Essex,
CM17 9SR
England
and Associated Companies throughout the world.

pearsonELT.com/goldexperience

First published 2019

Second impression 2019

ISBN: 978-1-292-19448-6

Set in Camphor Pro

Printed in Great Britain by CPI Group (UK) Ltd, Croydon, CR0 4YY

Acknowledgements
The publishers would like to thank the following people for their contribution to this title: Angela Bandis, Louise Manicolo, Billie Jago and Cait Hawkins.

Picture Credits

The publisher would like to thank the following for their kind permission to reproduce their photographs:

123RF.com: aleksanderdn 111, 113, auremar 120, belchonock 111, 113, Cathy Yeulet 148, 151, Graham Oliver 147, 151, Ivá Vagnerová 111, 113, ljupco 111, 113, sapocka 119; **Getty Images:** 186, DGLimages / iStock / Getty Images Plus 186, PhotoInc / iStock / Getty Images Plus 186; **Pearson Education Ltd:** Gareth Boden 103, 106, Jules Selmes 103, 106; **Shutterstock.com:** 186, Africa Studio 111, 113, Mike Flippo 111, 113, rikkyall 111, 113

Cover Image: *Front:* **Getty Images: Artur Debat**

Illustrated by:
Daniel Limon (Beehive Illustration) pp 21(3,6), 21(3,6), 24(3,6), 133(6), 140(6); Dusan Pavlic (Beehive Illustration) pp 71(1,4,6), 74(1,4,6), 133(1,2,3,4,5), 140(1,2,3,4,5); Amit Tayal (Beehive Illustration) pp 21(1,2,4,5), 24(1,2,4,5), 71(2,5), 74(2,5), 121, 123, 129(picnic, barbecue), 131(picnic, barbecue), 149, 152; Matt Ward (Beehive Illustration) (in the style of Simon Rumble) pp 129(sushi, salad), 131(sushi, salad).

OVERVIEW OF THE ASSESSMENT PACKAGE

The Gold Experience Assessment Package provides a wide range of tests which can be used at different points in the course. Each level has:

- A and B Diagnostic Test
- 9 x A and B Unit Tests
- 3 x A and B Review Tests
- A and B End of Year Test

Assessment *of* learning or Assessment *for* learning?

Any test can be used either as assessment *for* learning or assessment *of* learning. Assessment *of* learning usually takes place after the learning has happened and provides information about what the student is achieving. The student is usually given a mark or a grade. You can also use the tests as assessment *for* learning by using the tests to provide information on how well students have understood new language or skills, and then providing them with specific feedback and suggestions for improvement as part of the continual learning process.

A combination of both types of assessment can provide powerful tools for helping your students' progress.

Teacher's Resources site

In addition to the tests in this Teacher's Resource Book, the tests are also provided on the Teacher's Resources site in both PDF and Word format. We recommend using them in the PDF version, as they are. However, if you do need to edit the tests, this should be possible in the Word version.

The audio files accompanying the listening exercises in the Skills and End of Year tests can also be found on the Teacher's Resources site.

The access code for the Teacher's Resources site is in the front of your Teacher's Book.

Versions of tests

Most tests have two versions: A and B. Versions A and B are designed to be at exactly the same level of difficulty and feature the same task types, however, the test items in each are different. For listening tests, the tasks are different but the audio is the same in both A and B versions, making it easy to administer.

You can use the A/B tests in two ways:

- give half of the class A versions and half of the class B versions – this helps to deter cheating.
- give all students the A test and then use the B test either for students who missed the test or as a re-test or remedial work for students whose score shows they need a little more work on the unit objectives.

On the Teacher's Resources site, there is also a version of the tests adapted for students with dyslexia. See the next section for more information.

Assessment for dyslexic students

One of the most effective ways of checking classroom work and the teaching programme is through testing. Tests can show which learning materials work best for individual students, so teachers need to be able to select the most appropriate tests for their students. The two most important aspects of a test concern a) validity: whether or not the test measures what it is supposed to measure and b) reliability: whether it would produce similar results when used with a similar group under the same conditions at a different time.

When we consider validity, it is evident that tests written to measure reading comprehension, vocabulary, grammar or communication, will fail to obtain valid test results for dyslexic students. The type of reading difficulties dyslexic students experience in processing print affects all language skills and consequently will not provide valid information about their actual knowledge or skills. The same problem affects the reliability of a test. Obviously, if the same written test is used with dyslexic students and non-dyslexic students from the same class, the results will be significantly different for the two groups.

The Gold Experience Assessment Package offers alternative versions of tests for dyslexic learners. While the language content and linguistic level of the material tested is the same as in the main tests, a number of changes make it easier for dyslexic students to process. For example, these tests have a larger point size with increased spacing between the lines, and tasks which require multi-tasking have been reduced in complexity. See the introduction to the adapted tests for more detail.

Exam preparation

As your students are going to be working towards a final high-stakes exam, the tests also provide regular opportunities for them to try exam-style tasks in a low-stakes test environment, which should help them feel more confident going into the final exam.

We would recommend using past papers or practice papers in addition as you get close to the date of the exam. There is one full practice test in Unit 10 of the Workbook, and two further complete practice exams are available in the Exam Practice booklet.

Expected outcomes

We would expect all students who have completed the instructional material to score at least 50%, and the best students to score 90–100% on any given test. We have deliberately included more challenging questions in each test so as to help you identify students performing above the level.

TEST FORMAT

The Unit, Review and End of Year tests have several parts to them. This helps makes them flexible and allows you to assign only the parts you want to or have time to administer and mark. In addition to the tests in this Teacher's Resource Book, the tests are also provided on the Teacher's Resources site in both PDF and Word format. We recommend using them in the PDF version, as they are. However, if you do need to edit the tests, this should be possible in the Word version.

Assessment type	Quantity	Total marks	Timing
Diagnostic Test (A/B)	1 (at start of course)	100	45 mins
Unit Tests			
Language: Grammar and Vocabulary (A/B)	9 (after each main unit)	50	25–30 mins
Skills: Listening and Reading (A/B)	9 (after each main unit)	50	20–30 mins
Review Tests			
Grammar and Vocabulary (A/B)	3 (after every three units)	50	30 mins
Writing	3 (after every three units)	25	30 mins
Speaking (A/B/Teacher)	3 (after every three units)	25	10–15 mins per pair
End of year Test			
Listening and Reading (A/B)	1 (at end of course)	50	45 mins
Writing	1 (at end of course)	25	45 mins
Speaking (A/B/Teacher)	1 (at end of course)	25	10–15 mins per pair

For practice Cambridge exams, please see Unit 10 of the Workbook and the separate Exam Practice booklets.

Diagnostic Test

The main purpose of the Diagnostic Test is to help you identify any general areas of strength or weakness across the class. This will help you tailor your lessons to your class and maximise your time with your students. The Diagnostic Test will also help to place students at the right level of the Gold Experience series. The test contains 100 multiple-choice questions and is designed to last for 45 minutes.

To help score and analyse the Diagnostic Test, groups of questions are labelled by language topic in the answer key. Mark your students' test papers, and use the following guide to help you decide what to do next:

- If students get fewer than 10% of the answers right, they may not have the basic language knowledge required for this level. Consider starting with the level below.
- If students get 10–49% correct, assess their answers to check where remediation or extra help is required. Focus extra help on topics from questions 1–25.
- If students score 50–74%, assess their scores and, if they score at the upper end of this, consider an additional oral interview to decide whether this is the most appropriate level for them, or whether they would gain more from the next level (perhaps with some additional help).
- If they get more than 75% of the answers right, consider starting them at the level above.

Unit Tests

There are nine Unit Tests, which test the learning objectives from each main unit (after Unit 10, students would take the End of Year test). These should be administered after each respective unit check.

Each Unit Test has two parts: Language (Grammar and Vocabulary); and Skills (Listening and Reading). Both parts have A and B versions. There is also a version of the A tests for students with dyslexia.

You can assign both or neither of these, depending on the time available. If you are including the Listening test, it is best to run the Listening audio first, and then students can do the other sections in their own time.

The tests will take approximately:

- Language: Grammar and Vocabulary: 25–30 minutes
- Skills: Listening and Reading: 20–30 minutes

The Unit Test as a whole is out of 100 marks. The parts of the test are split as follows:

- Language: Grammar and Vocabulary: 50 marks
- Skills: Listening and Reading: 50 marks

Review Tests

There are three Review Tests (one every three units). These are cumulative achievement tests, and so test the learning objectives from all units so far in the course, but with a heavier focus on the most recent units:

- Review Test 1: Units 1–3
- Review Test 2: Units 4–6
- Review Test 3: Units 7–9

Depending on your school year, you may wish to do all of these or just some of them.

Each test has three parts: Grammar and Vocabulary; Writing; Speaking. Grammar and Vocabulary papers have A and B versions, as well as a version of the A tests for students with dyslexia. There is only one version of the Writing task. Students do the Speaking tasks in pairs, and there are separate materials for Students A and B, as well as a version for the teacher with questions.

As with the Unit Tests, you can assign all or none of the parts of the test, depending on the time available.

The tests will take approximately:

- Grammar and Vocabulary: 30 minutes
- Writing: 30 minutes
- Speaking: 10–15 minutes per pair of students

The Review Tests as a whole are out of 100 marks. The parts of the test are split as follows:

- Grammar and Vocabulary: 50 marks
- Writing: 25 marks
- Speaking: 25 marks

End of Year Test

The End of Year Test provides a skills-based test covering learning objectives from the whole course.

The test has three parts: Listening and Reading; Writing; Speaking. Grammar and Vocabulary papers have A and B versions, as well as a version of the A tests for students with dyslexia. There is only one version of the Writing task. Students do the Speaking tasks in pairs, and there are separate materials for Students A and B, as well as a version for the teacher with questions.

You can assign all or none of the parts of the test, depending on the time available.

The tests will take approximately:

- Listening and Reading: 45 mins
- Writing: 45 minutes
- Speaking: 10–15 minutes per pair of students

The End of Year Test as a whole is out of 100 marks. The parts of the test are split as follows:

- Listening and Reading: 50 marks
- Writing: 25 marks
- Speaking: 25 marks

Marking the tests

The Language test answer keys include references to specific Student's Book pages for revision.

Writing and Speaking tests have detailed mark schemes out of 25 (see pages 177–178), similar to the Cambridge mark schemes, to help you mark consistently, and to help you give students meaningful feedback. If you prefer to use the actual mark scheme for the exam your students will ultimately take, these are available online.

Whichever mark scheme you use, it can be very useful to go through it with your students before they take the test so they know what they are going to be marked against. You can then refer back to these marking criteria and bands in your feedback.

GOLD experience A2+
2ND EDITION
Preliminary for Schools

Name: ____________________

Class: ____________________

DIAGNOSTIC TEST A

Choose the correct answer (A, B, C or D).

1 I .... a sandwich for lunch.
A have usually **B** have often **C** have never **D** usually have

2 She .... cooks because she doesn't like cooking.
A never **B** usually **C** often **D** sometimes

3 Jason started .... comics when he was eight, and now he's got hundreds of them.
A taking **B** spending **C** collecting **D** caring

4 We can't go out now because ....
A it rained **B** it raining **C** it's raining **D** it rains

5 My .... is very old and the letters on it aren't easy to read.
A mouse **B** keyboard **C** webcam **D** playlist

6 If you want to read more about the subject, just .... this link.
A click on **B** visit **C** download **D** go

7 The maths lesson .... five minutes ago.
A ended **B** ends **C** has ended **D** will end

8 Max went to the party, but he .... fun.
A hasn't had **B** doesn't have **C** can't have **D** didn't have

9 We do our homework in our .... and then give them to our teacher.
A notes **B** notebooks **C** marks **D** uniforms

10 A car is .... a bike, of course!
A more fast than **B** the fastest **C** faster than **D** faster from

11 Which is .... band in the world?
A the most popular **B** more popular than **C** the popular **D** most popular

12 When I buy something online, I always use my mum's ....
A receipt **B** sale **C** price **D** card

13 How much did your new phone .... ?
A sell **B** pay **C** buy **D** cost

14 It .... when I woke up this morning.
A hasn't rained **B** isn't raining **C** wasn't raining **D** doesn't rain

15 Some of the singers in this TV show are .... ! They shouldn't sing at all!
A exciting **B** terrible **C** successful **D** scary

16 The students .... an exam tomorrow.
A are going to have **B** can have **C** were having **D** have had

17 I always .... the bus to school in the morning, but I walk home.
A take **B** go **C** travel **D** drive

18 I'm a good singer – I .... sing very well.
A could **B** can **C** have to **D** had to

19 I .... do the shopping. Mum has done it.
A can't **B** don't have to **C** shouldn't **D** couldn't

20 Alex .... swimming three times a week and he's very good at it.
A goes **B** plays **C** makes **D** does

Name: ______________________

Class: ______________________

21 Lucy isn't here. She .... to the library.
A will go **B** has been **C** was gone **D** has gone

22 I .... octopus. Is it tasty?
A wasn't eating **B** am not eating **C** didn't eat **D** have never eaten

23 From the top of the .... I could see the coast far away.
A forest **B** hill **C** ocean **D** iceberg

24 I'll help you if you .... me.
A asked **B** will ask **C** ask **D** are asking

25 You .... eat a lot of sweets. They're not good for you.
A don't have to **B** won't **C** can't **D** shouldn't

26 My name's Pat and I'm .... student.
A the **B** – **C** an **D** a

27 Can I ask you .... questions?
A much **B** a little **C** any **D** a few

28 Tourists visit this town because it's very ....
A dull **B** noisy **C** attractive **D** industrial

29 On Sunday we're going to a lovely restaurant .... the sea.
A by **B** in **C** at **D** on

30 Helen is at the shopping centre. She .... there every Saturday.
A go **B** goes **C** is going **D** went

31 The girls aren't at home. They .... a scary film at the cinema.
A watch **B** watching **C** are watching **D** have watched

32 What kind of music .... ?
A do you like **B** you like **C** you do like **D** like you

33 If you want to .... part in a team sport, try basketball. It's a lot of fun!
A get **B** take **C** make **D** spend

34 Ben is a very .... boy. He always says please and thank you.
A clever **B** quiet **C** careful **D** polite

35 I'm sorry, I .... you. Can you say that again, please?
A don't hear **B** am not hearing **C** didn't hear **D** haven't heard

36 It started to rain while I .... ready for bed.
A got **B** have got **C** am getting **D** was getting

37 This town is boring because there isn't .... to do here.
A something **B** anything **C** everything **D** nothing

38 Don't drop that vase! It's very ....
A exciting **B** ordinary **C** valuable **D** wooden

39 I've been at work all day. I need to rest because I'm .... !
A starving **B** fantastic **C** furious **D** exhausted

40 Tim .... us tomorrow because he isn't well.
A doesn't meet **B** isn't going to meet **C** hasn't met **D** won't meet

Name: ___________________

Class: ___________________

DIAGNOSTIC TEST A

41 Do you think all cars .... electric in the future?
A are **B** are going to be **C** will be **D** are being

42 Chris and Harry aren't sure, but they .... visit us later.
A might **B** can **C** must **D** have to

43 Don't worry if you .... a mistake. It's a good way to learn.
A do **B** have **C** make **D** get

44 I'm studying .... at school and I'm learning about the government of my country.
A PE **B** politics **C** science **D** dance

45 Six months ago Jim and Cathy .... a cake shop in the centre of the town.
A opened **B** made **C** developed **D** began

46 Our new house is .... our old one.
A bigger from **B** the biggest **C** more big than **D** bigger than

47 I have two exams today – it's .... day of the year!
A worse **B** the worst **C** worse than **D** the worse

48 For me, football isn't .... basketball.
A as exciting as **B** exciting as **C** more exciting as **D** the most exciting as

49 My sisters are fourteen – they're .... to go to university.
A young enough **B** too old **C** too young **D** old enough

50 I'm not .... to lift this heavy box.
A strong enough **B** too strong **C** enough strong **D** as strong as

51 Alice only wears .... when she goes out. She doesn't wear it every day.
A glasses **B** braces **C** freckles **D** make-up

52 Liam saw a great jacket in a shop. He .... and it looked good, so he bought it.
A dressed it up **B** checked it out **C** tried it on **D** saved it up

53 You .... buy any juice. There's a carton in the fridge.
A mustn't **B** can't **C** might not **D** don't have to

54 You .... be quiet in the library because other people are studying.
A can **B** must **C** may **D** might

55 Did you and Alex make this pizza .... ?
A himself **B** yourselves **C** itself **D** yourself

56 .... a good film on TV tonight. Do you want to watch it?
A It's **B** Is there **C** There's **D** It has

57 Look! Is that a .... in the tree? What is it holding?
A frog **B** penguin **C** monkey **D** wolf

58 Sharks are scary because they have lots of .... teeth!
A sharp **B** soft **C** clear **D** empty

59 Lions .... other animals to eat them.
A climb **B** hunt **C** dive **D** land

60 Oranges are my favourite fruit because they're sweet and ....
A salty **B** crispy **C** juicy **D** spicy

Name: ______________________

Class: ______________________

DIAGNOSTIC TEST A

61 Do we have any bread? I'd like to make some .... for breakfast.
A fries B curry C butter D toast

62 Anna .... to the beach – she's there now.
A goes B has been C was going D has gone

63 Ben has .... played cricket, but he wants to try it.
A never B ever C already D just

64 We haven't finished our homework ....
A then B yet C already D now

65 Mr Smith has taught English at our school .... twenty years.
A already B since C for D from

66 The girls have been at the library .... two o'clock.
A at B since C already D for

67 When my cousins flew to Australia, we drove them to the .... to say goodbye.
A journey B reception C platform D airport

68 When I went on holiday to Greece, I wrote about everything I saw and did in my ....
A journey B booking C diary D guidebook

69 We found a good hotel online and .... a reservation for our holiday.
A took B made C closed D did

70 When it's hot, they .... to the beach.
A go B will go C are going D have gone

71 If I go to the supermarket later, I .... to buy milk.
A won't forget B don't forget C haven't forgotten D didn't forget

72 We .... to have a summer holiday this year.
A enjoy B hope C like D love

73 It was late, but he .... walking around the city.
A decided B continued C arranged D planned

74 Would you rather .... or stay at home today?
A went out B to go out C going out D go out

75 Is there somewhere in this café where I can .... my phone?
A delete B search C charge D download

76 Are you .... on extreme sports?
A brilliant B interested C keen D excited

77 .... sport is very good for your health.
A Play B Plays C To play D Playing

78 We had a pizza after .... the match.
A watched B watching C watch D to watch

79 I can't .... this word. Can you say it for me, please?
A pronounce B explain C speak D mean

80 A: I don't have Nick's phone number.
B: It's OK. I .... it to you.
A will give B am giving C am going to give D gives

Name: ______________________

Class: ______________________

DIAGNOSTIC TEST A

81 Look at all the cars on the road. We .... late!
A are **B** are being **C** will be **D** are going to be

82 **A:** I'm bored.
B: .... going for a walk?
A We could **B** Shall we **C** How about **D** Why don't we

83 When the alarm .... this morning, I didn't want to get out of bed.
A plugged in **B** went off **C** switched on **D** set up

84 You can .... your printer to your computer very easily.
A install **B** tap **C** upload **D** connect

85 Maria is working hard. She .... four essays this week.
A writes **B** wrote **C** has written **D** is writing

86 The runners were on the ...., ready for the race to begin.
A track **B** court **C** locker **D** coach

87 My team is the best and no other team can .... it this year!
A win **B** catch **C** beat **D** train

88 If I .... a car, I would drive to the beach.
A have **B** had **C** have had **D** will have

89 I can't go out .... I finish my homework first.
A if **B** unless **C** in case **D** when

90 At the end of the play, the audience .... loudly.
A entertained **B** clapped **C** performed **D** reviewed

91 Our car .... last night!
A was stealing **B** has stolen **C** was stolen **D** stole

92 English .... in many countries around the world.
A speaks **B** has spoken **C** is speaking **D** is spoken

93 I .... by Dr Jones.
A have my eyes checked **B** check my eyes **C** am checking my eyes **D** have checked my eyes

94 This is the office .... my aunt works.
A that **B** which **C** where **D** who

95 Greece has many beautiful beaches, so it's a popular .... for summer holidays.
A flight **B** travel **C** destination **D** tour

96 I'm looking for the post office. Can you tell me .... ?
A where is it **B** where it is **C** it is where **D** is it where

97 Tom is .... about photography and he talks about it all the time.
A creative **B** intelligent **C** sociable **D** passionate

98 I didn't watch the film because I .... it before.
A have seen **B** saw **C** was seeing **D** had seen

99 Jane and her family .... in London, but they don't now.
A used to live **B** live **C** are living **D** have lived

100 I meet my friends at the youth club. That's where we usually ....
A go for **B** hang out **C** put together **D** deal with

Total:		100

GOLD experience A2+ 2ND EDITION Preliminary for Schools

Name: ____________________

Class: ____________________

DIAGNOSTIC TEST B

Choose the correct answer (A, B, C or D).

1 The bus .... late.
A never is **B** sometimes is **C** is often **D** usually is

2 Harry .... buys things online – he never goes to the shops.
A sometimes **B** always **C** often **D** never

3 These photos are great! Did you .... them on your holiday?
A make **B** do **C** have **D** take

4 The girls .... basketball at the moment.
A are playing **B** play **C** have played **D** played

5 There's a problem with the .... in my computer and I can't hear any videos.
A speakers **B** tablet **C** screen **D** printer

6 With this app, you can .... music to your phone and listen to it later.
A send **B** play **C** download **D** put on

7 Jake .... me a text message an hour ago.
A sends **B** has sent **C** is sending **D** sent

8 Grace isn't well, so she .... to the party last night.
A doesn't go **B** didn't go **C** isn't going **D** hasn't gone

9 There is information about the next school trip on the .... You can read about it there.
A noticeboard **B** timetable **C** desk **D** ruler

10 Our classroom is .... yours.
A the biggest **B** biggest than **C** bigger than **D** more big

11 Tim thinks physics is .... subject of all.
A more difficult than **B** most difficult **C** the more difficult **D** the most difficult

12 When I go out, my dad usually gives me some .... for bus tickets and food.
A cash **B** goods **C** sales **D** receipts

13 Before Kevin got a new phone, he .... his old one online for €50.
A paid **B** spent **C** sold **D** shopped

14 The girls were at home, but they .... when I called them.
A weren't studying **B** aren't studying **C** didn't study **D** haven't studied

15 That actor is .... All of the films he's in are really great too.
A kind **B** boring **C** strange **D** excellent

16 Pat .... her friends tomorrow afternoon.
A meets **B** has met **C** is going to meet **D** met

17 Let's .... the train. I don't want to pay for a taxi.
A ride **B** catch **C** drive **D** travel

18 Sam .... swim when he was three years old.
A can **B** should **C** has to **D** could

19 I .... wear a uniform at my school. It wasn't necessary.
A couldn't **B** shouldn't **C** didn't have to **D** can't

20 I don't .... cycling if it's raining.
A do **B** make **C** go **D** play

Name: ______________________

Class: ______________________

DIAGNOSTIC TEST B

21 Marc and Ben .... to the shops, but they'll be back soon.
A go B have gone C have been D will go

22 My grandpa .... a computer. He doesn't know how.
A has never used B never used C didn't use D isn't using

23 Are there any fish in this .... ?
A mountain B desert C forest D lake

24 We'll come to your party if you .... us.
A invite B invited C will invite D have invited

25 Chris .... ride his skateboard at night. It isn't safe.
A can't B shouldn't C doesn't have to D couldn't

26 Jo can play .... guitar very well.
A – B a C the D an

27 I watched .... good films last week.
A a few B lot of C all D a little

28 The town becomes very .... in the summer when many people visit it.
A lively B happy C safe D traditional

29 My aunt and uncle are staying at a hotel .... the coast.
A in B on C by D at

30 Let's hurry because the post office .... at five o'clock.
A closes B is closing C close D closed

31 Sorry, but I can't go out with you today – I .... for an exam.
A study B studied C have studied D am studying

32 Where .... at the weekend?
A Tom plays B does Tom play C Tom does play D plays Tom

33 Stop watching TV. You're .... time and you need to study for your exams.
A losing B spending C wasting D doing

34 Katy always tells the truth. She's a very .... person.
A confident B friendly C serious D honest

35 I .... that. Can you do it again?
A didn't see B haven't seen C don't see D wasn't seeing

36 Did they listen to music while they .... ?
A work B have worked C were working D are working

37 I didn't see .... from my class at the concert
A no one B everyone C someone D anyone

38 The objects in this museum are .... Some of them are more than 2,000 years old.
A ancient B useful C modern D scary

39 I can't eat all of this pizza on my own. It's .... !
A starving B delighted C huge D tiny

40 I'm not hungry. I .... lunch.
A don't eat B am not going to eat C am not eating D won't eat

Name: ____________________

Class: ____________________

DIAGNOSTIC TEST B

41 I'm sure Jack .... great music at his party tomorrow!
A is having B is going to have C will have D has

42 Lucy .... go out with us. She'll call me when she decides.
A may B has to C can D must

43 What are you going to do? Have you .... up your mind?
A thought B made C got D decided

44 The students who are studying .... are going to be actors in the school play.
A history B maths C art D drama

45 My uncle is a doctor and he .... a lot of money.
A takes B brings C makes D gets

46 I think today is .... it was yesterday.
A more hot than B hotter than C hotter from D the hottest

47 You have a lot of video games. Which game is .... ?
A better than B the best than C the better D the best

48 The film wasn't .... the book.
A boring as B as boring C as boring as D more boring as

49 This T-shirt is .... for me. I need a bigger size.
A too small B large enough C small enough D too large

50 I can't drink this tea. It's .... for me.
A sweet enough B too sweet C as sweet as D enough sweet

51 I don't have to wear my .... all the time, only when I watch TV.
A braces B make-up C glasses D freckles

52 Julie is .... her money to buy a pair of gold earrings.
A checking out B saving up C trying on D standing out

53 Tell George he .... come to the meeting today if he's busy.
A can't B doesn't have to C mustn't D may not

54 When you drive, you .... stop at a red light.
A must B might C can D may

55 My brothers painted their room by ....
A myself B itself C themselves D himself

56 .... cold and windy this morning.
A There's B It's C It has D Is

57 While we were on the ferry boat, we saw a .... swimming in the sea.
A dolphin B bee C fox D koala

58 The old horse was .... – it couldn't see at all.
A powerful B friendly C blind D bright

59 Some birds can .... into the sea to catch fish.
A bite B jump C climb D dive

60 The dentist took out one of my teeth and I can only eat .... food for a few days.
A hard B dry C burned D soft

Name: ______________________

Class: ______________________

DIAGNOSTIC TEST B

61 **A:** What are we having for lunch?
B: I'll cook us some ....
A jam **B** pasta **C** butter **D** yoghurt

62 I .... to Italy before and I loved it.
A have been **B** have gone **C** go **D** was going

63 'Have you .... eaten octopus?' 'Yes, I have.'
A never **B** yet **C** since **D** ever

64 Alex hasn't called me ....
A already **B** yet **C** just **D** now

65 I have known Alice .... a very long time.
A for **B** already **C** just **D** since

66 We've lived in this street .... 2010.
A before **B** already **C** since **D** after

67 They missed their train because they were waiting for it at the wrong ....
A platform **B** visa **C** customs **D** airport

68 The .... we bought had a lot of useful information about things to see in London.
A diary **B** guidebook **C** digital camera **D** charger

69 Next weekend, my friends and I are .... a trip to the countryside.
A taking **B** doing **C** making **D** going

70 Jo gets good marks at school when she ....
A will study **B** studies **C** is studying **D** studied

71 You .... a part-time job if you don't look for one!
A don't find **B** didn't find **C** won't find **D** haven't found

72 Tim .... to help me with my geography project.
A suggested **B** said **C** enjoyed **D** promised

73 I'll .... cleaning the house later.
A finish **B** help **C** want **D** try

74 Would they rather .... to the city centre or take the bus?
A to walk **B** walked **C** walk **D** walking

75 I'm going to .... some of the party photos because I don't like them.
A charge **B** download **C** forget **D** delete

76 He doesn't play in the garden because he's .... of spiders.
A frightened **B** bored **C** fed up **D** terrible

77 .... time with my friends is fun.
A Spend **B** To spend **C** Spending **D** I spend

78 Luke always has dinner before .... his homework.
A do **B** doing **C** does **D** to do

79 I have an app on my phone that .... from English into Spanish.
A understands **B** repeats **C** talks **D** translates

80 'This box is heavy.' 'Don't worry. I .... you carry it.'
A am helping **B** help **C** will help **D** am going to help

Name: ____________________

Class: ____________________

DIAGNOSTIC TEST B

81 The score is 5–0 and there are two minutes left in the match. My team .... !
A loses B will lose C is losing D is going to lose

82 A: It's hot in this room.
B: .... opening the windows?'
A Why don't you B How about C You could D Shall we

83 Can you .... the sound on the TV, please? I can't hear it very well.
A set up B turn up C plug in D go off

84 We bought a new dishwasher and someone came to our house to .... it.
A tap B connect C install D upload

85 I don't see Max very often, but I .... him twice this month.
A see B saw C have seen D was seeing

86 When the match ended, the tennis players left the ....
A locker B changing room C track D court

87 How many countries .... in the football World Cup?
A compete B kick C practise D beat

88 If we .... in the countryside, we would be happier.
A live B lived C will live D have lived

89 .... we get two tickets, we can't go to the concert.
A In case B When C If D Unless

90 During the concert, the fans in the .... sang and danced.
A choir B audience C orchestra D stage

91 My favourite books .... by Charles Dickens.
A were written B were writing C wrote D have written

92 These classrooms .... for art lessons.
A are using B are used C use D have used

93 I .... every two months.
A am cutting my hair B have cut my hair C was cutting my hair D have my hair cut

94 Is that the club .... you play tennis?
A who B that C where D which

95 We had to show our passports at the .... before we could enter the country.
A destination B check-in C location D border

96 Do you know .... ?
A I am B who I am C who am I D I am who

97 Kerry is very .... She believes that she will pass all of her exams.
A patient B creative C optimistic D sociable

98 Peter came to my party because I .... him.
A was inviting B have invited C had invited D will invite

99 Before he stopped working, my grandfather .... maths.
A used to teach B was teaching C has taught D could teach

100 A: Are you .... the concert, Tim?
B: Yes, I am! It's going to be fantastic!'
A going for B dealing with C hanging out D looking forward to

Total:		100

Name: ______________________

Class: ______________________

UNIT 1: LANGUAGE TEST A

GRAMMAR

Task 1

Complete the text with *a*, *an*, *the* or –.

My name's Erika and I'm from **(1)** .... Germany. I live in Berlin, which is **(2)** .... capital. It's **(3)** .... great city for people who love cultural activities. We have lots of excellent museums and some of them are very unusual. One of these is **(4)** .... German Currywurst Museum. I think it's **(5)** .... amazing place. It's **(6)** .... exhibition about 'currywurst' – a popular snack of sausage with curry ketchup. It sounds strange, but it's really delicious! **(7)** .... German people love it. **(8)** .... tourists think it's good, too. So if you visit my country, don't be afraid to try it!

[ ] 8

Task 2

Complete the sentences with one word in each gap.

9 Dad, I need a .... advice and I think you can help me.
10 Are there .... interesting things for visitors to see in your town?
11 Sorry, I can't meet you on Saturday. I've got a .... of homework to do.
12 Your backpack is heavy! How .... books have you got in it?
13 .... the information I have for my project is from the internet. I hope it's correct.
14 I have a .... good friends in my neighbourhood, including my best friend Tom.
15 Hurry up, Pat! We don't have .... time before our train leaves.
16 I don't know .... famous people, but I'd love to meet my favourite singer.

[ ] 8

Task 3

Choose the correct answer.

17 .... good friends are important to have.
A The **B** A **C** –

18 These are .... photos I took on my holiday in France.
A some **B** any **C** every

19 Do you have .... money?
A many **B** any **C** a lot

20 There are .... canals in Amsterdam.
A a lot **B** lot of **C** a lot of

21 There are a .... really nice cafés in the town square.
A little **B** few **C** lot

22 There isn't .... bread at all, so I can't make a sandwich.
A little **B** much **C** any

23 How .... pressure are you under when you have exams?
A much **B** many **C** any

24 Let's listen to .... music while we do our homework.
A some **B** little **C** any

25 .... students worry about their exams.
A A lot **B** All **C** Every

[ ] 9

Name: ....

Class: ....

VOCABULARY

Task 1

Complete the sentences with these words.

apartment bin centre crossing department gallery lift park rack seat stop

26 I'm going to the art .... to see a photography exhibition.
27 Don't leave that bottle on the grass. Put it in the rubbish ....
28 Let's leave our bikes at the bike .... and take the train.
29 I have basketball training twice a week at the sports ....
30 Harry lives on the tenth floor of a(n) .... block.
31 We can meet at the bus .... at four o'clock. Don't be late!
32 Is there a skate .... near the high school?
33 I'm going to the .... store to buy a present for my sister.
34 Mum, I'm late for school. Can you give me a .... ?
35 Cars must stop at a .... if people are waiting there.
36 The bus was full this morning, so I didn't have a ....

	11

Task 2

Choose the correct words to complete the sentences.

37 There's a bathroom **between** / **by** my room and my brother's room. We share it.
38 I didn't see Fred because he was **under** / **behind** the door.
39 I'm busy now, **because** / **but** I'll be free at six o'clock. Call me then.
40 It's a lot colder **in** / **on** the north of the country than the south.
41 This is a funny photo! Who is the tall boy **at** / **on** the left?
42 Carlos is from Figueres in Spain. It's **near** / **by** the border with France.
43 How often do you hang **out** / **up** with your friends?
44 Brighton is a city **in** / **on** the coast, so lots of people go there in the summer.

	8

Task 3

Match 45–50 with A–F to make sentences.

45 I prefer to sit at ....
46 Sam is in front ....
47 We have a house by ....
48 The library is next ....
49 The video games are on ....
50 All the students are in ....

A to the school.
B of me in this photo.
C the classroom.
D the front of the bus.
E the floor.
F the sea.

	6

Total:		50

Name: ____________________

Class: ____________________

UNIT 1: LANGUAGE TEST B

GRAMMAR

Task 1

Complete the text with *a*, *an*, *the* or –.

I'm Jake and I'm from Melbourne, in **(1)** .... Australia. **(2)** .... sport is an important part of life here. **(3)** .... Australian people love it! Every year, there are big sports competitions in Melbourne. That's one reason why it's **(4)** .... exciting city to live in. In January there is **(5)** .... Australian Open tennis tournament. The best players in **(6)** .... world compete. In March we have the Formula One Grand Prix race. There is **(7)** .... lake in the city and the drivers race around it. We also have amazing stadiums in **(8)** .... centre of the city for soccer, cricket and Australian football. It's the best place for sports fans!

	8

Task 2

Complete the sentences with one word in each gap.

9 I don't have .... brothers or sisters – I'm an only child.
10 My parents give me a .... of good advice.
11 How .... friends do you have at school?
12 Here is a .... information about life in Holland.
13 What do you want to do for your birthday? Do you have .... ideas?
14 Wow! .... the clothes in this shop are really cool!
15 I always study for a .... hours every day.
16 We don't have .... homework tonight – only one exercise.

	8

Task 3

Choose the correct answer.

17 .... young people want to have fun in the holidays.
A Every **B** All **C** A lot

18 How .... free time do you have at the weekend?
A many **B** any **C** much

19 There is .... water on the floor. What happened?
A some **B** a lot **C** little

20 This is a popular video game and .... my friends play it.
A lots **B** a lot of **C** a lot

21 My mum drinks her tea with a .... milk, but no sugar.
A little **B** lot **C** any

22 These days, ... teens like to feel that they are independent.
A – **B** The **C** A

23 Is there .... orange juice in the fridge?
A many **B** any **C** little

24 I have a .... hobbies that I enjoy doing.
A many **B** some **C** few

25 There are .... interesting comments on your blog.
A every **B** much **C** some

	9

Name: ______________________

Class: ______________________

UNIT 1: LANGUAGE TEST B

VOCABULARY

Task 1

Complete the sentences with these words.

bin block centre crossing gallery lift park rack seat stop store

26 Do you live in a house or in an apartment .... ?
27 Can I give you a .... to the shops?
28 My friends and I go to the skate .... every weekend.
29 Please put these old newspapers in the rubbish ....
30 Sit here – there's a .... next to me.
31 I love the paintings in this art .... – they're so beautiful.
32 It started raining when I was at the bus .... and I got wet.
33 There's a bike .... at school where we leave our bikes.
34 Let's go to the sports .... and watch the volleyball game.
35 The police stopped the driver because he didn't stop at the ....
36 You can find lots of different things to buy at a department ....

| | 11 |

Task 2

Choose the correct words to complete the sentences.

37 There are a lot of things to see in California **and** / **so** the beaches are amazing.
38 The city of London is **at** / **in** the south of England.
39 Maria and Elena always sit **at** / **by** the front of the classroom.
40 Max wants to go to Barcelona, **but** / **because** he loves the football team.
41 The post office is **between** / **under** the supermarket and the bank.
42 Is your house **next** / **near** the school that you go to?
43 We usually spend our holidays **on** / **to** the coast.
44 Let's sit **on** / **under** a tree in the park and have our lunch.

| | 8 |

Task 3

Match 45–50 with A–F to make sentences.

45 That's my sister on .... **A** the living room.
46 I often hang .... **B** the right.
47 Jo sits in front .... **C** the sea.
48 It's nice to walk by .... **D** of me in class.
49 The girls are in .... **E** to the door.
50 There's a chair next .... **F** out here.

| | 6 |

Total: | | 50 |

Name: ______________________

Class: ______________________

UNIT 1: SKILLS TEST A

DICTATION

You are going to listen to a recording about Dutch teenagers. Listen to the whole recording once. Then you will hear the recording again with pauses for you to write down what you hear. Make sure you spell the words correctly.

....

....

....

/10

LISTENING

Task 1

You are going to listen to six conversations. For questions 1–6, choose the answer (A, B or C) which fits best according to what you hear.

1 What is the boy doing?

A B C

2 What should the students take with them?

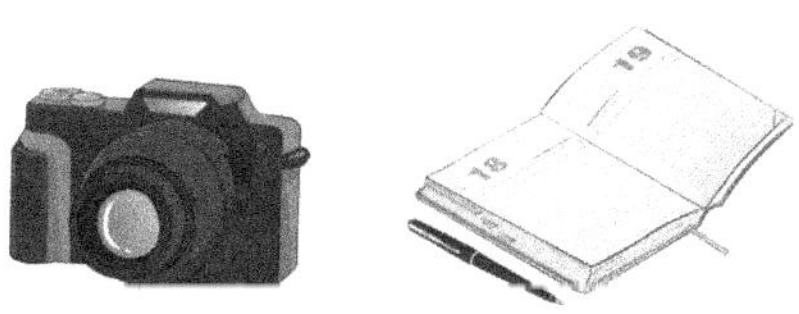

A B C

3 When will the girl go to the photography club?

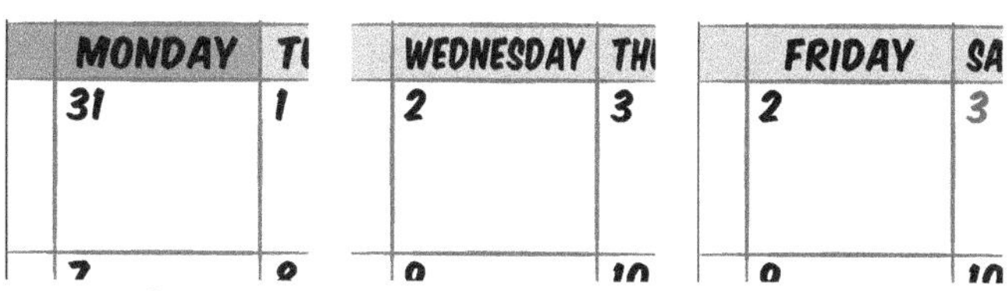

A B C

4 What did the girl and her cousins do together?

A B C

5 How does the girl keep fit?

A B C

6 What do they decide to eat?

A B C

/18

Name: ____________________

Class: ____________________

Task 2

You are going to listen to the last conversation again. Are the sentences true (T) or false (F)?

7 The girl asked the boy to go the cinema with her. ....

8 The boy suggests they do something after the film. ....

| | 2 |

READING

Task 1

Read the blog about what makes teenagers happy. Decide if the sentences are true (T) or false (F). If there is not enough information, write DS (doesn't say).

9 Teens are happy when they own nice things. ....

10 Young people should spend less time with their friends. ....

11 Teens use the internet because that's what their friends do. ....

12 Most teens are online for more than a few hours a day. ....

13 There are times when teenagers want their parents to leave them alone. ....

14 Teens feel good when they can discuss school with their parents. ....

15 Students who prepare well for exams get good marks. ....

16 It makes teens unhappy to ask for money. ....

| | 16 |

Task 2

Read the blog again and answer the questions in your own words.

17 Why is it important for young people to spend time with their friends?

....

18 How do exams make young people unhappy?

....

| | 4 |

Total: | | 50 |

What makes teens happy?

I'm Ana. Welcome to my blog.
Or 'Willkommen' as we say in German!

Recently, my teacher told us about some reports on teen happiness. What do you think makes teens happy? Is it money, going out or owning things? No, you're wrong. The reports show that teens are happy when they have good relationships with their friends and families.

Everyone needs friends, but young people seem to be with their friends all the time! That's OK – young people need to spend time with their friends because it helps them to learn how to be around other people. We see our friends at school all day, and when we get home, we go online to chat there. Going online for an hour or two isn't a problem. Most teens understand this and don't spend all of their time online. The internet makes us happy and we must have it because our friends have it, but we're happier when we go out with our friends in real life.

How do we feel about our parents? The reports say teens think their parents are annoying sometimes, for example, when they text too much or ask too many questions, but teens are pleased to have their parents' help and love. Happy teens have parents who often spend time with them, eating as a family and talking about what's happening at school. In fact, spending time just talking is the number one activity to do with parents at home that makes teens happy.

And what makes us unhappy? Exams! We often worry that exams will be difficult and our marks will be bad. Many students are worried about tests that they have prepared well for! We also worry about money – we want to have enough for the things we enjoy, but we don't want to ask our parents for it all the time. It also makes us unhappy when our parents don't understand us. But we can just sit down at the dinner table and talk about it. Problem solved!

GOLD experience A2+ 2ND EDITION Preliminary for Schools

Name: ______________________

Class: ______________________

UNIT 1: SKILLS TEST B

DICTATION

You are going to listen to a recording about Dutch teenagers. Listen to the whole recording once. Then you will hear the recording again with pauses for you to write down what you hear. Make sure you spell the words correctly.

....

....

....

/ 10

LISTENING

Task 1

You are going to listen to six conversations. For questions 1–6, choose the answer (A, B or C) which fits best according to what you hear.

1 What does the girl want to do?

A

B

C

2 What do the students need for their school trip?

A

B

C

3 Which day should the best photographers go to the club?

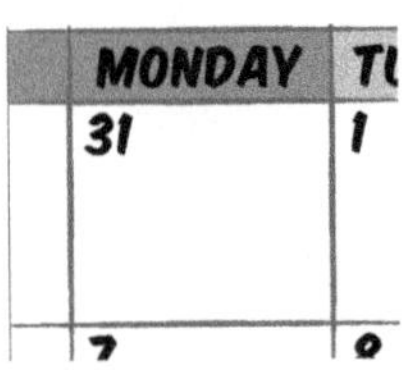

A

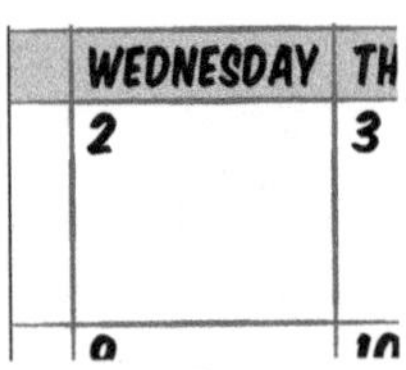

B

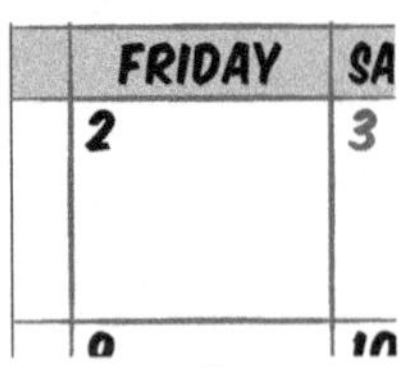

C

4 Where did the girl and her cousins not go?

A

B

C

5 Which activity does the girl enjoy the most?

A

B

C

6 What does the girl not want to eat?

A

B

C

/ 18

Task 2

You are going to listen to the last conversation again. Are the sentences true (T) or false (F)?

7 The girl paid for the popcorn. ....

8 They won't eat anything after the film. ....

	2

READING

Task 1

Read the blog about what makes teenagers happy. Decide if the sentences are true (T) or false (F). If there is not enough information, write DS (doesn't say).

9 Teens are happy when they own nice things. ....

10 Young people should spend less time with their friends. ....

11 Teens use the internet because that's what their friends do. ....

12 Most teens are online for more than a few hours a day. ....

13 There are times when teenagers want their parents to leave them alone. ....

14 Teens feel good when they can discuss school with their parents. ....

15 Students who prepare well for exams get good marks. ....

16 It makes teens unhappy to ask for money. ....

	16

Task 2

Read the blog again and answer the questions in your own words.

17 According to the report, what do young people think about parents?

....

18 Why is it important for young people to spend time with their friends?

....

	4

Total:		50

What makes teens happy?

I'm Ana. Welcome to my blog. Or 'Willkommen' as we say in German!

Recently, my teacher told us about some reports on teen happiness. What do you think makes teens happy? Is it money, going out or owning things? No, you're wrong. The reports show that teens are happy when they have good relationships with their friends and families.

Everyone needs friends, but young people seem to be with their friends all the time! That's OK – young people need to spend time with their friends because it helps them to learn how to be around other people. We see our friends at school all day, and when we get home, we go online to chat there. Going online for an hour or two isn't a problem. Most teens understand this and don't spend all of their time online. The internet makes us happy and we must have it because our friends have it, but we're happier when we go out with our friends in real life.

How do we feel about our parents? The reports say teens think their parents are annoying sometimes, for example, when they text too much or ask too many questions, but teens are pleased to have their parents' help and love. Happy teens have parents who often spend time with them, eating as a family and talking about what's happening at school. In fact, spending time just talking is the number one activity to do with parents at home that makes teens happy.

And what makes us unhappy? Exams! We often worry that exams will be difficult and our marks will be bad. Many students are worried about tests that they have prepared well for! We also worry about money – we want to have enough for the things we enjoy, but we don't want to ask our parents for it all the time. It also makes us unhappy when our parents don't understand us. But we can just sit down at the dinner table and talk about it. Problem solved!

Name: ______________________________

Class: ______________________________

GRAMMAR

Task 1

Choose the correct words to complete the text.

(1) Do you like / Are you liking really exciting activities? **(2) Do you look for / Are you looking for** a new challenge? What about wall climbing? It **(3) seems / is seeming** scary the first time you do it, but after that, it's great. My friend and I often **(4) go / are going** to a gym with a climbing wall. The wall we usually **(5) climb / are climbing** is ten metres high, but this week we **(6) don't go up / aren't going up** that wall – we **(7) try / are trying** something more difficult. It's a fifteen-metre wall, but we aren't worried about it. The special equipment we use keeps us safe. I **(8) love / am loving** climbing! Maybe it's the right hobby for you, too.

[ ] 8

Task 2

Complete the sentences with the present simple or present continuous form of the verbs in brackets.

9 The girls aren't here. They .... (play) football at the moment.

10 I .... (not believe) Jim. He's telling lies again!

11 Anna is tired so she .... (not go) to the cinema tonight.

12 Yuk! I can't drink this tea! It .... (need) more sugar in it.

13 My friends and I .... (spend) a lot of time outdoors in the summer.

14 .... you .... (think) taekwondo is a fun activity?

15 I never .... (listen) to the radio, but my parents enjoy it.

16 Jim isn't a fan of cricket. In fact, he .... (hate) it!

17 I'm sorry, Grandma. .... I .... (walk) too fast?

18 Jack .... (not like) video games – he says they're boring.

[ ] 10

Task 3

Choose the correct answer.

19 During the holidays, I .... bored at home.
- **A** usually am
- **B** am often
- **C** always am

20 She goes to parties, but she ....
- **A** dances often
- **B** dances usually
- **C** never dances

21 Ben .... loses swimming races.
- **A** hardly ever
- **B** hardly never
- **C** ever hardly

22 I don't live near the sea, so .... swimming.
- **A** rarely I go
- **B** I rarely go
- **C** I go rarely

23 Who .... a new tennis racket?
- **A** is having
- **B** does have
- **C** has

24 What .... in your free time?
- **A** do you do
- **B** you doing
- **C** you do

25 Why .... late?
- **A** do they
- **B** they are
- **C** are they

[ ] 7

Name: ______________________

Class: ______________________

VOCABULARY

Task 1

Match 26–33 with A–H to make sentences.

26 Harry wants to take ....
27 It's good to spend ....
28 The team is getting ....
29 Try hard and you can do ....
30 You will make ....
31 Keep practising until you get ....
32 I'm searching online ....
33 When things don't go ....

A well in the competition.
B for the address of the youth club.
C time doing things you enjoy.
D it right.
E progress, I'm sure.
F part in the school play.
G well, try again.
H good results with the new coach.

[ ] 8

Task 2

Complete the sentences with these words.

careful clever confident friendly honest polite quiet serious

34 Anna always tells the truth. She's very ....
35 Martin never forgets to say 'please' and 'thank you'. He's a .... boy.
36 I'm .... because I don't want to make any mistakes.
37 Freda is a .... girl. She's always smiling and everyone likes her.
38 You're the best student in the class. You're very .... !
39 Kelly doesn't talk a lot because she's a .... girl.
40 Alana doesn't do anything silly because she's a very .... person.
41 Ben is sure he can pass all his exams. He's a very .... student.

[ ] 8

Task 3

Choose the correct words to complete the sentences.

42 YouTube is the best **site** / **space** for videos.
43 Do you **share** / **give** photos on social media?
44 Just **go** / **follow** this link to my new blog.
45 Where can I find a free computer **program** / **programme** for chess?
46 Tom is interested in snowboarding. **He likes** / **He'd like** to try it.
47 Find the book you want in this online shop and then **hold** / **press** 'Buy' to pay for it.
48 What can I do to **do** / **get** better at basketball?
49 I don't want to **waste** / **pass** time playing video games.
50 There's something wrong with the TV – it doesn't **go** / **work**.

[ ] 9

Total: [ ] 50

Name: ____________________

Class: ____________________

GRAMMAR

Task 1

Choose the correct words to complete the text.

How **(1) do you usually spend / are you usually spending** your free time? **(2) Do you look for / Are you looking for** a fun new hobby? Try wall climbing! For this activity, you **(3) use / are using** your hands and feet to climb up and down a wall. It's like being outdoors on a rock, but you're safe because it never **(4) rains / is raining** inside, and special equipment holds you so you **(5) don't fall / aren't falling**. I **(6) start / am starting** this week with my friend Emma and we **(7) look forward to / are looking forward to** it very much! It **(8) looks / is looking** a little scary, but it isn't really. Just keep calm and keep climbing!

| | 8 |

Task 2

Complete the sentences with the present simple or present continuous form of the verbs in brackets.

9 I .... (agree) with you about taekwondo – it's a lot of fun!

10 Dan .... (not run) in the race today because he isn't well.

11 I'm sorry, but I .... (not understand) this. Can you explain it to me?

12 Dad .... (watch) his favourite TV show every Wednesday night.

13 .... Pat .... (know) what time the youth club opens?

14 .... your brothers .... (learn) some new card tricks?

15 We .... (love) these photos. They're amazing!

16 Jill .... (not do) puzzles very often.

17 .... you .... (want) to go to the sports centre tomorrow?

18 Oh no! .... it .... (rain) again? We can't go hiking!

| | 10 |

Task 3

Choose the correct answer.

19 I want to watch the race. When .... ?
- **A** it's starting
- **B** it starts
- **C** does it start

20 Who .... to the chess club every weekend?
- **A** goes
- **B** does go
- **C** is going

21 Where .... , Anita?
- **A** you are living
- **B** do you live
- **C** you live

22 Alex .... online.
- **A** occasionally is chatting
- **B** occasionally chats
- **C** chats occasionally

23 Jane .... hard – she's very lazy.
- **A** rarely tries
- **B** rarely she tries
- **C** tries rarely

24 We .... go to the theatre to see a play.
- **A** hardly never
- **B** hardly ever
- **C** never hardly

25 Tim .... for football practice.
- **A** is always late
- **B** often is late
- **C** is ever late

| | 7 |

Name: ______________________

Class: ______________________

VOCABULARY

Task 1

Match 26–33 with A–H to make sentences.

26 I practise every day to do ....
27 You can make ....
28 We often spend ....
29 He needs to get ....
30 The girls are taking ....
31 Practise every day and you will get ....
32 They're searching ....
33 When things go ....

A for information about the race.
B part in the concert next week.
C well, I'm really happy.
D well in my taekwondo class.
E time making videos to put online.
F it right, I'm sure.
G progress when you work hard.
H good results in the chess competition.

	8

Task 2

Complete the sentences with these words.

careful clever confident friendly honest polite quiet serious

34 Jim doesn't like to talk very much – he prefers to listen. He's a .... person.
35 Lisa is very .... She knows a lot of people and she likes hanging out with them.
36 I know I can win this tennis match. I'm very ....
37 We know the answers to all of the teacher's questions – we're .... !
38 Marc works hard and always prepares for his lessons – he's a .... student.
39 You must always say 'please' when you ask for something – be ....
40 Sandra is the best chess player – she's always .... and she never makes mistakes.
41 Will doesn't tell lies – he's a very .... person.

	8

Task 3

Choose the correct words to complete the sentences.

42 Just **follow** / **go** this link and it will take you to the club's web page.
43 He's working hard and he's **getting** / **going** better at football.
44 Don't worry if it doesn't **make** / **work** the first time.
45 I want to show you a new computer **program** / **programme** for photographers.
46 YouTube is my favourite **page** / **site**. Which is yours?
47 Find a song you like and **press** / **push** 'Play' to listen to it – it's really easy.
48 Please don't **pass** / **waste** time online – go out and play sport!
49 My friends and I **give** / **share** videos and photos online all the time.
50 I think karate looks like a lot of fun – **I like** / **I'd like** to try it.

	9

Total:		50

Name: ....

Class: ....

DICTATION

You are going to listen to a recording about improving skills. Listen to the whole recording once. Then you will hear the recording again with pauses for you to write down what you hear. Make sure you spell the words correctly.

....

....

....

....

....

....

....

....

....

....

....

....

....

/ 10

LISTENING

Task 1

You are going to listen to a talk about summer events at a youth club. Complete the notes. Write the correct answer in each gap.

Clayton Youth Club

Here are some ideas for fun **(1)** .... and day trips.

Paintballing:

The centre opens **(2)** .... of the week.

It costs **(3)** .... pounds on Monday and Tuesday and £8 from Wednesday to Sunday

We can leave the youth club at nine o'clock in the morning and play for two **(4)** .... until twelve o'clock.

After that, we can return to the youth club or have **(5)** .... in town.

Everyone must bring old **(6)** .... and shoes and change at the centre.

/ 18

Task 2

Are the sentences true (T) or false (F)?

7 The members of the youth club will do more than one activity during the summer holidays. ....

8 They have already decided when they will go paintballing. ....

/ 2

Name: ______________________

Class: ______________________

READING

Task 1

Read the texts (9–11) and choose the correct answer (A, B or C).

9

> All students:
>
> Adventure Camp
>
> Your parents must fill in the forms.
>
> Return them by Tuesday.

A Students can give the forms to the school on Monday.

B Students will return from the camp on Tuesday.

C Students should complete the forms themselves.

10

> From: Lena
>
> To: Stan
>
> I'm thinking of having sailing lessons and I'd like some information about the sailing club you go to. Can we meet next week?

Lena is writing because

A she wants Stan to teach her how to sail.

B she wants to ask Stan about his club.

C she wants to go sailing with Stan.

11

> Jane
>
> The bus is late. I'll meet you at the jewellery-making class. Please tell the teacher I'm sorry and explain what's happened. Thanks!
>
> Nicky

What should Jane do?

A wait for Nicky's bus to arrive

B ask the teacher to wait for Nicky

C go to the class without Nicky

[ ] 6

Task 2

Read the article about trying new hobbies. Match the sentences (12–16) with the hobbies: juggling (J), blogging (B) or music videos (M).

12 This can be a group project. ....

13 You need to keep doing this to get better. ....

14 It teaches you a skill that you can use in the future. ....

15 It's a good activity for your body. ....

16 You can get help from people who have done this. ....

[ ] 10

Task 3

Read the article again and answer the questions in your own words.

17 What is the best thing to write a blog about?

....

18 Where can you film your music video?

....

[ ] 4

Total: [ ] 50

Try something new!

Here are some great ideas about things you can do in your free time! They're fun and they're free!

What: Juggling

How: It's easier than you think! You don't need balls to learn this – you can start with supermarket plastic bags. You don't believe me? Go online and search for 'learn how to juggle'. You'll be amazed at how simple the basic movements are. Keep practising and, eventually, you'll be quick enough to throw and catch the bags while they're in the air. Once you've got some confidence, you can juggle balls or rings.

Why: Juggling is an exercise that doesn't feel like an exercise. It's great for your hands, arms and shoulders. But it also exercises your brain. That's because it makes you focus on what you're doing.

What: Blogging

How: Don't worry. You don't need special computer knowledge to start a blog. There's lots of advice online from successful bloggers about how they started. They'll also tell you to blog about something you enjoy and make it interesting for others to read. If people like your blog, they'll want to discuss your opinions with you and they'll leave comments on your blog.

Why: First of all, it's fun! It's creative and it allows you to talk about things that are important to you. It also greatly improves your writing skills, and those skills will stay with you forever. The more you write, the better you will communicate with other people.

What: Music videos

How: You'll need equipment for this. You can use a video camera or the video on your phone. Choose a song that you like and think about the video you can add to it. It could be dancing, or a story. Ask your friends to help you and to appear in the video. You can make costumes and do your hair and make-up, too. Also, think about where you want to film it – it could be at home or somewhere in your town.

Why: Videos are a fantastic way for friends to spend time together and, when you finish, you'll all have something to remember the experience and watch again and again, even when you're a lot older!

Name: ______________________

Class: ______________________

UNIT 2: SKILLS TEST B

DICTATION

You are going to listen to a recording about improving skills. Listen to the whole recording once. Then you will hear the recording again with pauses for you to write down what you hear. Make sure you spell the words correctly.

....

....

....

....

....

....

....

....

....

....

....

....

/ 10

LISTENING

Task 1

You are going to listen to a talk about summer events at a youth club. Complete the notes. Write the correct answer in each gap.

Clayton Youth Club

Here are some ideas for fun activities and day **(1)** ....

Paintballing

The centre is open every day of the week.

It **(2)** .... £5 on Monday and Tuesday and **(3)** .... pounds from Wednesday to Sunday.

We can leave the youth club at nine o'clock in the morning and play for **(4)** .... hours until twelve o'clock.

After that, we can return to the youth club or have lunch in the **(5)** ....

Everyone must bring old clothes and **(6)** ...., and change at the centre.

/ 18

Task 2

Are the sentences true (T) or false (F)?

7 The members of the youth club don't want to do any unusual activities. ....

8 They won't be at the paintball course in the afternoon. ....

/ 2

Name: ....

Class: ....

READING

Task 1

Read the texts (9–11) and choose the correct answer (A, B or C).

9

> Jane
>
> The bus is late. I'll meet you at the jewellery-making class. Please tell the teacher I'm sorry and explain what's happened. Thanks!
>
> Nicky

What should Jane do?

A wait for Nicky to arrive at the bus stop

B go to the jewellery-making class without Nicky

C tell the teacher Nicky can't come to the class

10

> All students:
>
> Adventure Camp
>
> Your parents must fill in the forms.
>
> Return them by Tuesday.

A Parents should go to the school with the forms.

B Students will return from the camp on Tuesday.

C Students can give the forms to the school on Monday.

11

> From: Lena
>
> To: Stan
>
> I'm thinking of having sailing lessons and I'd like some information about the sailing club you go to. Can we meet next week?

Lena is writing because

A she wants to ask Stan about his club.

B she wants Stan to teach her how to sail.

C she wants to go sailing with Stan.

	6

Task 2

Read the article about trying new hobbies. Match the sentences (12–16) with the hobbies: juggling (J), blogging (B) or music videos (M).

12 It's a way to express your opinion. ....

13 There are many places where you can do this hobby. ....

14 Watch videos to learn this skill. ....

15 You can change the equipment after you make progress. ....

16 This isn't an activity you can do alone. ....

	10

Task 3

Read the article again and answer the questions in your own words.

17 Why is juggling a good activity for your body?

....

18 What advice can other bloggers give?

....

	4

Total:		50

Try something new!

Here are some great ideas for fun, free hobbies you can do at home!

What: Juggling

How: It looks difficult, but it isn't, and you can start right now! Surprisingly, supermarket plastic bags are the best things to start with. It's true! Go online and search for videos about how to juggle. It's amazing how simple the basic movements are. Just keep doing them and soon, you'll be to throw and catch the bags quite easily while they're in the air. When you become more confident and you no longer drop the bags, you can try juggling balls or rings.

Why: Juggling is fantastic exercise for your hands, arms and shoulders. But just as importantly, it's good exercise for your brain. Why? Because it makes you think hard about what you're doing.

What: Blogging

How: If you can use a computer to do your homework or write emails, you can blog! No special computer knowledge is necessary. Go online for useful advice from other bloggers. They can give you information about how to start your blog. The most important thing is to blog about something you enjoy doing. That makes it interesting for your readers and they'll want to give their own opinions in the comments they leave.

Why: It's fun and creative. You can talk about things you think are important. Also, it improves a skill you'll always need – writing. Keep writing and you'll communicate better with other people.

What: Music videos

How: A video camera or the video on your phone are all you need. Find a song that you love – maybe your favourite – and create a dance or a story that can go with it. Make it funny or serious. Your friends can be your actors. Think about costumes, hair and make-up, too. Where are you going to film your video? How about an interesting place in your town, in your home or in your garden?

Why: Making videos is a great way to spend time with your friends. And when you finish, everyone will have something cool to remember the experience, and to watch again and again when you're older!

Name: ________________

Class: ________________

GRAMMAR

Task 1

Choose the correct words to complete the sentences.

1 We **sat** / **were sitting** on the beach when suddenly it **started** / **was starting** to rain.
2 I **chatted** / **was chatting** to my friend while we **waited** / **were waiting** for the bus.
3 Jack **read** / **was reading** a comic when I **called** / **was calling** him at three o'clock yesterday.
4 While the boys **played** / **were playing** cricket in the garden, they **broke** / **were breaking** a window.
5 Lionel **kicked** / **was kicking** the ball hard and **scored** / **was scoring** an incredible goal.
6 Where **did Pat sit** / **was Pat sitting** while you **listened** / **were listening** to music?
7 Harry **didn't meet** / **wasn't meeting** his friends yesterday because he **studied** / **was studying** then.
8 It was a cold night. It **rained** / **was raining** and the wind **blew** / **was blowing**.

| | 8 |

Task 2

Complete the sentences with the past simple or past continuous form of the verbs in brackets.

9 Gill .... (not watch) the TV show, so she changed the channel.
10 .... (you / buy) anything while you were shopping at the market?
11 Mum was having lunch with her friends in the town while dad .... (do) the housework.
12 I ordered a pizza and then .... (pay) for it when it arrived.
13 .... (she / drive) fast when the accident happened?
14 The lights .... (go out) last night while Beth was reading an interesting story.
15 Someone knocked on the door, but when I .... (open) it, no one was there.
16 I .... (not go) to the shops when you saw me this morning.

| | 8 |

Task 3

Complete the sentences with these words. You will need to use one word twice.

anyone anything everyone everything no one nothing someone something

17 I didn't see .... that I liked at the shops, so I looked online.
18 All of my friends are busy today – there's .... to go swimming with me.
19 I did my homework quickly. I finished .... in an hour.
20 .... sent me a text message, but I don't know who the sender is.
21 Did you see .... interesting on your holiday?
22 There's .... in the box – it's empty.
23 It was quiet in the library because .... was studying.
24 Ouch! There's .... in my eye!
25 Do you know .... who can speak German?

| | 9 |

Name: ____________________

Class: ____________________

VOCABULARY

Task 1

Match 26–33 with A–H to make sentences.

26 My brother broke my camera!	....	**A**	I'm exhausted.
27 I'm spending the summer in Greece.	....	**B**	I'm freezing.
28 I studied all night for my English exam.	....	**C**	It's delicious.
29 I didn't eat lunch today.	....	**D**	It's useful.
30 This old house is very cold.	....	**E**	It's terrible.
31 Can I have another piece of cake?	....	**F**	I'm furious.
32 I don't know why you like this stupid show.	....	**G**	I'm starving.
33 This website has lots of information.	....	**H**	I'm delighted.

/ 8

Task 2

Complete the sentences with a word from A and a word from B.

A

ancient dark dull huge ordinary

B

exciting light modern special tiny

34 I don't look good in .... colours, like black. That's why I always wear .... ones.
35 The match wasn't .... and we were bored. It ended 0–0 and was really .... to watch.
36 The archaeologists used some .... technology to find the .... coins buried in the ground.
37 Today isn't an .... day. It's a .... day – it's my birthday!
38 Ants are ...., but elephants are .... !

/ 10

Task 3

Put the words in brackets in the correct order to complete the sentences.

39 This .... is the most important in the museum. (painting / valuable / Italian)
40 A .... wrote this story. (young / writer / brilliant)
41 My parents gave me a .... for my birthday. (beautiful / ring / gold)
42 My uncle drives a .... (German / fantastic / sports car).
43 Milly watched a .... and then had a bad dream. (black and white / film / scary)
44 When I opened the door, a(n) .... was standing there. (man / strange / old)
45 I mixed the milk, flour, eggs and sugar with a .... (wooden / spoon / long)

/ 7

Total: / 50

Name: ______________________

Class: ______________________

GRAMMAR

Task 1

Choose the correct words to complete the sentences.

1 Tom **showed** / **was showing** us his holiday photos on his phone, when suddenly he **dropped** / **was dropping** it.
2 I **found** / **was finding** some money under my bed when I **looked** / **was looking** for my football boots.
3 Bobby **went** / **was going** to the sports centre when I **called** / **was calling** him at three o'clock.
4 While Anita **skied** / **was skiing**, she **fell** / **was falling** and hurt her leg.
5 The girls **didn't invite** / **wasn't inviting** me to their party because they **forgot** / **were forgetting**.
6 **Did you sit** / **Were you sitting** in your room while you **read** / **were reading** the story?
7 We **didn't cycle** / **weren't cycling** to school today because it **rained** / **was raining**.
8 When I woke up, the sun **shone** / **was shining** and the birds **sang** / **were singing**.

	8

Task 2

Complete the sentences with the past simple or past continuous form of the verbs in brackets.

9 Nick .... (not listen) to the teacher during the lesson and she got angry.
10 .... (you / take) a break while you were studying last night?
11 Mum was having lunch with her friends in the town while dad .... (do) the housework.
12 They went to France and .... (visit) Paris.
13 .... (you / have) lunch when the letter arrived?
14 I was tidying my room on Saturday when Mum .... (come) home with the shopping.
15 The boys .... (go) to the cinema and then had a snack at a café.
16 It.............................. (not snow) when I got up this morning.

	8

Task 3

Complete the sentences with these words. You will need to use one word twice.

anyone anything everyone everything no one nothing someone something

17 I know .... who writes stories for teenagers – she's a great writer.
18 The picnic was fantastic and .... had a great time.
19 We were bored during the holidays because we didn't have .... to do.
20 It was a difficult question and .... knew the answer.
21 Mum, here's the shopping. I got .... that was on the list you gave me.
22 Are they doing .... at the moment?
23 Did you see .... that you knew at the party?
24 Let's go to a restaurant – there's .... to eat at home.
25 I want .... to drink. Is there any lemonade?

	9

Name: ____________________

Class: ____________________

UNIT 3: LANGUAGE TEST B

VOCABULARY

Task 1

Match 26–33 with A–H to make sentences.

26 Someone stole my phone!	....	**A**	It's useful.
27 I'm going to the beach today.	....	**B**	I'm starving.
28 I worked hard all day.	....	**C**	It's freezing.
29 I didn't eat anything this morning.	....	**D**	It's terrible.
30 Our classroom is very cold in winter.	....	**E**	I'm delighted.
31 Did you make this pizza?	....	**F**	I'm exhausted.
32 Yuk! I can't drink this coffee.	....	**G**	It's delicious.
33 I have a laptop that I take with me.	....	**H**	I'm furious.

[ ] 8

Task 2

Complete the sentences with a word from A and a word from B.

A

ancient dark dull huge ordinary

B

exciting light modern special tiny

34 .... Roman art is so beautiful. I think it's more interesting than the .... art people create today.

35 These rooms are .... because they have big windows, but the rest of the house is .... and not very nice.

36 Russia is the biggest country in the world – it's .... ! The smallest is Vatican City – it's ....

37 Our summer holiday wasn't .... We went to an adventure camp and every day was .... ! We never got bored.

38 You need a .... bike to cycle in races. You can't ride the .... bike you use every day.

[ ] 10

Task 3

Put the words in brackets in the correct order to complete the sentences.

39 My brother was watching a(n) .... last night. (American / film / funny)

40 I sat in a(n) .... (wooden / uncomfortable / chair)

41 My grandmother has some .... (gold / jewellery / valuable)

42 Who is your .... ? (tennis player / young / favourite)

43 Someone left a .... in the classroom. (bottle / blue / strange)

44 Santorini is a(n) .... and I want to go there. (island / incredible / Greek)

45 I think she's a(n) .... (singer / brilliant / opera)

[ ] 7

Total: [ ] 50

Name: ______________________

Class: ______________________

DICTATION

You are going to listen to a recording about reading while travelling. Listen to the whole recording once. Then you will hear the recording again with pauses for you to write down what you hear. Make sure you spell the words correctly.

....

....

....

....

....

....

....

....

....

....

....

....

	10

LISTENING

Task 1

You are going to listen to a radio interview with Molly talking about her online book club. For questions 1–6, choose the answer (A, B or C) which fits best according to what you hear.

1 Why did Molly start the online club?
A to help students with their projects
B to show book reviews by students
C to discuss books with other students

2 What else can members do at the club?
A read a blog
B get ideas about what to read
C meet some writers

3 What was surprising for Molly?
A Reading is a hobby that teenagers enjoy.
B Some people think reading is boring.
C Students improved their schoolwork.

4 Why does Molly enjoy reading?
A Reading changes her life.
B It's an activity she can do anytime.
C She sounds clever when she reads.

5 How are audio books useful?
A You only need headphones to enjoy them.
B They can improve your spelling.
C They teach you to say words properly.

6 What must new members do?
A give some information online
B get permission from their school
C pay some money to join

	18

Task 2

Are the sentences true (T) or false (F)?

7 Molly's book club began because she couldn't find anything similar online. ....

8 The book club has nearly 1,000 members, but not many people are joining it now. ....

	2

Name: ______________________

Class: ______________________

READING

Task 1

Read the blog. Choose from the sentences (A–J) the one which fits each gap (9–14). There are four extra sentences which you do not need to use.

A Everything came out, then everything went back in.

B First you show your passport and then you get on the plane.

C The eight-and-a-half-hour flight from the UK to India is the easy part!

D The look on her face changed from worry to happiness.

E Without them, we couldn't return to the UK.

F But my mum wasn't sure where to look for them.

G We don't live far from the airport in London.

H Everything was incredible for the two weeks we were there.

I So he decided to look in the suitcases again.

J It looked like he was doing a silly dance.

	18

Task 2

Read the blog again and answer the question in your own words.

15 How does the family get from the UK to the village in India?

....

	2

Total:		50

Mandy's holiday disaster!

My parents and I enjoy travelling and we usually go away once a year. My dad is English and my mum's from India, so when we visit her family it's a long trip! **(9)** .... After we land in New Delhi, the capital city, we always take a taxi to the train station. From there, we travel to a town near my grandparents' village, and finally a bus. We're exhausted when we arrive, but excited to be there too.

All of our Indian holidays have been awesome, but the first one was nearly a disaster! **(10)** .... On the last day we returned to New Delhi by bus and train. At the airport, my dad asked my mum for our passports. 'No, you've got them,' she said. He then started putting his hands in all of his pockets – jacket, shirt, jeans (front and back!). **(11)** .... I wanted to laugh, but the situation was too serious.

Next, my parents searched through our small bags and the suitcases. **(12)** .... Nothing was found. They looked at each other and there was panic in their eyes.

You don't need to show a ticket to fly – the information is in the airline's computer system, but passports aren't. **(13)** .... So where were they? On the bus, the train or in the taxi? How could we check? It seemed impossible.

At that moment, Mum's phone rang and she answered it. **(14)** .... My grandmother was calling to tell her our passports were in a plastic bag on her kitchen table! Yes, we missed our flight, but we didn't care! My uncle brought us the passports the next day and we spent more time in India!

Name: ______________________

Class: ______________________

DICTATION

You are going to listen to a recording about reading while travelling. Listen to the whole recording once. Then you will hear the recording again with pauses for you to write down what you hear. Make sure you spell the words correctly.

....

....

....

....

....

....

....

....

....

....

....

....

/10

LISTENING

Task 1

You are going to listen to a radio interview with Molly talking about her online book club. For questions 1–6, choose the answer (A, B or C) which fits best according to what you hear.

1 What was Molly looking for before she started the online club?

A a site where she could discuss a book
B someone to help her do her project
C some reviews that students had written

2 What information can club members get?

A ideas on how to read for enjoyment
B ideas for blogs
C ideas about which writers to read

3 What didn't surprise Molly?

A that reading is so popular with teenagers
B the reason why students joined the club
C that teenagers read and also do other activities

4 Why is reading good?

A It teaches you new words.
B It makes you more clever.
C It gives you a new life.

5 What can audio books help to improve?

A listening to words
B saying words
C spelling words

6 What must you do to join the club?

A say where you live
B tell your school about it first
C give some personal details

/18

Task 2

Are the sentences true (T) or false (F)?

7 The only discussions on the site are about books the members study in school. ....

8 More teenagers enjoy reading than Molly thought they did. ....

/2

Name: ______________________

Class: ______________________

READING

Task 1

Read the blog. Choose from the sentences (A–J) the one which fits each gap (9–14). There are four extra sentences which you do not need to use.

A You don't need to show a ticket to travel by plane.

B On the last day we said goodbye and left for New Delhi.

C There were clothes, shoes and souvenirs on the floor around us.

D We didn't know how to contact any of them.

E When we visit their families, it's a long trip!

F He didn't want to talk to anyone so he gave it to me.

G Maybe they were somewhere on the train.

H After we arrived, we slept for two days.

I The trains stop at a lot of stations.

J Of course, we're exhausted when we arrive.

	18

Task 2

Read the blog again and answer the question in your own words.

15 Where did they look for the passports?

....

	2

Total:		50

A holiday to remember!

My parents and I enjoy travelling and we usually go away every summer. We live in London, but my parents are from India. **(9)** .... The flight from the UK to India is nearly nine hours, but it's comfortable. After we land in the capital city – New Delhi – a taxi takes us to the train station. We travel to a town near my grandparents' village, and finally get on a bus. **(10)** .... But it's exciting to be there too.

Our holidays in India are always amazing, but the first one nearly ended badly! The two weeks we spent there were awesome. **(11)** .... At the airport, my mum asked my dad for our passports. 'I gave them to you last night,' she said. First, he looked surprised. Then he started checking all the pockets in his jacket and jeans. He checked them a second time. No, the passports weren't there.

Next, my parents looked through our small bags and then they opened our suitcases and took everything out. **(12)** .... My dad's face was red and my mum was nearly crying. This was serious!

Where could the passports be? Did we lose them on the bus from the village? **(13)** .... Or could they be in the taxi that brought us to the airport? We didn't know. But without them, it was impossible to fly.

Suddenly, Dad's phone rang. **(14)** .... My grandfather was calling to say he had found our passports in the house. We missed our flight, but we felt very lucky too! My dad's brother brought us the passports a few days later. It was great because we spent a few more days in India.

Name: ______________________

Class: ______________________

GRAMMAR

Task 1

Choose the correct answer.

1 We .... a maths test next week and I'm worried about it!
- **A** have
- **B** are having
- **C** are going to have

2 He .... for a job when school finishes.
- **A** looks
- **B** is looking
- **C** is going to look

3 The history lesson .... at nine o'clock. It's always at ten o'clock.
- **A** doesn't start
- **B** isn't starting
- **C** isn't going to start

4 They .... married next month.
- **A** get
- **B** are getting
- **C** are going to get

5 Let's go to the cinema. When .... ?
- **A** does the film start
- **B** is the film starting
- **C** is the film going to start

6 .... the dance club this year?
- **A** Do you join
- **B** Are you joining
- **C** Are you going to join

7 I .... in the race tomorrow. I hope I win!
- **A** run
- **B** am running
- **C** am going to run

8 The buses to London .... three times a day.
- **A** leave
- **B** are leaving
- **C** are going to leave

	8

Task 2

Choose the correct words to complete the sentences.

9 My parents **may** / **will** be happy when I pass all my exams.

10 Lucy **may** / **will** go out tonight, but she's not sure.

11 I know it **might not** / **won't** rain today – look at the sunny sky.

12 Don't believe everything you read on the internet – it **might** / **will** not be true.

13 I promise I **may** / **will** send you a postcard from Italy.

14 Alex **might** / **will** come with us, but he doesn't know yet.

15 Are you sure that the schools of the future **may** / **will** be online?

16 My sister isn't certain – she **may not** / **won't** go swimming later.

17 Jenny **might** / **will** win the race – she's the fastest runner.

18 Nick could help us, but he **may** / **will** be busy right now. Let's find out.

	10

Task 3

Complete the sentences with the verbs in brackets. Use the present simple, present continuous, *going to* and *will*.

19 .... (you / make) lunch when you get home later?

20 Don't worry. I'm sure everything .... (be) OK.

21 The girls .... (go) to the football match tomorrow. They have their tickets.

22 When .... (you / start) school every day?

23 Do you promise you .... (help) me with my homework?

24 They .... (have) a party on Saturday night.

25 The music festival .... (end) on Sunday night.

	7

Name: ______________________

Class: ______________________

VOCABULARY

Task 1

Choose the correct answer.

Revising for exams is stressful. There's pressure on you to do well and **(26)** .... good grades. So you sit **(27)** .... at your desk and spend hours preparing, often until quite late. But that's not the best way to study. In fact, it's probably the worst! You need to take regular breaks. That means getting **(28)** .... from your desk and doing something else. You could go outside and walk **(29)** .... your garden or do some light exercise. Ten minutes later, you'll be ready to settle **(30)** .... and start revising again. **(31)** .... it a try and you'll see that your ability to think clearly and remember important information will improve. So what are you waiting for? Jump **(32)** .... and move **(33)** .... !

26 A have	**B** take	**C** get
27 A in	**B** down	**C** around
28 A up	**B** off	**C** out
29 A down	**B** out	**C** around
30 A off	**B** down	**C** up
31 A Make	**B** Take	**C** Give
32 A up	**B** in	**C** off
33 A down	**B** around	**C** out

| | 8 |

Task 2

Match 34–41 with A–H to make sentences.

34 Jack wants to start ....
35 He needs to make ....
36 I fancy ....
37 She has to manage ....
38 The teacher will tell ....
39 He should have ....
40 Try to develop ....
41 You should take ....

A a business plan before you do anything else.
B 100 people at the company where she works.
C up his mind about what to study at university.
D a go and see what happens.
E advice from someone who already has a business.
F his own business when he is older.
G you off if you are noisy in class.
H going for a walk after my exam.

| | 8 |

Task 3

Choose the correct words to complete the sentences.

42 How can we **make** / **have** a lot of money from our business?
43 Alex wants to **open** / **start** a shop that sells sports equipment.
44 He spelt the word incorrectly, so the teacher crossed it **out** / **off**.
45 Don't be afraid to **get** / **take** a chance – you could become successful.
46 He doesn't know how to **work** / **run** a business at all!
47 I noted **down** / **out** the book she told me about and found it in the library.
48 She was running **off** / **around** all day and she's tired now.
49 If you're careful, you won't **make** / **do** any mistakes.
50 I like your idea for a new shop. It **hears** / **sounds** really good!

| | 9 |

Total: | | 50 |

Name: ____________________

Class: ____________________

GRAMMAR

Task 1

Choose the correct answer.

1 I'm sorry, but the library .... early on Saturdays.
- **A** doesn't open
- **B** isn't opening
- **C** isn't going to open

2 I hope I have time to see the art exhibition. When .... ?
- **A** does it end
- **B** is it ending
- **C** is it going to end

3 They .... on a school trip this Wednesday – that's why they're so excited.
- **A** go
- **B** are going
- **C** are going to go

4 .... Jack a present for his birthday next week?
- **A** Do you buy
- **B** Are you buying
- **C** Are you going to buy

5 She .... a famous athlete one day.
- **A** becomes
- **B** is becoming
- **C** is going to become

6 I'm so happy! I .... a new computer tomorrow!
- **A** get
- **B** am getting
- **C** am going to get

7 They're so lucky. They .... to Rome tomorrow!
- **A** fly
- **B** are flying
- **C** are going to fly

8 Hurry up! The show .... in ten minutes and I don't want to be late.
- **A** starts
- **B** is starting
- **C** is going to start

	8

Task 2

Choose the correct words to complete the sentences.

9 I **might** / **will** meet you later, but I can't promise you.

10 Students definitely **may not** / **won't** use books in twenty years because of technology.

11 It's possible that Jane **might** / **will** know the answer.

12 We promise we **may** / **will** call you when we arrive.

13 Our friends **may** / **will** go to the concert, but they don't know yet.

14 I think Chris **might** / **will** get excellent grades – he's the best student.

15 We **may not** / **won't** lose the game – I'm sure of it!

16 'Are you going to Anna's party?' 'I don't know. I **might** / **will** not.'

17 Don't worry. Ben **may** / **will** help you – he can fix anything!

18 You **may** / **will** not know this, but Tim's mum is a famous scientist!

	10

Task 3

Complete the sentences with the verbs in brackets. Use the present simple, present continuous, *going to* and *will*.

19 .... (Andy / walk) home after school today?

20 Listen to this song. I know you .... (love) it.

21 We .... (look) forward to our summer holiday!

22 Oh no! The shop is closed. When .... (it / open)?

23 I promise I .... (tidy) my room, Mum.

24 All of my friends .... (come) to my party next week.

25 The next bus .... (come) in twenty minutes.

	7

Name: ________________

Class: ________________

VOCABULARY

Task 1

Choose the correct answer.

Do you feel stressed when you revise for exams? You're not alone. Lots of students are under pressure to do well. Is this how you study? You settle **(26)** .... at your desk with your books and everything you have noted **(27)** .... in class. You spend hours trying to solve problems in maths, for example, but you **(28)** .... mistakes and lose confidence. You're studying in the wrong way! To **(29)** .... good grades, you need to take a break every hour. So stand **(30)** .... and move away from your desk. Do something totally different. Listen to music for ten minutes or throw **(31)** .... the rubbish! When you sit **(32)** .... again to study, you'll realise that you can think more clearly than you did before. Why don't you **(33)** .... it a try?

26 A down	**B** in	**C** off
27 A out	**B** around	**C** down
28 A take	**B** make	**C** have
29 A get	**B** give	**C** do
30 A around	**B** up	**C** in
31 A out	**B** down	**C** off
32 A around	**B** up	**C** down
33 A give	**B** take	**C** make

/8

Task 2

Match 34–41 with A–H to make sentences.

34 Your idea sounds ....
35 You have to develop ....
36 Remember to hand ....
37 You should cross ....
38 You can't start ....
39 You should take ....
40 It's hard to manage ....
41 I want to make ....

A a business if you don't have any money.
B in your history homework tomorrow.
C all the people in a big company.
D out all the mistakes and write it again.
E a business plan and follow it.
F a chance and not be scared.
G money and give it to people who need it.
H really good, so you should do it.

/8

Task 3

Choose the correct words to complete the sentences.

42 Do you **like** / **fancy** going to the cinema tonight?
43 When did you **make** / **take** up your mind about going to university?
44 The teacher told Danny **off** / **out** because he wasn't listening to her.
45 My parents are going to **start** / **open** a computer shop.
46 Why don't you **have** / **give** a go and see if you like working in a café?
47 I'm going to walk **off** / **around** outside for a few minutes.
48 My dad was right, but I didn't **take** / **give** his advice.
49 When we saw a mouse in the classroom, we all jumped **up** / **in**!
50 I don't think Sam **runs** / **works** his business very well.

/9

Total: /50

Name: ....

Class: ....

DICTATION

You are going to listen to a recording about making an important decision. Listen to the whole recording once. Then you will hear the recording again with pauses for you to write down what you hear. Make sure you spell the words correctly.

....

....

....

....

....

....

....

....

....

....

....

....

/ 10

LISTENING

Task 1

You are going to listen to six conversations. For questions 1–6, choose the answer (A, B or C) which fits best according to what you hear.

1 You will hear a girl telling her friend about a problem with a school project. Why is she worried?

A She has too much school work.
B She must talk to her teacher.
C She thinks she won't finish her project.

2 You will hear a boy, Tom, talking to his teacher about his homework. The teacher

A understands Tom's problem.
B is very worried about Tom's health.
C tells Tom off.

3 You will hear a brother and sister talking about cooking. How does the boy feel about cooking?

A He wants to make amazing food.
B He prefers eating to cooking
C He only cooks when he's hungry.

4 You will hear two friends preparing for an exam. What do they both agree to do?

A have a rest from work
B ask and answer questions
C write in their books

5 You will hear two friends talking about their lessons. What do they enjoy about them?

A learning more than they did last year
B bringing just a few things to class
C using computers in their lessons

6 You will hear two friends talking about a maths test. Why is the boy upset?

A The maths test was difficult.
B He didn't check his answers.
C He did badly in his test.

/ 18

Task 2

You are going to listen to the last conversation again. Answer the question in your own words.

7 How does the girl check her answers?

....

/ 2

Name: ____________________

Class: ____________________

READING

Task 1

Read the article and choose the answer (A, B, C or D) which you think fits best according to the text.

8 How did Regina experience life in Britain?
- **A** She went there with her family at age 15.
- **B** She visited a school there.
- **C** She lived like a local person.
- **D** She compared it to Brazil.

9 How did Regina feel when she was away from her family?
- **A** She was kind to the Browns.
- **B** She was a little unhappy at the start.
- **C** She didn't like the new place.
- **D** She understood her feelings.

10 When Regina first saw the Brown family
- **A** she met Charlie's sister Charlotte.
- **B** she realised Charlie and Max were twins.
- **C** she found out all their names.
- **D** she knew she was wrong about something.

11 How is Regina's school in Brazil different to her British school?
- **A** There is more space at the school in Brazil.
- **B** More students go to the British school.
- **C** The school in Britain has more buildings.
- **D** There are a lot of stairs at the school in Brazil.

12 What does Regina say about school uniforms?
- **A** She didn't know that ties were part of the uniform.
- **B** She believes it's a good idea for students wear them.
- **C** She thinks they aren't as nice as fashionable clothes.
- **D** She prefers to wear jeans when she goes to school.

13 How did Regina feel on her last day in Britain?
- **A** sad
- **B** upset
- **C** excited
- **D** surprised

	18

Task 2

Read the article again and answer the question in your own words.

14 Describe Regina's friendship with Charlie.

....

	2

Total:		50

Name: ________________

Class: ________________

Regina Flores talks about her year abroad as an exchange student

When I went to Britain last year, I was a fifteen-year-old student from Brazil who didn't know a lot about life outside of my country because I'd never been overseas before. It was time to experience a new lifestyle and culture. So, for a year, I lived with a British family and went to a local school.

The Browns were really kind and helpful. They realised that I felt a bit scared and uncertain because I was in a new place and far away from my own family. There are three children – fifteen-year-old twins Charlie and Max, and ten-year-old Holly.

When I first got the information about the family, I thought Charlie was a boy because that's a boy's name. But when we had a video call I found out 'he' is a 'she'! Her real name is Charlotte. She became my best friend. We shared her bedroom and we often talked for ages before we fell asleep.

My school in Brazil is very different to the one in Britain. In Brazil, it's big. There are a lot of students and the area the school is on is huge. The buildings are all on one level. But in Britain my classroom was on the second floor so I had to walk up and down the stairs a lot!

Also, I wore a uniform – with a tie! – for the first time in my life. It felt really strange at first because I wear jeans to school in Brazil. After a week, I realised my day began better when I didn't have to think about what to wear! And everyone is equal – I think that's what I like best about the uniform. Back in Brazil, young people like to look fashionable all the time and it makes some students feel bad because they don't have nice clothes.

On my last day at school, my classmates surprised me with a present and a card that they all wrote messages in. I cried when I said goodbye! The next day, the Browns drove me to the airport in London. I didn't cry then. Do you want to know why? Because Charlie is coming to stay with me in Brazil next month. It's her turn to live and study in another country for a year! Hooray!

Name: ____________________

Class: ____________________

DICTATION

You are going to listen to a recording about making an important decision. Listen to the whole recording once. Then you will hear the recording again with pauses for you to write down what you hear. Make sure you spell the words correctly.

....

....

....

....

....

....

....

....

....

....

....

....

/10

LISTENING

Task 1

You are going to listen to six conversations. For questions 1–6, choose the answer (A, B or C) which fits best according to what you hear.

1 You will hear a girl telling her friend about a problem with a school project. Why is she worried?

A She needs to work hard on the project.

B She's too busy to do her project.

C She has to practise for a competition.

2 You will hear a boy, Tom, talking to his teacher about his homework. The teacher

A wants to help Tom.

B is angry with Tom.

C thinks Tom isn't alright.

3 You will hear a brother and sister talking about cooking. How does the boy feel about cooking?

A Cooking is too difficult for him.

B He enjoys cooking the dishes from the TV show.

C Cooking isn't something he wants to do.

4 You will hear two friends preparing for an exam. What do they both agree to do?

A have a drink

B take a break

C test each other

5 You will hear two friends talking about their lessons. What do they enjoy about them?

A the laptops they use

B what they are learning

C the lessons are easier

6 You will hear two friends talking about a maths test. Why is the boy upset?

A He didn't pass a difficult test.

B His friend did badly in the test.

C He handed in his test without checking it.

/18

Task 2

You are going to listen to the last conversation again. Answer the question in your own words.

7 Why does the girl always check her answers?

....

/2

Name: ____________________

Class: ____________________

READING

Task 1

Read the article and choose the answer (A, B, C or D) which you think fits best according to the text.

8 How did Regina learn about life in Britain?
- **A** She learnt about the culture.
- **B** She made friends there.
- **C** She met a British family.
- **D** She lived and went to school there.

9 How did the Browns help Regina?
- **A** They became her family.
- **B** They explained why she was scared.
- **C** They understood her feelings.
- **D** They told her about the new place.

10 When Regina spoke with the Browns online
- **A** she found out something that surprised her.
- **B** she learnt there were twins in the family.
- **C** she became best friends with Charlie.
- **D** she thought Charlie and Max were girls.

11 What is true about Regina's classroom in Britain?
- **A** It was very big.
- **B** It was upstairs.
- **C** It was in a second building.
- **D** It was far to walk to.

12 What did Regina like most about her school uniform?
- **A** a tie was part of the uniform
- **B** it's more comfortable than jeans
- **C** she didn't need to choose clothes every day
- **D** all the students looked the same

13 What were Regina feelings on her last day in Britain?
- **A** She was excited.
- **B** She was surprised.
- **C** She was sad.
- **D** She was upset.

	18

Task 2

Read the article again and answer the question in your own words.

14 What does Regina say about students' clothes in Brazil?

....

	2

Total:		50

Regina Flores talks about her year abroad as an exchange student

The first time I went overseas was last year, when I was fifteen. Because I had never left my country, Brazil, I didn't know much about other places. So my parents sent me to Britain for a year, to live with a family and attend school. It was a great way to learn about a different lifestyle and culture.

The family I stayed with – the Browns – were helpful and kind. They knew I felt a little uncertain and scared because I was far away from my own family in a foreign country. The three children in the family are 15-year-old twins, Charlie and Max, and Holly who is ten.

When I first read about the family, I thought Charlie and Max were brothers because they have boys' names. But during our first video chat I found out that Charlie is a 'she', whose real name is Charlotte! We became best friends. I shared her bedroom and we spent a lot of time talking before bed.

My school I went to in Britain is very different to my school in Brazil. In Brazil, it's much bigger. There are a lot of students and the school is on a lot of land. There are more buildings, but the buildings aren't high. In Britain my classroom was on the second floor and I walked up and down the stairs a lot!

Also, I wore a school uniform for the first time in my life. It felt really strange wearing a jacket and tie at first because I wear jeans to school in Brazil. I soon realised life was easier when I didn't have to think about what to wear every day! But the thing I like best about the uniform is that everyone is equal. In Brazil, young people like to be fashionable at school, but some students don't have trendy clothes and they feel bad.

My last day at school in Britain was sad. I cried when my classmates gave me a present and a card. It was hard to say goodbye! The next day, the Browns took me to the airport, but I didn't cry because Charlie is coming to stay with me in Brazil next month. She's going to live with my family and study in my town for a year! Hooray!

Name: ....

Class: ....

GRAMMAR

Task 1

Choose the correct answer.

1 I admire Jake because he's .... student in my class.
- **A** good
- **B** better
- **C** the best

2 This jacket is .... the other one we saw.
- **A** dark
- **B** darker than
- **C** the darkest

3 These earrings .... those over there.
- **A** not as nice
- **B** aren't nice as
- **C** aren't as nice as

4 I thought the film was ....
- **A** as boring as
- **B** too boring
- **C** the most boring

5 These are .... boots of all in the shop.
- **A** the most expensive
- **B** more expensive
- **C** the more expensive

6 I don't like my hair – it isn't ....
- **A** too short
- **B** long enough
- **C** a bit short

7 Today isn't .... as cold as it was yesterday.
- **A** quite
- **B** much
- **C** a lot

8 She's .... in books than fashion.
- **A** much more interested
- **B** the most interested
- **C** much interested

	8

Task 2

Match 9–16 with A–H to make sentences.

9 He was quieter ....
10 Julie and Kate are the ....
11 My backpack is too ....
12 Grandma is the most ....
13 Louise is quite ....
14 Smartphones are much ....
15 Uncle Bob is the ....
16 My dad's wallet is a ....

A interesting person in the family.
B more expensive now.
C than the others in the room.
D funniest person I know.
E lot fatter than mine!
F shortest of the four girls.
G a bit taller than her brother.
H heavy with all my books.

	8

Task 3

Complete the sentences with the correct form of the words in brackets. Use *too* or *enough*.

17 Lily says her hair is .... (curly) and she wants to make it straight.

18 Let's stay at home today – it .... (not hot) for the beach.

19 These jeans are .... (big). They're falling off me!

20 Are you .... (talented) to be a successful fashion designer?

21 Trainers are great because they're ....(comfortable) to wear all day.

22 These clothes .... (not fashionable), so I don't want to wear them.

23 I broke my sister's glasses and now she's .... (angry) to talk to me.

24 Harry is .... (fast) to become a great runner one day.

25 I'm going to bed early tonight – I'm .... (tired) to stay up late.

	9

Name: ____________________

Class: ____________________

VOCABULARY

Task 1

Choose the correct words to complete the sentences.

26 If you want to find out about the latest fashions, **check** / **stand** out this website.

27 Why don't you **dress** / **save** up and buy that great jacket you saw?

28 I'd like to **put** / **try** on these jeans before I buy them.

29 What does the **pattern** / **slogan** on that T-shirt say? I can't read it.

30 Do you **fancy** / **like** going shopping with me tomorrow?

31 Her hair is very **fair** / **dark** – it's almost black.

32 He isn't tall or short – he's of **average** / **usual** height.

33 I'm sure I need **braces** / **glasses** – I can't see the board very well.

| | 8 |

Task 2

Complete the conversations with a word from A and a word from B.

A

how like look what who

B

curly freckles might personality probably

34 A: What's your best friend .... ?
B: She's great. She has an amazing ....

35 A: What does your brother .... like?
B: He's short with ....

36 A: .... do you look like?
B: My mum. We have the same .... hair.

37 A: .... does she like?
B: I'm not sure. She .... enjoy sport.

38 A: .... old do you think he is?
B: He's .... twelve or thirteen.

| | 10 |

Task 3

Choose the correct answer.

39 How can you .... that backpack everywhere? It's so heavy!
A carry
B fit
C have

40 I have to wash the .... off my face before I go to sleep.
A make-up
B freckles
C stripes

41 Emma is very .... for her age.
A high
B tall
C long

42 When did you start .... braces?
A trying
B carrying
C wearing

43 He never carries a .... He keeps his money in his pocket.
A wallet
B cap
C pattern

44 Are you going to dress .... for the party?
A on
B up
C out

45 A: Why isn't he watching the fashion show?
B: .... he's bored.
A Probably
B Might
C Maybe

| | 7 |

Total: | | 50 |

Name: ____________________

Class: ____________________

GRAMMAR

Task 1

Choose the correct answer.

1 This shampoo is .... of all for curly hair.
- **A** the best
- **B** good
- **C** better

2 I think going to real shops is .... shopping online.
- **A** the best
- **B** the better
- **C** better than

3 Alice .... Martha.
- **A** not as tall
- **B** isn't tall as
- **C** isn't as tall as

4 I think my hair is ....
- **A** too short
- **B** shorter than
- **C** as short as

5 She is one of .... fashion designers in the world.
- **A** the most famous
- **B** more famous
- **C** most famous

6 I don't go to that shop because the owner isn't ....
- **A** as friendly as
- **B** friendly enough
- **C** too friendly

7 I think baseball isn't .... as exciting as basketball.
- **A** more
- **B** quite
- **C** much

8 He's .... in jeans than a suit.
- **A** much more comfortable
- **B** the most comfortable
- **C** much comfortable

[ ] / 8

Task 2

Match 9–16 with A–H to make sentences.

9 I can't wear this – it's too ....
10 These are the most ....
11 Tim's hair is as ....
12 Our fans are the ....
13 Fashion is much more ....
14 My youngest cousin is quite ....
15 This is the most ....
16 Her style is more ....

A noisiest of all.
B modern than her friend's.
C beautiful dresses in the shop.
D important to teenagers than children.
E fair as his brother's.
F small for me.
G exciting match of the year.
H tall now.

[ ] / 8

Task 3

Complete the sentences with the correct form of the words in brackets. Use *too* or *enough*.

17 Is she .... (confident) to colour her hair green?

18 The clothes in this shop are .... (cheap) for teenagers to buy.

19 I can't drive a car yet because I'm .... (young)!

20 We can't sleep because the music from the party next door is .... (loud).

21 My homework .... (not good) and I have to do it all again!

22 These accessories are .... (old) – I need new ones.

23 I wear size thirty-nine shoes and these are size thirty-seven – they .... (not big).

24 We can't sleep. We're .... (excited) because we're going on holiday tomorrow.

25 Can you get that book on the top shelf? Are you .... (tall)?

[ ] / 9

Name: ____________________

Class: ____________________

VOCABULARY

Task 1

Choose the correct words to complete the sentences.

26 We're going to a party tonight so we're going to **dress** / **save** up.

27 She wears small sizes because she's very **long** / **slim**.

28 If you want to **check** / **stand** out, wear bright colours.

29 Don't sit in the sun for too long or you'll get **freckles** / **stripes**.

30 Excuse me. Where can I **put** / **try** on these dresses, please?

31 My dentist says I need **braces** / **glasses** to make my teeth straight.

32 I like wearing **make-up** / **accessories**, but I don't like washing it off!

33 Those circles make an interesting **pattern** / **slogan** on your scarf.

[ ] 8

Task 2

Complete the conversations with a word from A and a word from B.

A

how like look what who

B

average friendly maybe probably tall

34 A: .... does he look like?
B: His dad? They're both very ....

35 A: What's Lucas .... ?
B: He's really ....

36 A: What does your sister .... like?
B: She's of .... height.

37 A: .... old do you think that girl is?
B: .... she's fourteen.

38 A: .... does she like?
B: She wears nice clothes, so she .... likes fashion.

[ ] 10

Task 3

Choose the correct answer.

39 What do you think of these earrings? Do they .... me?
A go
B match
C suit

40 Do you .... going to the fashion show tonight?
A like
B enjoy
C fancy

41 He carries all his books in a big red ....
A wallet
B baseball cap
C backpack

42 I always .... my glasses when I watch TV.
A have
B wear
C carry

43 Anna is always nice to people – she has a lovely ....
A personality
B appearance
C style

44 Are you going to save .... for the smartphone you like?
A on
B up
C out

45 Nick .... be at home. Let's call him.
A might
B maybe
C probably

[ ] 7

Total: [ ] 50

Name: ....

Class: ....

DICTATION

You are going to listen to a recording about online shopping. Listen to the whole recording once. Then you will hear the recording again with pauses for you to write down what you hear. Make sure you spell the words correctly.

....

....

....

....

....

....

....

....

....

....

....

....

/10

LISTENING

Task 1

You are going to listen to some information about a model agency. Complete the notes. Write the correct answer in each gap.

Kidz Model Agency

The agency opened in **(1)** ....

A parent should **(2)** .... an online form.

The agency wants to know about your **(3)** .... and your interests.

You can't **(4)** .... if your parents don't give their permission.

The youngest actors at the agency are **(5)** .... years old.

In addition to money, child actors can get **(6)** .... like clothes, games and toys.

/18

Task 2

Are the sentences true (T) or false (F)?

7 You don't have to pay anything to join the agency. ....

8 Parents take all of the money that actors get for a job. ....

/2

Name: ______________________

Class: ______________________

READING

Task 1

Read the article. Decide which shop or online store (A–H) would be the most suitable for the young people (9–14).

9 ....

Luke is going on a relaxing island holiday with his family. He'll be at the beach every day. He's grown a lot in the last year and his clothes don't fit him. He doesn't want to spend too much because he's still growing.

10 ....

Sam loves designer fashions, but they're expensive. She has saved up money to buy something that she'll have for a long time, so she needs to choose well. It can be a piece of clothing or an accessory. She prefers plain colours and simple styles.

11 ....

Andy doesn't know what suits him, so his sister usually goes shopping with him. She's away at university now, and he needs help. His favourite band is playing in a few days and he needs something cool to wear to the concert.

12 ....

Holly has never been camping, but she's going on a school camping trip in two weeks. She needs warm, comfortable clothes and good boots that will keep her dry in wet weather. She doesn't want to spend too much because she doesn't think she'll go camping again.

13 ....

Jake is starting a part-time job at a computer shop in a few days and he wants to make a good impression. The assistants at the shop are not allowed to wear casual clothes. They don't have to wear a suit, but they should look neat and professional.

14 ....

Claire is sporty and always wears casual clothes, so she doesn't have anything suitable for her cousin's twenty-first birthday party. She'd like to find a pretty dress and accessories that she can wear for a few years. Because she's studying, she hasn't got time to go to the shops.

	18

Task 2

Read the article again and answer the question in your own words.

15 Why is it a good idea to buy quality items?

....

....

	2

Total:		50

Fashion blogger Milly Jones reviews the best places for teens to shop.

A Get the Look

When it's time to wear your best, there's no better site. Shop for dresses, bags, shoes and jewellery. Buy one or two items, or a whole look – there are great suggestions on the site. If you change your mind about something after you receive it, you can return or exchange it quite easily. Use the special bag that is included with your order and send it back within 30 days.

B Fine Fashions

There are no hoodies or trainers here! When you want to look nice, but it's not a formal event, try this site. Maybe you have a job interview or are going out for dinner with your family. For guys, there are shirts and trousers. Girls can find lovely skirts, tops and summer dresses. These are good quality clothes that you will wear again and again. Just download the app and start shopping.

C Explorer

At Explorer you'll find everything you need to enjoy life outdoors. There are jackets to protect you from wind and rain, as well as casual, running, hiking and walking shoes and boots. The winter sale is on now with 50% off many of their popular items. Use code EXPLORELIFE for another 10% off when you pay. For this week only, there is free delivery on all orders they receive.

D Wear It Once

Most of us can't afford to buy designer clothes, but that doesn't mean we can't wear the best. At Wear It Once, you can rent clothes, bags and shoes for a low price. It's certainly cheaper than buying them! Wear them to a special event and then take them back in good condition the next day. It's so easy! They're open seven days a week, with shops in cities across the country.

E Here and Now

If you want to look good for less money, try this shop. They've got great casual clothes for teens and young people – T-shirts, jeans, shorts, shoes, boots and trainers. There are always great deals. This month, you can get ready for summer – buy three T-shirts and get a fourth for free! You'll look great and feel comfortable too. The shops are open Monday to Saturday. More details are available online.

F Top Store

When you have to look your best, this is a great shop. They have the latest suits, shirts, ties and leather shoes by the most famous designers. For work or special events, you'll find everything you need. They offer excellent service too. If you're too busy to visit the shop, they'll come to you. Good quality costs more, but it's a small price to pay when you want to look and feel confident.

G Forever Style

Forget about fashion. Focus on style – it makes you stand out and feel special. Is it better to buy lots of cheap items in the season's patterns and colours that you'll wear a few times, or one amazing, high quality piece that you will enjoy forever? At Forever Style, you'll pay a bit more, but that's smart shopping. It's easy to find something you can afford – just choose how much you want to pay, and the app will do the rest.

H Teen Trends

This is one of the biggest online stores for teen fashions and there are loads of great bargains. If you're not sure what to wear, let them help you. Just tell them your size, height and what you're looking for. They'll put together a great collection of cool casual clothes for you to choose from. If you're in a hurry, don't worry! They offer next-day delivery to most areas.

Name: ______________________

Class: ______________________

DICTATION

You are going to listen to a recording about online shopping. Listen to the whole recording once. Then you will hear the recording again with pauses for you to write down what you hear. Make sure you spell the words correctly.

....

....

....

....

....

....

....

....

....

....

....

....

/10

LISTENING

Task 1

You are going to listen to some information about a model agency. Complete the notes. Write the correct answer in each gap.

Kidz Model Agency

The agency received an award in **(1)** ....

One of your parents can go **(2)** .... and fill in a form.

They will ask you about the things you are **(3)** .... doing.

During the **(4)** .... of an advertisement, one of your parents must be there.

The oldest actors at the agency are **(5)** .... years old.

Free gifts for young actors include the **(6)** .... , games and toys.

/18

Task 2

Are the sentences true (T) or false (F)?

7 The agency will definitely find you a job. ....

8 The agency gives most of the money to your parents. ....

/2

Name: ....

Class: ....

READING

Task 1

Read the article. Decide which shop or online store (A–H) would be the most suitable for the young people (9–14).

9 ....

Tom doesn't know what suits him, so his sister usually goes shopping with him. She's away at university now, and he needs help. His favourite band is playing in a few days and he needs something cool to wear to the concert.

10 ....

Alice is sporty and always wears casual clothes, so she doesn't have anything suitable for her cousin's twenty-first birthday party. She'd like to find a pretty dress and accessories that she can wear for a few years. Because she's studying, she hasn't got time to go to the shops.

11 ....

Ben is starting a part-time job at a computer shop in a few days and he wants to make a good impression. The assistants at the shop are not allowed to wear casual clothes. They don't have to wear a suit, but they should look neat and professional.

12 ....

Lucy loves designer fashions, but they're expensive. She has saved up money to buy something that she'll have for a long time, so she needs to choose well. It can be a piece of clothing or an accessory. She prefers plain colours and simple styles.

13 ....

Max is going on a relaxing island holiday with his family. He'll be at the beach every day. He's grown a lot in the last year and his clothes don't fit him. He doesn't want to spend too much because he's still growing.

14 ....

Annie has never been camping, but she's going on a school camping trip in two weeks. She needs warm, comfortable clothes and good boots that will keep her dry in wet weather. She doesn't want to spend too much because she doesn't think she'll go camping again.

	18

Task 2

Read the article again and answer the question in your own words.

15 Why is it better to buy one good item than lots of cheap ones?

....

....

	2

Total:		50

Fashion blogger Milly Jones reviews the best places for teens to shop.

A Shop Top

When you have to look your best, this is a great shop. They have the latest suits, shirts, ties and leather shoes by the most famous designers. For work or special events, you'll find everything you need. They offer excellent service too. If you're too busy to visit the shop, they'll come to you. Good quality costs more, but it's a small price to pay when you want to look and feel confident.

B Stylista

Forget about fashion. Focus on style – it makes you stand out and feel special. Is it better to buy lots of cheap items in the season's patterns and colours that you'll wear a few times, or one amazing, high quality piece that you will enjoy forever? At Stylista, you'll pay a bit more, but that's smart shopping. It's easy to find something you can afford – just choose how much you want to pay, and the app will do the rest.

C Good Looking

When it's time to wear your best, there's no better site. Shop for dresses, bags, shoes and jewellery. Buy one or two items, or a whole look – there are great suggestions on the site. If you change your mind about something after you receive it, you can return or exchange it quite easily. Use the special bag that is included with your order and send it back within 30 days.

D Cool Teen

This is one of the biggest online stores for teen fashions and there are loads of great bargains. If you're not sure what to wear, let them help you. Just tell them your size, height and what you're looking for. They'll put together a great collection of cool casual clothes for you to choose from. If you're in a hurry, don't worry! They offer next-day delivery to most areas.

E Adventurer

At Adventurer you'll find everything you need to enjoy life outdoors. There are jackets to protect you from wind and rain, as well as casual, running, hiking and walking shoes and boots. The winter sale is on now with 50% off many of their popular items. Use code ADVENTURENOW for another 10% off when you pay. For this week only, there is free delivery on all orders they receive.

F Fashion Forward

There are no hoodies or trainers here! When you want to look nice, but it's not a formal event, try this site. Maybe you have a job interview or are going out for dinner with your family. For guys, there are shirts and trousers. Girls can find lovely skirts, tops and summer dresses. These are good quality clothes that you will wear again and again. Just download the app and start shopping.

G Yours for a Day

Most of us can't afford to buy designer clothes, but that doesn't mean we can't wear the best. At Yours for a Day, you can rent clothes, bags and shoes for a low price. It's certainly cheaper than buying them! Wear them to a special event and then take them back in good condition the next day. It's so easy! They're open seven days a week, with shops in cities across the country.

H Best for Less

If you want to look good for less money, try this shop. They've got great casual clothes for teens and young people – T-shirts, jeans, shorts, shoes, boots and trainers. There are always great deals. This month, you can get ready for summer – buy three T-shirts and get a fourth for free! You'll look great and feel comfortable too. The shops are open Monday to Saturday. More details are available online.

Name: ....

Class: ....

GRAMMAR

Task 1

Choose the correct answer.

1 It's OK, he .... call me now – he can send me a text message later.
A can't
B mustn't
C doesn't have to

2 You .... go out with your friends, but don't come home late.
A can
B must
C have to

3 Mum says we .... go swimming today, so we'll go tomorrow.
A can't
B mustn't
C don't have to

4 You .... remember your passports when you go to the airport.
A can
B must
C have

5 .... warm and sunny today. Let's go to the park.
A It's
B It has
C There's

6 We can't play tennis now. .... some people on the tennis court.
A They are
B There are
C There have

7 Look! .... a dolphin in the water!
A It's
B It has
C There's

8 When you go hiking in the mountains, you .... leave the path because there are bears.
A can't
B mustn't
C don't have to

[ ] 8

Task 2

Complete the conversations with the correct reflexive pronoun.

9 A: Look! We painted the boat!
B: That's great! Did you really do it .... ?

10 A: That's a big box, Dan. Do you need some help?
B: No, thanks. I can carry it ....

11 A: Here's a photo from my holiday.
B: That fish is really big! Did you catch it .... ?

12 A: Are you going to pack your suitcase?
B: Of course. It isn't going to pack .... !

13 A: Is Kelly singing?
B: No, I think she's talking to ....

14 A: Let's help them with their tent.
B: I'm sure they can put it up ....

15 A: What happened to Jim?
B: He fell and hurt .... in the forest.

16 A: Did someone show you where the camp was?
B: No, we found it ....

[ ] 8

Task 3

Complete the sentences with one or two words. Use modal verbs for rules, reflexive pronouns and *it's*, *there is* and *there are*.

17 Elena .... bring a signed form from her parents before she goes on the trip.

18 .... a lot of people at the zoo today because it's Sunday.

19 We can fill in the forms to join the club .... We don't have to ask our parents.

20 You .... be late or you will miss the bus again.

21 I really enjoy hiking. I think .... a lot of fun.

22 Yesterday, I cleaned the house by .... and everyone was surprised when they got home.

23 .... a big park in the middle of New York – it's called Central Park.

24 We .... go to the adventure camp. Mum says it's OK.

25 Anna is staying at home today – she doesn't .... go to work.

[ ] 9

Name: ______________________

Class: ______________________

UNIT 6: LANGUAGE TEST A

VOCABULARY

Task 1

The letters of the words in bold are mixed up. Write them correctly.

26 Kangaroos can kick hard because they have **rewulpof** legs. ....

27 The water here is so **ecral** that I can see the sand and some small fish at the bottom. ....

28 Our cat is **dibln**, but she knows every part of the garden and she always finds her favourite places. ....

29 In winter, these beaches are **pymet** because it's too cold to swim, but in summer they're full of tourists. ....

30 My pet parrot is very **eclrev** – he can talk and he repeats everything I say to him. ....

31 In spring, the red, pink and yellow roses make the garden very **lucuorfol**. ....

32 It was late and I was asleep when a **dulo** noise woke me up. ....

33 Be careful with that **rasph** knife while you're cutting the vegetables. ....

	8

Task 2

Match 34–41 with A–H to make sentences.

34 It's amazing how some animals can land

35 Nigel's ball was in the tree, so he climbed

36 The monkeys were so funny as they jumped

37 Wild animals in nature have to hunt

38 The stars shining in the sky at night look

39 It's a lovely day and the sun feels

40 Big cities like London and New York seem

41 The man stood on the rock and then dived

A into the water. ....

B from tree to tree. ....

C warm on my face. ....

D on their feet. ....

E for food. ....

F very noisy. ....

G up very carefully. ....

H beautiful. ....

	8

Task 3

Choose the correct answer.

42 Farmers worry about .... because they try to eat their chickens.

A dolphins
B insects
C foxes

43 Kittens are so cute! They have sweet faces and soft ....

A feathers
B fur
C wings

44 **A:** Let's go camping next week.
B: That .... great!

A sounds
B feels
C looks

45 Don't go near the water! There are crocodiles and they could .... you!

A dive
B bite
C climb

46 The window was open and a very pretty purple .... flew into my room.

A penguin
B monkey
C butterfly

47 .... like to eat fruit. They sit in my cherry tree and eat all the cherries!

A Bats
B Wolves
C Bees

48 It's so .... in the countryside, far away from the noise of the city.

A cool
B bright
C peaceful

49 Dolphins look .... because they always seem to be smiling.

A wild
B friendly
C huge

50 I always feel happy when there aren't any clouds and the sun is ....

A bright
B silent
C calm

	9

Total:		50

Name: ____________________

Class: ____________________

GRAMMAR

Task 1

Choose the correct answer.

1 .... have some more cake, please?
A Do we have to
B Must we
C Can we

2 Alex .... come with us if he doesn't want to.
A doesn't have to
B mustn't
C can't

3 In Australia, you .... drive on the left side of the road.
A can
B must
C has to

4 Adam .... to do a maths test tomorrow.
A can
B has
C must

5 You .... talk in the library because people are trying to study.
A mustn't
B can't
C don't have to

6 .... a lake in the middle of the forest.
A It's
B There's
C There are

7 I love going to the countryside because .... so quiet there.
A there is
B it has
C it's

8 .... a lot of animals on my uncle's farm.
A There are
B There is
C It is

	8

Task 2

Complete the conversations with the correct reflexive pronoun.

9 A: When did Nelly have horse-riding lessons?
B: She didn't. She taught ....

10 A: I didn't know that you had so many roses in your garden.
B: Well, we planted them .... last year.

11 A: What did your brothers do in the holidays?
B: They went hiking by ....

12 A: Do you like our roof garden?
B: It's amazing. Did you do it all by .... ?

13 A: When is Nick going camping?
B: Why don't you ask him .... ?

14 A: I like your tree house, Fred!
B: Thanks, I built it by ....

15 A: This poor little bird fell out of the tree.
B: Oh, I hope it didn't hurt ....

16 A: Who put up the tent?
B: James did. He put it up ....

	8

Task 3

Complete the sentences with one or two words. Use modal verbs for rules, reflexive pronouns and *it's*, *there is* and *there are*.

17 .... cloudy. I think a storm is coming.

18 You .... go there at night – it's dangerous.

19 Oh, no! I think .... a bee in the house.

20 Leo doesn't .... get a new phone – he found the one he lost.

21 Tony .... be at school at nine o'clock.

22 My sister Julia prefers to go jogging by ....

23 .... too many people at the beach today – we have nowhere to sit.

24 The girls want to plan the holiday ....

25 .... I go to a summer camp this year, Dad?

	9

Name: ______________________

Class: ______________________

VOCABULARY

Task 1

The letters of the words in bold are mixed up. Write them correctly.

26 The dogs that help farmers to look after their sheep are very **verlec**. They understand their job and they do it well. ....

27 Wolves are wild dogs and they have very **phars** teeth that can hurt you badly. ....

28 Gorillas are strong and they have very **eowrflup** arms. ....

29 It was a cold rainy night and the streets were **tempy** – no one wanted to be outside in such bad weather. ....

30 The sky was **lacer** last night – there were no clouds and we could see all the stars. ....

31 Lions are very **lodu** – you can hear them from very far away when they roar. ....

32 My sister likes to draw **lofulcour** pictures of red and yellow flowers and green trees. ....

33 People who are **inbdl** have special dogs that can see for them and take them where they have to go. ....

	8

Task 2

Match 34–41 with A–H to make sentences.

34 Pets are lucky because they don't have to hunt
35 I'm not going to swim – the water feels
36 The dog chased the cat and it climbed
37 These birds catch fish by diving
38 We watched the frog as it jumped
39 That cat fell out of the tree, but it landed
40 The flowers in my grandmother's garden look
41 I'd like to try bungee jumping – it seems

A from rock to rock in the lake. ....
B very exciting. ....
C up a tree very quickly. ....
D on its feet. ....
E for their food. ....
F into the sea. ....
G very pretty. ....
H cold. ....

	8

Task 3

Choose the correct answer.

42 The people travelling on the ferry boat were pleasantly surprised to see .... in the sea.
A foxes
B dolphins
C lions

43 Birds have to move their .... up and down very quickly to fly.
A wings
B feathers
C fur

44 **A:** Why don't we go fishing?
B: Yes, that .... good.
A looks
B sounds
C feels

45 In the rainforest, there are dangerous snakes that can .... you!
A bite
B hunt
C jump

46 Although .... are birds, they can't fly, but they swim very well.
A butterflies
B penguins
C monkeys

47 .... are very important because they produce honey.
A Wolves
B Bats
C Bees

48 The sun is so hot! Let's sit under a tree – it'll be .... there.
A peaceful
B cool
C bright

49 Elephants are .... Did you know some weigh more than 5,000 kilograms?
A huge
B wild
C friendly

50 It was .... in the forest – we didn't hear any animals.
A social
B bright
C silent

	9

Total:		50

Name: ____________________

Class: ____________________

DICTATION

You are going to listen to a recording about cities. Listen to the whole recording once. Then you will hear the recording again with pauses for you to write down what you hear. Make sure you spell the words correctly.

....

....

....

	10

LISTENING

Task 1

You are going to listen to six conversations. For questions 1–6, choose the answer (A, B or C) which fits best according to what you hear.

1 What was the weather like last weekend?

A

B

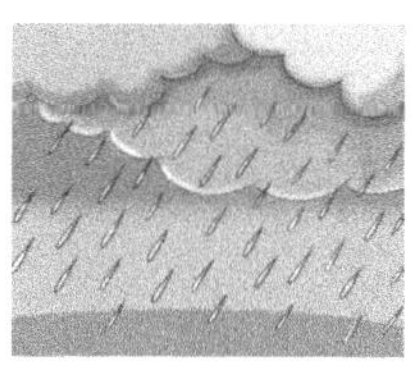
C

2 Where will they camp?

A

B

C

3 When will they arrive in the countryside?

A

B

C

4 Where does the girl go swimming?

A

B

C

5 What does the girl enjoy doing the most?

A

B

C

6 What did the boy forget to take with him on his trip?

A

B

C

	18

Task 2

Are the sentences true (T) or false (F)?

7 The boy's mum told him where his bottle was. ....

8 Apples are the girl's favourite snack. ....

	2

Name: ____________________

Class: ____________________

READING

Task 1

Read the article and choose the answer (A, B, C or D) which you think fits best according to the text.

9 People who live in cities like to spend time in
- **A** traffic.
- **B** green spaces only.
- **C** parks or squares.
- **D** parks far from the city.

10 What is the purpose of a square?
- **A** to replace a park
- **B** to bring people together
- **C** to have shops and cafés
- **D** to be a quiet place for people to relax

11 How did Julia feel about Xinghai Square?
- **A** She didn't believe it was really that big.
- **B** She thought it was a good place to play football.
- **C** She admired the tall buildings.
- **D** She enjoyed exploring it on foot.

12 What could people do at both the ancient Agora and the Forum?
- **A** go shopping
- **B** talk about politics
- **C** watch a play
- **D** see tourists

13 In the UK, the village green
- **A** is a small square.
- **B** has a long history.
- **C** is where animals still feed.
- **D** can only be used by locals.

14 What is the writer doing in the final paragraph?
- **A** telling people where they can meet locals
- **B** describing how people lived in the past
- **C** explaining which events are celebrated in the UK
- **D** recommending a place for visitors to see

	18

Task 2

Read the article again and answer the question in your own words.

15 What can visitors to Xinghai Square see and do there?

....

	2

Total:		50

In the heart of the city

Julia Bland, an architecture student, talks about public squares.

Big cities are busy, crowded and full of traffic. City people like to go to parks. Even though they're still in the city, it feels like they're far away from the traffic and chaos. But there are also public squares where they can relax. Squares aren't green spaces. In fact, they're the opposite because they're usually surrounded by shops and cafés. However, they're very important because they're social spaces. People go there to meet their friends, have a coffee or a meal, maybe to shop at an open market or see a concert.

A few years ago, I visited China and while I was there I went to Xinghai Square in the city of Dalian. I couldn't believe the size of the square – it's 1,760,000 square metres, which is about the size of 243 Wembley football fields! In fact, it's the largest square in the world. Most people in Dalian live in tall buildings and they really need a place where they can be outside and enjoy themselves. The square is by the sea and there are amusement parks, shopping malls and museums. It took me hours to walk all the way along it, but it was a cool experience!

Public spaces have been around for thousands of years. The ancient Greeks called theirs the 'Agora'. It was an open area in the most central part of the city where people bought food, did business and discussed politics. The Romans called their public space the 'Forum' and it had shops, markets and theatres. The ancient sites in Athens and Rome still exist, though, these days, they're full of tourists, not shoppers and shopkeepers! But if you go there, you can get an idea of how the ancients lived.

Even villages have a public area where the local people can meet. It might be a small square or an actual grassy area that is known as the 'village green' in the UK. Hundreds of years ago, people took their animals to eat the grass on the green. It was also used to celebrate important events such as May Day – in many places, it still is. If you're ever in the UK, don't miss the opportunity to visit one of these beautiful little villages. You'll be really glad you did!

Name: ______________________

Class: ______________________

UNIT 6: SKILLS TEST B

DICTATION

You are going to listen to a recording about cities. Listen to the whole recording once. Then you will hear the recording again with pauses for you to write down what you hear. Make sure you spell the words correctly.

....

....

....

	10

LISTENING

Task 1

You are going to listen to six conversations. For questions 1–6, choose the answer (A, B or C) which fits best according to what you hear.

1 What will the weather be like on Saturday?

A

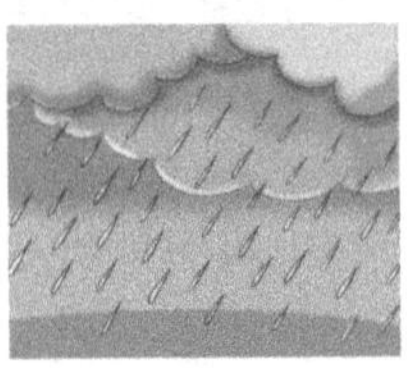
B

C

2 Where are the boys going to camp?

A

B

C

3 When will they catch the bus?

A

B

C

4 Where will the girl not swim?

A

B

C

5 Which activity does the girl like best?

A

B

C

6 What was the boy looking for?

A

B

C

	18

Task 2

Are the sentences true (T) or false (F)?

7 The boy called his mum from the village. ....

8 The girl believes she is a very good painter. ....

	2

Name: ____________________

Class: ____________________

READING

Task 1

Read the article and choose the answer (A, B, C or D) which you think fits best according to the text.

9 Where can people who live in cities relax?

A in parks far from the city
B in parks or squares
C in green spaces only
D in traffic

10 Why are public squares important?

A They bring people together.
B They are a quiet place for people to relax.
C They can replace parks.
D They have shops and cafés.

11 How did Julia feel about Xinghai Square?

A She was happy that people had somewhere to go.
B She didn't believe it was the biggest in the world.
C She had a good time exploring the place.
D She thought it took too long to see it all.

12 What can people do now at both the ancient Agora and the Forum?

A watch a play
B learn about the past
C talk about politics
D go shopping

13 The village greens in the UK

A have been a part of life for many years.
B are squares with grass in the centre.
C are only used for important events.
D are full of animals.

14 What is the writer doing in the final paragraph?

A telling us where some villages are
B giving details about important celebrations
C encouraging visitors to see a place
D explaining how locals lived in the past

	18

Task 2

Read the article again and answer the question in your own words.

15 What can city people do in a square?

....

	2

Total:		50

Name: ______________________

Class: ______________________

In the heart of the city

Julia Bland, an architecture student, talks about public squares.

Big cities are busy, crowded and full of traffic. City people like to go to parks. Even though they're still in the city, it feels like they're far away from the traffic and chaos. But there are also public squares where they can relax. Squares aren't green spaces. In fact, they're the opposite because they're usually surrounded by shops and cafés. However, they're very important because they're social spaces. People go there to meet their friends, have a coffee or a meal, maybe to shop at an open market or see a concert.

A few years ago, I visited China and while I was there I went to Xinghai Square in the city of Dalian. I couldn't believe the size of the square – it's 1,760,000 square metres, which is about the size of 243 Wembley football fields! In fact, it's the largest square in the world. Most people in Dalian live in tall buildings and they really need a place where they can be outside and enjoy themselves. The square is by the sea and there are amusement parks, shopping malls and museums. It took me hours to walk all the way along it, but it was a cool experience!

Public spaces have been around for thousands of years. The ancient Greeks called theirs the 'Agora'. It was an open area in the most central part of the city where people bought food, did business and discussed politics. The Romans called their public space the 'Forum' and it had shops, markets and theatres. The ancient sites in Athens and Rome still exist, though, these days, they're full of tourists, not shoppers and shopkeepers! But if you go there, you can get an idea of how the ancients lived.

Even villages have a public area where the local people can meet. It might be a small square or an actual grassy area that is known as the 'village green' in the UK. Hundreds of years ago, people took their animals to eat the grass on the green. It was also used to celebrate important events such as May Day – in many places, it still is. If you're ever in the UK, don't miss the opportunity to visit one of these beautiful little villages. You'll be really glad you did!

Name: ____________________

Class: ____________________

GRAMMAR

Task 1

Choose the correct words to complete the sentences.

1 He's the chef **who** / **which** is on the TV cooking show.
2 The thing **who** / **which** I like most about this café is the free Wi-Fi!
3 Cooking is something **who** / **which** I really enjoy doing.
4 Penny is the girl with red hair **who** / **which** is sitting in the corner.
5 A difficult dish **who** / **which** I know how to make is paella.
6 If you want to learn how to cook, the person **who** / **which** can teach you is Grandma.
7 Chris is a friend of mine **who** / **which** is training to become a chef.
8 This is the cookbook **who** / **which** I bought last week.
9 Are you someone **who** / **which** loves fast food or do you prefer healthy food?
10 Here are some easy recipes **who** / **which** you can cook at home.

	10

Task 2

Complete the text with *who* or *which*.

The history of pasta

Pasta is one of the most popular foods **(11)** .... you can eat. You can find it in any supermarket and it's cheap. There are a lot of people **(12)** .... make fresh pasta at home, too. The ingredients **(13)** .... you need are flour, salt and eggs or water.

Nearly every country has its own kind of pasta. In Italy, some of the different kinds of pasta **(14)** .... they have are spaghetti, lasagne and fettucine. In Germany and Hungary they cook spaetzle. In Poland, they eat pierogi **(15)** .... are very similar to Italian ravioli.

Many people believe that it was the Chinese **(16)** .... invented the first kind of pasta. Marco Polo was the Italian explorer **(17)** .... brought the idea of pasta to Europe, from China, in the 13th century.

During the 1800s and 1900s, many Italians went to America, Canada and Australia to start a new life. They were the ones **(18)** .... made pasta a common food in those countries and around the world.

	8

Task 3

Complete the sentences with the correct form of the words in bold.

19 Be **careful**! You need to mix the flour and the water very ....
20 Pizza is so **easy** to make. Anyone can make it quite .... at home.
21 Gordon Ramsay is a very **good** chef. He's famous because he cooks very ....
22 Owning a restaurant is **hard**. You have to work .... and be there every day.
23 The waiters here are **quick**. After you order your meal, they bring it to you ....
24 Why is the chef so **rude**? I can hear him speaking .... to the kitchen workers.
25 She makes **beautiful** cakes and she decorates them ....

	7

Name: ____________________

Class: ____________________

UNIT 7: LANGUAGE TEST A

VOCABULARY

Task 1

Choose the correct words to complete the sentences.

26 Chips are **crispy** / **burned** – you make a lot of noise when you eat them!
27 I always make a mess when I eat oranges because they're so **raw** / **juicy**.
28 The old man hasn't got many teeth so he can only eat **soft** / **hard** foods.
29 The chef cooked the meat for too long and it was **fried** / **dry**.
30 My grandma doesn't like **sweet** / **roast** tea, so she doesn't put any sugar in it.
31 I don't eat **hard** / **salty** food very often because it isn't good for my health.
32 This pizza is really **cooked** / **tasty**. Can I have another slice, please?
33 I don't know anyone who eats lemons – they're too **sour** / **spicy**!

	8

Task 2

Complete the sentences with these words. There are four extra words that you do not need to use.

butter curry jam lemons marshmallow paella pasta popcorn sushi toast tortillas yoghurt

34 We went to a traditional Spanish restaurant for dinner and we ate ....
35 That Mexican restaurant makes the best .... in town.
36 I have a great recipe for an Indian .... dish that I found online.
37 Instead of ice cream, why don't we have some healthy .... with fruit?
38 The pizzas and .... at that restaurant are made using traditional Italian recipes.
39 Let's go to a Japanese restaurant and have some .... for lunch.
40 Have we got any bread? I want to make some .... for breakfast.
41 We always get a big bucket of .... when we go to the cinema and we eat it while we watch the film.

	8

Task 3

Complete the words in the conversations.

42 A: Is Liz is **v** _ _ _ _ _ _ _ _ _?
B: Yes, she is. She doesn't eat meat, **f** _ _ _ or **c** _ _ _ _ _ _.
43 A: I love this fast food restaurant. The **b** _ _ _ _ _ _ are really tasty.
B: The **f** _ _ _ _ are my favourite. I always get the large size!
44 A: That French restaurant is very **e** _ _ _ _ _ _ _ _.
B: I know. A meal there costs a **f** _ _ _ _ _ _.
45 A: Where can we eat that's cheap? I'm a bit **s** _ _ _ _ of money this week.
B: There's a **p** _ _ _ _ _ _ _ _ at the local pizza restaurant – buy one pizza and get a second for half price.

	9

Total:		50

Name: ______________________

Class: ______________________

GRAMMAR

Task 1

Choose the correct words to complete the sentences.

1 This is the cooking show **who** / **which** I watch every week.
2 At the cooking school, the teacher **who** / **which** is the best is Mrs Jones.
3 The waiter **who** / **which** brought us our food was very friendly.
4 This is usually a good restaurant, but the dish **who** / **which** I had today was awful.
5 Is that the boy from your class **who** / **which** works at a fast food restaurant?
6 I like to feed the animals **who** / **which** my uncle has on his farm.
7 Mozzarella is the cheese **who** / **which** you put on a pizza.
8 Do you know anyone **who** / **which** has eaten snails?
9 This isn't the café **who** / **which** makes the best sandwiches in town.
10 I know someone **who** / **which** writes reviews about restaurants.

	10

Task 2

Complete the text with *who* or *which*.

The history of pasta

People **(11)** .... love Italian food eat a lot of pasta! It's a food **(12)** .... doesn't cost a lot to buy and you can get it at any shop or supermarket. Anyone **(13)** .... has made pasta at home says it's very easy. Flour, salt and eggs or water are the only things **(14)** .... you need. This freshly made pasta only takes a few minutes to cook.

Most countries have their own type of pasta. The kinds **(15)** .... are popular in Italy include spaghetti, lasagna and fettucine. In Hungary and Germany they call theirs spaetzle. In Poland, it's called pierogi, and is very similar to Italian ravioli.

It was the Chinese **(16)** .... invented the first kind of pasta, many hundreds of years ago. In the West we call Chinese pasta 'noodles'. Many people believe it was the Italian explorer Marco Polo **(17)** .... introduced pasta to Europe in the 13th century, after visiting China.

Much later, in the 19th and 20th centuries, Italians went to America, Canada and Australia to begin new lives. It was their arrival in these countries **(18)** .... made pasta popular around the world.

	8

Task 3

Complete the sentences with the correct form of the words in bold.

19 The waiters here are **slow**. They always work ....
20 I'm always **polite** to the customers. I speak to them ....
21 The chairs in this café are so **comfortable**. Are you sitting .... ?
22 Why are you so **noisy** in the kitchen? You always cook .... !
23 He's not a **fast** walker, but he has to walk .... today or he'll be late for work.
24 Be **careful** with the glasses! Wash them .... so that you don't break them.
25 My aunt is a **good** cook. She cooks .... and we always look forward to eating at her house.

	7

Name: ____________________

Class: ____________________

UNIT 7: LANGUAGE TEST B

VOCABULARY

Task 1

Choose the correct words to complete the sentences.

26 This meat isn't **cooked** /**raw**. It's still red inside.
27 You can't eat bread that's more than a few days old – it's too **sour** / **hard**.
28 The dish was so **spicy** / **sweet** that my face turned red and I needed to drink a lot of water!
29 I'm sorry! I forgot the cake in the oven and it's **salty** / **burned**!
30 You can put **raw** / **fast** vegetables like tomatoes and onions in a salad.
31 On Sunday, we had **soft** / **roast** chicken with potatoes for lunch. It was delicious!
32 After I went to the dentist, I could only eat **soft** / **crispy** food for a few days.
33 I sometimes have **sour** / **fried** eggs for breakfast.

| | 8 |

Task 2

Complete the sentences with these words. There are four extra words that you do not need to use.

burger chilli curry fries kebabs lemons marshmallows peanuts pineapples scones steak sushi

34 .... are my favourite fruit because they're sweet and juicy.
35 I cooked my .... well because I didn't want it to be raw.
36 Cathy ordered a .... because she loves fast food.
37 It's east to make Turkish .... at home – you just put pieces of meat on sticks and cook them.
38 I love the hot chocolate drink at this café because they put lots of sweet .... on top.
39 When I visited Tokyo, I learnt to make ...., a traditional Japanese dish.
40 In Britain, people like to eat .... with jam and cream.
41 My favourite dishes are Mexican because there's a lot of .... in them, which makes them very spicy!

| | 8 |

Task 3

Complete the words in the conversations.

42 A: How about we go to the **p** _ _ - _ _ café for coffee?
B: OK, and let's have something sweet too, like a **c** _ _ _ _ _ _.
43 A: Let's find a place that doesn't **c** _ _ _ a fortune for lunch.
B: OK. There's a fast food **c** _ _ _ _ near here that has a special **p** _ _ _ _ _ _ _ _. We can get free fries with our meal.
44 A: Shall I make some **t** _ _ _ _ for breakfast? There's enough bread for us both.
B: Yes, please. But don't put any **b** _ _ _ _ _ on mine – I prefer it without.
45 A: I don't want to go to an **e** _ _ _ _ _ _ _ _ restaurant for dinner.
B: Neither do I because I'm short of **m** _ _ _ _ this week. Let's cook at home.

| | 9 |

| Total: | | 50 |

Name: ____________________

Class: ____________________

DICTATION

You are going to listen to a recording about a type of TV show. Listen to the whole recording once. Then you will hear the recording again with pauses for you to write down what you hear. Make sure you spell the words correctly.

....

....

....

....

....

....

....

....

....

....

....

....

/ 10

LISTENING

Task 1

You are going to listen to people talking in six different situations. For questions 1–6, choose the answer (A, B or C) which fits best according to what you hear.

1 You will hear a girl and her father talking about a restaurant. Why can't the girl eat paella?

A It isn't a vegetarian dish.

B She doesn't like chicken.

C It isn't very tasty.

2 You will hear a woman explaining a recipe for a cake. What do you need to make the cake?

A something you usually cook on

B something you usually eat your food on

C something you usually drink from

3 You will hear a girl ordering food at a fast food restaurant. What does she buy?

A a burger, fries and a drink

B a burger and fries

C a burger and a drink

4 You will hear a boy talking to his sister. Why doesn't he feel well?

A He ate too much.

B He's very ill.

C He ate bad food.

5 You will hear a woman and a man talking about what to eat. What will they do?

A order a takeaway meal

B go to a restaurant

C eat at home

6 You will hear a girl and boy talking about some biscuits he cooked. What happened to the biscuits?

A They burnt while he was doing his homework.

B They were in the oven for too long.

C He threw them out because they smelled bad.

/ 18

Task 2

Are the sentences true (T) or false (F)?

7 The boy tried to get rid of the smell. ....

8 The boy's friend is going to have a party. ....

/ 2

Name: ______________________

Class: ______________________

READING

Task 1

Read the article. Choose from the sentences (A–J) the one which fits each gap (9–14). There are four extra sentences which you do not need to use.

A And, in France, it is not allowed on public transport – just like durian in Singapore.

B If it was, passengers on trains and buses would complain.

C Most people buy it at food markets around the country.

D Perhaps you don't like the taste or the smell of a certain food.

E They weren't sure how to describe the taste.

F However, most people agree that it tastes better than it smells.

G Of course, the older cheeses have stronger smells than the younger ones.

H An unpleasant smell tells us that something is bad and shouldn't be eaten.

I Sweet foods such as ice cream and chocolate are the most popular.

J Lots of gases develop in the tins and this can be dangerous.

| | 18 |

Task 2

Read the article again and answer the question in your own words.

15 Why do some children not enjoy eating vegetables?

....

| | 2 |

| Total: | | 50 |

Smelly foods!

We all have our favourite foods, and we also have foods that we don't like at all! **(9)** .... Children, for example, often don't like eating vegetables. But that's probably because they would rather eat something tastier like pizza!

When it comes to what we eat, smell is very important. **(10)** .... However, did you know that there are very smelly foods that some people love to eat?

One of these is the durian, which is the smelliest fruit in the world. It has such a strong smell that it's not allowed on public transport in Singapore. **(11)** .... Even taxis have signs to let passengers know they cannot travel with the fruit.

People find it difficult to describe the taste and the smell of durian. There is no food in the world that you can compare it to. Many who have smelled it describe it as 'old socks' or 'rubbish'. **(12)** .... It's very creamy and if you can forget about the smell, is quite pleasant to eat.

Cheese is another food that can be quite smelly. Napoleon Bonaparte's favourite cheese, Époisses, is famous for its strong smell. **(13)** .... Another French cheese, Vieux-Boulogne, was found to be the smelliest in the world. It was chosen by a group of human testers and an 'electronic nose' at a UK university. The machine analysed the different chemical smells from the cheese and rated it as the worst smelling.

Finally, let's talk about surströmming, a fish dish from northern Sweden that smells like rotten eggs, vinegar and bad butter. The fish is kept in barrels for a few months, then put into tins before being sold. **(14)** .... For this reason, some airlines do not allow passengers to carry the tins because they could explode. It's best to open the tin in water, wash the fish well and eat it outdoors. Otherwise, your house won't smell very pleasant.

If you want to experience some truly unusual flavours, try these unique foods!

Name: ______________________

Class: ______________________

DICTATION

You are going to listen to a recording about a type of TV show. Listen to the whole recording once. Then you will hear the recording again with pauses for you to write down what you hear. Make sure you spell the words correctly.

....

....

....

....

....

....

....

....

....

....

....

....

	10

LISTENING

Task 1

You are going to listen to people talking in six different situations. For questions 1–6, choose the answer (A, B or C) which fits best according to what you hear.

1 You will hear a girl and her father talking about a restaurant. Why can't the girl eat paella?

A She doesn't like vegetables.

B It contains something she can't eat.

C She doesn't think it's a tasty dish.

2 You will hear a woman explaining a recipe for a cake. What do you need to make the cake?

A sugar

B eggs

C chocolate

3 You will hear a girl ordering food at a fast food restaurant. What does she buy?

A small fries

B regular fries

C large fries

4 You will hear a boy talking to his sister. Why does his stomach hurt?

A He's seriously ill.

B He had a lot of food.

C He drank too much lemonade.

5 You will hear a woman and a man talking about what to eat. What does the man enjoying eating the most?

A pasta

B curry

C sushi

6 You will hear a girl and boy talking about some biscuits he cooked. Why were the biscuits burnt?

A He forgot to check them.

B He was doing his homework.

C He was getting ready for a party.

	18

Task 2

Are the sentences true (T) or false (F)?

7 The boy didn't keep any of the biscuits. ....

8 The boy called his friend Maddy. ....

	2

Name: ______________________

Class: ______________________

READING

Task 1

Read the article. Choose from the sentences (A–J) the one which fits each gap (9–14). There are four extra sentences which you do not need to use.

A For this reason, some airlines do not allow passengers to carry the tins because they could explode.

B Children, for example, often don't like eating vegetables.

C It was chosen by a group of human testers and an 'electronic nose' at a UK university.

D For a lot of people in Asia, the fruit is too expensive to buy.

E Many who have smelled it describe it as 'old socks' or 'rubbish'.

F Certainly cheese has to be one of the smelliest foods.

G It has such a strong smell that it's not allowed on public transport in Singapore.

H But of all the fish, this one is the best known.

I However, did you know that there are very smelly foods that some people love to eat?

J I wonder why it's sold in supermarkets around the country.

	18

Task 2

Read the article again and answer the question in your own words.

15 Why is smell important?

....

	2

Total:		50

Name: ______________________

Class: ______________________

Smelly foods!

We all have our favourite foods, and we also have foods that we don't like at all! Perhaps you don't like the taste or the smell of a certain food. **(9)** .... But that's probably because they would rather eat something tastier like pizza!

When it comes to what we eat, smell is very important. An unpleasant smell tells us that something is bad and shouldn't be eaten. **(10)** ....

One of these is the durian, which is the smelliest fruit in the world. **(11)** .... If it was, passengers on trains and buses would complain. Even taxis have signs to let passengers know they cannot travel with the fruit.

People find it difficult to describe the taste and the smell of durian. There is no food in the world that you can compare it to. **(12)** .... However, most people agree that it tastes better than it smells. It's very creamy and if you can forget about the smell, is quite pleasant to eat.

Cheese is another food that can be quite smelly. Époisses cheese is famous for its strong smell. And, in France, it is not allowed on public transport – just like durian in Singapore. Another French cheese, Vieux-Boulogne, was found to be the smelliest in the world. **(13)** .... The machine analysed the different chemical smells from the cheese and rated it as the worst smelling.

Finally, let's talk about surströmming, a fish dish from northern Sweden that smells like rotten eggs, vinegar and bad butter. The fish is kept in barrels for a few months, then put into tins before being sold. Lots of gases develop in the tins and this can be dangerous. **(14)** .... It's best to open the tin in water, wash the fish well and eat it outdoors. Otherwise, your house won't smell very pleasant.

If you want to experience some truly unusual flavours, try these unique foods!

Name: ______________________

Class: ______________________

GRAMMAR

Task 1

Complete the sentences with the present perfect simple form of the verbs in brackets.

1 I .... (buy) some nice T-shirts and shorts for my summer holiday.

2 Sally loves adventure holidays and she .... (decide) to go on another one this year.

3 The girls .... (not try) mountain biking, but they're looking forward to it.

4 .... (Tom / go) to the airport with Dad to wait for Milly?

5 We .... (find) a good place to stay in France for the summer.

6 The rain that we had during the night .... (delay) all of the buses.

7 I .... (not speak) with Kim today. Do you know where she is?

8 .... (they / see) this travel show about China?

	8

Task 2

Complete the conversations with these words. You will need to use one word twice.

already ever for just never since yet

9 A: I've .... stayed in an expensive hotel, but I'd like to. What about you?
B: No, I haven't, but I think it would be great.

10 A: Who were you talking to on the phone?
B: My friend Holly. She's .... invited me to her end-of-year party!

11 A: Has it .... snowed on this island?
B: Actually, it has, but it was a very long time ago.

12 A: Are you excited about going to summer camp next month?
B: Yes. In fact, I've .... packed my backpack!

13 A: Has your brother been water skiing on his holiday?
B: No, he hasn't done any water sports ....

14 A: How long have you known Kelly?
B: We've been friends .... the fourth grade.

15 A: Hi, Alex. What are you doing outside the cinema?
B: I'm waiting for Sam and I've been here .... half an hour!

16 A: Have the art classes started .... ?
B: No, there's still time to sign up if you want to join.

	8

Task 3

Complete the email with the present perfect simple form of the verbs in brackets.

From:	Jake
To:	Ellie

Hi Ellie,

Here I am in Crete! We arrived last week and we **(17)** .... (already see) and done so much. The beaches are amazing – I **(18)** .... (never swim) in such clear warm water. The sun **(19)** .... (shine) every day and we **(20)** .... (spend) all our time outdoors. It **(21)** .... (not rain) once!

Oh, and the food is fantastic! **(22)** .... (you ever eat) Greek food? It's delicious! My sister **(23)** .... (not stop) eating cheese pies. In fact, she **(24)** .... (just have) another one!

I hope you're having fun at your adventure camp. **(25)** .... (you / make) lots of friends?

Write soon,
Jake

	9

Name: ______________________

Class: ______________________

VOCABULARY

Task 1

Choose the correct words to complete the sentences.

26 Millions of **guests** / **tourists** visit Paris every year.

27 I'd like a return **fare** / **ticket** to Bristol, please.

28 Have you **booked** / **closed** your accommodation yet?

29 I'm writing about my holiday in my **guidebook** / **diary**.

30 The bus stopped **sudden** / **suddenly** and I nearly fell over.

31 Let's **make** / **take** a boat trip at the weekend – the weather will be very nice, I think.

32 Before we get on the plane, we have to **go through** / **go on** security.

33 My cousins **caught** / **went** the train at ten o'clock this morning.

	8

Task 2

Match the sentences (34–40) with (A–G).

34 I'm going to a tennis camp this summer. ....

35 You don't need to call the hotel. ....

36 My friends are going on a long journey. ....

37 Alex has a great idea for a new sport. ....

38 You don't have to pay the full fare. ....

39 You must show your ID before you travel. ....

40 We have to go to reception first. ....

A They're travelling through Africa.

B That's where we'll get our room key.

C You're under eighteen so it's less for you.

D I need to improve my skills.

E Usually, that means a passport.

F He wants to develop water volleyball!

G You can make a reservation online.

	7

Task 3

Complete the words in the sentences.

41 I had nowhere to sit on the bus this morning because there were so many **p** _ _ _ _ _ _ _ _ _.

42 This is an excellent **g** _ _ _ _ _ _ _ _ – it's got so much useful information.

43 The **c** _ _ _ _ _ _ **o** _ _ _ _ _ _ at the airport asked us if we had any food in our bags.

44 To enter some countries, you need to have a passport and a **v** _ _ _.

45 There is a **c** _ _ _ _ _ of two different rooms at the hotel – one has a view of the beach and the other is next to the garden.

46 There are a lot of people waiting on the **p** _ _ _ _ _ _ _ for the train to arrive.

47 Horse riding doesn't look easy. In fact, it seems very **c** _ _ _ _ _ _ _ _ _ _, but I want to learn one day.

48 I'm travelling alone and I'd like a **s** _ _ _ _ _ room for three nights, please.

49 It's very sunny today, so I'll need to wear my **s** _ _ _ _ _ _ _ _ _ when I drive.

50 Hello. My name's John Smith. I have a **b** _ _ _ _ _ _ for a double room.

	9

Total:		50

Name: ______________________

Class: ______________________

GRAMMAR

Task 1

Complete the sentences with the present perfect simple form of the verbs in brackets.

1 My sister .... (read) *Travels With My Aunt* and she loves it.

2 Oh no! I think I .... (lose) my keys. I can't find them anywhere.

3 We .... (not meet) the manager of the hotel.

4 .... (Lou / take) a taxi to the airport?

5 .... (she / keep) the postcards that I sent her?

6 It's noisy outside the hotel at night and we .... (not sleep) well.

7 What .... (you / do) today?

8 The bad weather .... (delay) all of the flights at the airport.

	8

Task 2

Complete the conversations with these words. You will need to use one word twice.

already ever for just never since yet

9 A: How long have the boys been at the beach?
B: They've been there .... hours!

10 A: Is Marco having skiing lessons?
B: Yes, he is, and he's .... improved.

11 A: Helen has .... travelled in a plane.
B: I know. She's scared of flying.

12 A: Are you going to a summer camp this year?
B: I'm not sure. I haven't decided ....

13 A: I'm excited to see my friends. They've .... come back from their holiday.
B: Where did they go?

14 A: I love Rome! We've been to so many wonderful places.
B: Have you visited the Colosseum .... ?

15 A: How long have the Smiths lived here?
B: They've lived here .... 2012.

16 A: Have you .... been to a water park?
B: No, I haven't. Have you?

	8

Task 3

Complete the email with the present perfect simple form of the verbs in brackets.

From:	Lily
To:	Ben

Hi Ben,

I'm writing to you from the Greek island of Rhodes! We arrived a few days ago and we **(17)** .... (already explore) a lot of the island. The beaches are incredible – I **(18)** .... (never see) such clear blue water. It **(19)** .... (be) hot and sunny every day, so we **(20)** .... (not stay) indoors at all. Our hotel is in the oldest part of the island and it's got a lot of history – we **(21)** .... (visit) an amazing museum too.

The food is great! **(22)** .... (you ever have) octopus? I tried it yesterday. It's a bit unusual, but I really like it. My sister loves the Greek yoghurt – she **(23)** .... (eat) it every morning at breakfast.

Are you having a good time in Scotland? I hope it **(24)** .... (not rain)! **(25)** .... (you / take) any photos? Please send me some!

Bye for now,
Lily

	9

Name: ______________________

Class: ______________________

UNIT 8: LANGUAGE TEST B

VOCABULARY

Task 1

Choose the correct words to complete the sentences.

26 There are seats for fifty **passengers** / **guests** on this bus.

27 Excuse me. How much does a full **fare** / **ticket** cost?

28 Hello. I'd like to **book** / **make** a reservation for two nights, please.

29 According to the **diary** / **guidebook**, the museum is open every day.

30 It **final** / **finally** stopped raining on the last day of our holiday!

31 They **went on** / **took** a very long journey across Canada.

32 When you arrive at the hotel, **go to** / **go through** reception first.

33 We must leave now or we won't **catch** / **get** our flight.

| | 8 |

Task 2

Match the sentences (34–40) with (A–G).

34 What happens when you go through security? ....

35 Let's go to the mountains this weekend. ....

36 Tanya wants to develop a new game. ....

37 Should we buy return tickets to London? ....

38 We need to book a hotel soon. ....

39 I'm not very good at drawing ....

40 Can you show me your ID, please? ....

A Good idea. It's been ages since we took a trip.

B Really? Is it going to be like Monopoly?

C Of course. Here's my passport.

D I know, I'm looking for one with a swimming pool.

E They check your passport.

F You can improve if you have lessons.

G Yes, it's cheaper to buy a ticket to go there and come back.

| | 7 |

Task 3

Complete the words in the sentences.

41 Every summer, thousands of **t** _ _ _ _ _ _ _ come to this island.

42 The train to Manchester leaves from **p** _ _ _ _ _ _ _ four in ten minutes.

43 I always wear **f** _ _ _ **f** _ _ _ _ when I go to the beach.

44 At night, before I go to sleep, I write about my day in my **d** _ _ _ _.

45 That hotel is very popular. You need a **b** _ _ _ _ _ _ to stay there – you can't just walk in and ask for a room.

46 We use a website called WorldHotels4U to find **a** _ _ _ _ _ _ _ _ _ _ _ _ before we go on holiday.

47 At **c** _ _ _ _ _ _, there are signs that tell you what you're not allowed to bring on the plane.

48 We stayed in two **d** _ _ _ _ _ rooms – one for my parents and one for me and my sister.

49 Do I need a **v** _ _ _ to visit the USA, or just my passport?

50 You have a **c** _ _ _ _ _ of twenty different activities at our summer camp.

| | 9 |

| Total: | | 50 |

Name: ______________________

Class: ______________________

DICTATION

You are going to listen to a recording about holidays in space. Listen to the whole recording once. Then you will hear the recording again with pauses for you to write down what you hear. Make sure you spell the words correctly.

....

....

....

....

....

....

....

....

....

....

....

....

/10

LISTENING

Task 1

You are going to listen to a radio interview with a boy called Adam who travelled around the world with his family. For questions 1–6, choose the answer (A, B or C) which fits best according to what you hear.

1 What problem did the family have when they were planning their trip?

A They wanted to visit a lot of foreign countries.

B It was a difficult trip to plan for four people.

C They couldn't agree where to go.

2 Why did they choose the round-the-world ticket?

A It was cheaper than flying to Australia.

B It allowed them to see more countries.

C There was a lot of information online.

3 What was surprising about Japan?

A the difference between life in the city and the countryside

B how modern Tokyo was

C the traditions in the countryside

4 Why did they stay in Australia for two weeks?

A They explored all the amazing beaches.

B Adam wanted to spend more time surfing.

C It took time to go from one place to another.

5 Why were they lucky when they visited the desert in Chile?

A They saw the flowers in the desert.

B They experienced the driest place on earth.

C It started raining while they were there.

6 In which country did they spend the most time?

A Japan

B the USA

C Australia

/18

Task 2

Are the sentences true (T) or false (F)?

7 Adam's family visited Japan, Australia, Chile and the USA. ....

8 Adam was looking forward to swimming in Australia. ....

/2

Name: ______________________

Class: ______________________

READING

Task 1

Read the article. Decide which club (A–H) would be the most suitable for the young people (9–14).

9 ....

Liam enjoys being outdoors and he's keen to try something unusual that he's never done before. He'd like to do a group activity such as a team sport that will help him to get fit too.

10 ....

Alice doesn't have much free time because she's got a part-time job in a shop this summer. However, she wants to do something for fun in the free time that she has. She's thinking about learning a useful skill that is also creative.

11 ....

Jason likes outdoor activities. He's done mountain biking before and he loved it because it was challenging. This summer, he'd like to try a different sport. If he gets to a good level, he'd like to continue with the sport.

12 ....

Kate enjoys doing puzzles and watching films. This summer, she'd like to do a group activity that isn't a sport, and which also doesn't cost much. She loves talking about different topics with her friends.

13 ....

Simon has just moved to the town and he would like to make some friends before school starts. He'd like to join a club that is popular with lots of teenagers. He's interested in all kinds of new technology. He's free every day.

14 ....

Monica loves nature and enjoys spending time in the countryside. She'd like to learn more about the environment and do something to protect it. She also loves spending time with animals and she is a volunteer at an animal shelter.

| | 18 |

Task 2

Read the article again and answer the question in your own words.

15 Which activity is best for people who enjoy adventure? Why?

....

| | 2 |

| Total: | | 50 |

Summer clubs

Are you staying at home this summer? You don't have to go on a holiday to have fun. We review some popular clubs where you can enjoy activities with other teenagers.

A Page Turner

Do you think sport is boring? Are you a thinker not a doer? If your idea of a perfect afternoon is sitting down with a good book, then this is the club for you. Read the classics of world literature and then discuss them with the other members of the book club. By the end of the summer, you'll be a lot smarter! The club has its own library so you don't need to buy anything. Just come to the weekly discussions.

B Nature Calls

When school ends, the best way to enjoy the summer is outside in the fresh air. So turn off the TV, shut down your computer and join the many happy teens at Nature Calls – a club for green teens. At the club, you'll learn what you can do to help nature and take part in activities that really make a difference, like cleaning up local beaches and collecting glass, paper and aluminium for recycling.

C Fast and Furious Frisbee

Ultimate Frisbee has been played for over fifty years, but you probably haven't heard of it. You can play it on grass with two teams of seven players each, or on the beach with teams of five each. All you need is a frisbee – a flat disc. During a game, the the team with the disc throws it to others on their team to score goals. It's fast and fun, and you don't stop running!

D Zip It

If excitement and adventure are for you, try zip lining, an activity that combines speed and nature.
You'll slide down the wire faster than you can run.
Don't do it if you're scared of being in high places!
This is an exciting activity that will put a big smile on your face. The instructors will show you how it's done and the club provides all the equipment you need.

E Splash

Nothing's better than being at the beach on a hot summer's day, so join in the fun at Splash. You can improve your swimming and learn to scuba dive, sail or ski. Classes are available for beginners, intermediate and advanced teens. You'll get a certificate when you successfully complete a level. But the fun doesn't stop when summer ends. Classes continue until November.

F Data Dudes

Every day, the Preston Youth Club opens its doors to teens from across the area. There are many activities on offer including sports, art and drama, but be quick and sign up now if you want to take part in the computer classes. They're enjoyed by many teens who are learning about computer programming. It's a fun way to meet new people and, who knows, you could become the next Bill Gates.

G On the Stage

Do you have hidden talents? At On the Stage, you can find out! The club has drama lessons for young people. This is a great activity for shy teens. They can meet new people in a friendly place and have a lot of fun acting scenes from well-known films and plays. The club meets every day and, at the end of the summer, members give a performance.

H Shake and Bake

One day, when you're older, you'll have to look after yourself. You'll definitely need to cook! At Shake and Bake, you start with basic dishes like salads and omelettes, and then move on to more challenging food like cakes. Show your artistic talents and decorate a birthday cake for a friend or a member of your family. They'll be amazed at what you can do!

Name: ____________________

Class: ____________________

DICTATION

You are going to listen to a recording about holidays in space. Listen to the whole recording once. Then you will hear the recording again with pauses for you to write down what you hear. Make sure you spell the words correctly.

....

....

....

....

....

....

....

....

....

....

....

....

/10

LISTENING

Task 1

You are going to listen to a radio interview with a boy called Adam who travelled around the world with his family. For questions 1–6, choose the answer (A, B or C) which fits best according to what you hear.

1 Why was it difficult for the family to plan their trip?

A They had different opinions about where to go.

B No one was sure where to go.

C They didn't like travelling together.

2 What did they find out about round-the-world tickets?

A It is easier to research them online.

B The fares are cheaper than flying to the USA.

C They aren't as expensive as they thought they would be.

3 What surprised Adam about Japan?

A the modern cities

B the different ways that people lived

C the buildings in the countryside

4 What was Adam looking forward to doing in Australia?

A surfing

B exploring the country

C going to the beaches

5 What was unusual about the desert in Chile when they visited?

A It started raining.

B There were flowers.

C It was very dry.

6 In which country did they spend the least time?

A the USA

B Australia

C Japan

/18

Task 2

Are the sentences true (T) or false (F)?

7 Adam's holiday began in Australia and ended in the USA. ....

8 Adam's family travelled to New York by car. ....

/2

Name: ....

Class: ....

READING

Task 1

Read the article. Decide which club (A–H) would be the most suitable for the young people (9–14).

9 ....

Liam likes spending time outdoors and he's interested in trying something unusual that he's never done before. He wants to take part in a team sport that will help him to improve his fitness.

10 ....

Alice is working part-time in a shop this summer so she doesn't have a lot of free time for activities. However, she'd like to do something interesting when she isn't at work. She wants to learn a practical skill which is also creative.

11 ....

Jason is a fan of outdoor activities. Last summer he did rock climbing, which he enjoyed because it was challenging. This year, he'd like to do another sport. If he likes it, he wants to keep doing it and improve.

12 ....

Kate loves old films, doing quizzes and playing board games. She's thinking about doing a group activity that isn't a sport or other physical activity and is free. She enjoys talking with her friends about different topics.

13 ....

Simon is starting at a new school after the summer and he wants to make some friends in the area. He's very interested in technology and would like to join a club with lots of other teens who have the same interest. He's available every day of the week.

14 ....

Monica prefers to spend her time in the countryside, enjoying nature. She loves studying plants and watching birds. Protecting the environment is also very important to her, and she'd like to meet other young people who share her opinions.

	18

Task 2

Read the article again and answer the question in your own words.

15 Which club does something that helps the local area? What does it do?

....

	2

Total:		50

Name: ______________________

Class: ______________________

Summer clubs

Are you staying at home this summer? You don't have to go on a holiday to have fun. We review some popular clubs where you can enjoy activities with other teenagers.

A Taste Test

One day, when you're older, you'll have to look after yourself. You'll definitely need to cook! At Taste Test, you start with basic dishes like salads and omelettes, and then move on to more challenging food like cakes. Show your artistic talents and decorate a birthday cake for a friend or a member of your family. They'll be amazed at what you can do!

B Read It

Do you think sport is boring? Are you a thinker not a doer? If your idea of a perfect afternoon is sitting down with a good book, then this is the club for you. Read the classics of world literature and then discuss them with the other members of the book club. By the end of the summer, you'll be a lot smarter! The club has its own library so you don't need to buy anything. Just come to the weekly discussions.

C Green Team

When school ends, the best way to enjoy the summer is outside in the fresh air. So turn off the TV, shut down your computer and join the many happy teens at Green Team – a club for green teens. At the club, you'll learn what you can do to help nature and take part in activities that really make a difference, like cleaning up nearby beaches and collecting glass, paper and aluminium for recycling.

D Whoosh!

If excitement and adventure are for you, try zip lining, an activity that combines speed and nature. You'll slide down the wire faster than you can run. Don't do it if you're scared of being in high places! This is an exciting activity that will put a big smile on your face. The instructors will show you how it's done and the club provides all the equipment you need.

E Frisbee Freaks

Ultimate Frisbee has been played for over fifty years, but you probably haven't heard of it. You can play it on grass with two teams of seven players each, or on the beach with teams of five each. All you need is a frisbee – a flat disc. During a game, the the team with the disc throws it to others on their team to score goals. It's fast and fun, and you don't stop running!

F Hit the Water

Nothing's better than being at the beach on a hot summer's day, so join in the fun at Hit the Water. You can improve your swimming and learn to scuba dive, sail or ski. Classes are available for beginners, intermediate and advanced teens. You'll get a certificate when you successfully complete a level. But the fun doesn't stop when summer ends. Classes continue until November.

G Keyboard Kids

Every day, the Preston Youth Club opens its doors to teens from across the area. There are many activities on offer, including sports, art and drama. But be quick and sign up now if you want to take part in the computer classes! They're enjoyed by many teens who are learning about computer programming. It's a fun way to meet new people and, who knows, you could become the next Bill Gates.

H Act One

Do you have hidden talents? At Act One, you can find out! The club has drama lessons for young people. This is a great activity for shy teens. They can meet new people in a friendly place and have a lot of fun acting scenes from well-known films and plays. The club meets every day and, at the end of the summer, members give a performance.

Name: ....

Class: ....

GRAMMAR

Task 1

Complete the zero conditional and first conditional sentences with the verbs in brackets.

1 When I .... (play) too many video games, my eyes .... (hurt).

2 If you .... (want) any help, ... (ask) me.

3 Karen .... (come) to your party if you .... (invite) her.

4 If we .... (decide) to go the cinema, we .... (call) you.

5 If it .... (rain) later, we .... (not go out).

6 If you .... (mix) yellow and blue, you .... (get) green.

7 If Jane .... (call), please .... (tell) her to meet me at the café.

8 When I .... (arrive) in London tomorrow, I .... (send) you a text message.

	8

Task 2

Choose the correct words to complete the sentences.

9 I would prefer **to play** / **playing** a sport than a computer game!

10 Can you imagine **to win** / **winning** a lot of money?

11 In the summer holidays, I hate **to miss** / **missing** my friends from school.

12 Did your friends agree **to go** / **going** to the beach with you tomorrow?

13 I want **to speak** / **speaking** to the manager, please.

14 Be careful! It's important not **to drive** / **driving** too fast.

15 He doesn't mind **to get up** / **getting up** early every day!

16 I'm interested in **to watch** / **watching** documentaries – you can learn a lot.

	8

Task 3

Complete the second sentence so that that is has a similar meaning to the first sentence using the word given. Do not change the word given. Use between two and four words, including the word given.

17 It's necessary that we pay for our tickets.

NEED

We .... for our tickets.

18 I need to use my map app to find the restaurant.

IF

I won't find the restaurant .... my map app.

19 Do you want to go swimming?

WE

Shall .... swimming?

20 Take my old phone if you don't want to buy a new one.

GIVE

If you don't want to buy a new phone, I .... you my old one.

21 I tried, but I couldn't fix my computer.

TRIED

I .... my computer, but I couldn't.

22 I'll leave without them if they're late.

WAIT

If they're late, I .... for them.

23 Eat now or you'll be hungry later.

EAT

If you .... now, you'll be hungry later.

24 Sam is a good writer and he's going to become a journalist.

AT

Sam is good .... and he's going to become a journalist.

25 If you don't want to fail your exams, you should study.

IF

You will fail your exams ....

	9

Name: ______________________

Class: ______________________

VOCABULARY

Task 1

Choose the correct answer.

26 To find the information you need, just .... a search online.
- **A** go
- **B** do
- **C** get

27 We're going to .... a sleepover!
- **A** make
- **B** do
- **C** have

28 I can't get a .... here because we're in the mountains.
- **A** signal
- **B** Wi-Fi
- **C** link

29 Ballet is fun. You should .... it a go!
- **A** make
- **B** try
- **C** give

30 'What are you listening to?' 'It's a new ....'
- **A** website
- **B** podcast
- **C** app

31 I often watch TV shows .... demand.
- **A** on
- **B** in
- **C** with

32 I'm going to .... all the files that I don't need.
- **A** run out of
- **B** delete
- **C** charge

33 He uses a lot of .... on his phone.
- **A** memories
- **B** links
- **C** apps

	8

Task 2

Match the sentence halves 34–42 with A–I.

34 My sister does ....
35 I love watching ....
36 They have ....
37 You play ....
38 He's writing his ....
39 You should download the ....
40 Let's go to ....
41 She needs to charge ....
42 I've arranged ....

- **A** new app.
- **B** the guitar very well.
- **C** exciting action films.
- **D** to meet my friends.
- **E** Wi-Fi at this café.
- **F** ballet at a school.
- **G** her battery.
- **H** football blog now.
- **I** the music festival tomorrow.

	9

Task 3

Complete the sentences with these verbs.

do download forget have leave
listen to play run out of

43 Can you teach me to .... chess?
44 I .... a good connection so I can use my phone here.
45 This is a fun quiz! You should .... it.
46 I've .... memory on my phone.
47 Oh no! Did I .... my phone at home?
48 Try not to .... your username and password!
49 Let's .... some tracks to our phones.
50 We can .... a live band at the school concert.

	8

Total:		50

Name: ....

Class: ....

GRAMMAR

Task 1

Complete the zero conditional and first conditional sentences with the verbs in brackets.

1 If it .... (be) warm today, we .... (go) to the beach.

2 When you .... (put) ice in hot water, it .... (melt).

3 If the boys .... (want) to eat a pizza, we .... (order) one.

4 He .... (not finish) his homework if he .... (play) video games tonight.

5 My little sister .... (cry) when she .... (get) upset.

6 If you .... (not know) what a word means, ... (check) in a dictionary.

7 If your arm .... (hurt), ... (see) a doctor.

8 Ben and I .... (visit) lots of museums if we .... (travel) to Italy.

	8

Task 2

Choose the correct words to complete the sentences.

9 Do you enjoy **to play** / **playing** the piano?

10 Ariel is tired of **to watch** / **watching** TV.

11 My mum has promised **to buy** / **buying** me a new phone.

12 Don't forget **to take** / **taking** your umbrella with you today.

13 Thanks for **to cook** / **cooking** lunch today, Mark.

14 Nick can't stand **to listen** / **listening** to rap music.

15 It's possible **to relax** / **relaxing** in the countryside.

16 My brother has decided **to start** / **starting** a vlog.

	8

Task 3

Complete the second sentence so that that is has a similar meaning to the first sentence using the word given. Do not change the word given. Use between two and four words, including the word given.

17 Alex says he'll become a doctor.

PLANS

Alex .... a doctor.

18 You must remember to call us later.

FORGET

Please .... us later.

19 Do you want to play tennis or basketball?

RATHER

Would .... tennis or basketball?

20 If the train isn't here soon, we'll be late.

ARRIVE

We'll be late if the train .... soon.

21 Hopefully, I can improve my English in London.

HOPE

I .... my English in London.

22 If you don't eat good food, you'll get sick.

IF

You won't get sick .... good food.

23 Finding the answer will be impossible if you don't understand the question.

FIND

If you don't understand the question, you .... the answer.

24 He doesn't think it's interesting to travel.

IN

He isn't ....

25 You can't charge your phone without a charger.

HAVE

If you ...., you can't charge your phone.

	9

Name: ____________________

Class: ____________________

VOCABULARY

Task 1

Choose the correct answer.

26 I can't .... this quiz. It's too difficult!
- **A** do
- **B** play
- **C** make

27 Does this cafe .... free Wi-Fi?
- **A** give
- **B** have
- **C** get

28 I'm .... a very interesting blog for teenagers.
- **A** listening to
- **B** watching
- **C** reading

29 Chess is great fun. Why don't you give it a .... ?
- **A** play
- **B** go
- **C** make

30 Do you want to .... this podcast with me?
- **A** listen to
- **B** watch
- **C** play

31 We ordered a pizza and watched a TV show .... demand.
- **A** for
- **B** at
- **C** on

32 He can't store any more photos on his phone because he has .... memory.
- **A** deleted
- **B** left
- **C** run out of

33 I've .... all the apps I need to my new phone.
- **A** clicked
- **B** downloaded
- **C** followed

[ ] 8

Task 2

Match the sentence halves 34–42 with A–I.

34 I'm listening to ....
35 Let's download ....
36 I hope you have ....
37 It isn't difficult to make ....
38 I do ....
39 I need to be quiet, so I'm using ....
40 He's often ....
41 I have to charge ....
42 Louise will arrange ....

A online in the evening.
B my headphones.
C a video with your phone.
D a film and watch it later.
E to go out with her friends.
F a good time tonight.
G a great song on the radio at the moment.
H my phone right now – the battery is dead.
I judo every Monday.

[ ] 9

Task 3

Complete the sentences with these verbs.

delete do forget get have leave play watch

43 We can find the address of the shop if we .... a search online.

44 For my birthday, I want to .... a sleepover with my friends.

45 I wonder why I can't .... a signal on my phone.

46 I usually .... half of the photos that I take.

47 Don't .... your password or you won't be able to log in.

48 Make sure you don't .... your tennis racket at the club.

49 It's fun to .... travel vlogs and learn about different places.

50 Let's .... a board game. How about Scrabble or Monopoly?

[ ] 8

Total: [ ] 50

Name: ....

Class: ....

DICTATION

You are going to listen to a recording about using social media. Listen to the whole recording once. Then you will hear the recording again with pauses for you to write down what you hear. Make sure you spell the words correctly.

....

....

....

....

....

....

....

....

....

....

....

....

/10

LISTENING

Task 1

You are going to listen to a talk about an event to raise money for charity. Complete the notes. Write the correct answer in each gap.

Offline – log off and have fun!

Offline is an event that lasts for **(1)** .... hours and raises money for charity.

By joining in the event, young people can have a **(2)** .... from technology.

The event is planned for two days in the month of **(3)** ....

Offline starts and ends at **(4)** .... o'clock.

The money raised is used to buy **(5)** .... for African schools.

Friends, family or **(6)** .... in the area can become sponsors.

/18

Task 2

Are the sentences true (T) or false (F)?

7 First, students fill in a form and then they find sponsors. ....

8 The school that raises the most money will receive a computer. ....

/2

Name: ______________________

Class: ______________________

READING

Task 1

Read the article and choose the answer (A, B, C or D) which you think fits best according to the text.

9 Max left social media because some companies
- **A** have become very rich.
- **B** had his private information.
- **C** don't help us to communicate.
- **D** aren't honest with users.

10 After he deleted the apps, Max
- **A** checked his phone without thinking.
- **B** decided he wanted to use them again.
- **C** thought they were silly.
- **D** received some notifications.

11 Why did Max join social media?
- **A** He hoped people would like him.
- **B** He was copying what other people did.
- **C** He enjoyed writing updates.
- **D** He wanted to get attention.

12 Sally was worried about her exams because she
- **A** couldn't stop using social media.
- **B** didn't spend enough time studying.
- **C** wasn't able to remember information.
- **D** hadn't deleted the apps on her phone.

13 What happened when Sally stopped using social media?
- **A** She didn't see her friends.
- **B** She wanted to sleep more.
- **C** She no longer used her phone.
- **D** She rested and studied well.

14 What would be a good introduction to this article?
- **A** Teenagers live their lives on social media. Max and Sally tell us why it's so important for them to be online.
- **B** Do young people understand how social media can affect their lives? Meet two teenagers who found out and did something about it.
- **C** Leaving social media isn't difficult. Max and Sally explain how they did it and how living without it has changed their lives.
- **D** Is social media good or bad for young people? Two teenagers give us their opinions on this important question.

	18

Task 2

Read the article again and answer the question in your own words.

15 How do Max and Sally use social media now?

....

	2

Total:		50

TEEN TIME OUT

Max, 15

I read about social media companies that were selling the information of their users. It made me angry because I hadn't agreed to that! These huge companies say their purpose is to bring people together and make communication easier, but actually, we – the users – are just products that they sell to make lots of money. So I deleted my accounts and never went back.

It wasn't easy, though. For the first few days, I kept looking at my phone for notifications. It was silly because I no longer had the apps! That's when I realised it had become a bad habit. I asked myself why I used social media. At first, it was because most of my friends were on Facebook. Then, as time passed, I wanted to be liked. I wrote and rewrote my updates and posts many times, hoping I seemed clever or funny to get more attention. The truth is, we care what people think about us and want them to like us. Social media makes those feelings stronger. When social media starts to control your life like that, it's time to leave!

Sally, 14

My exams were a few weeks away and it was important for me to work hard. I had started to panic because although I was studying every night, I forgot so much. It was really strange! Then my mum suggested something that I didn't like: to remove the social media apps from my phone. Why? Because I was always looking at my phone. I just couldn't pay attention to anything else.

I promised my mum I would stop until my exams finished. To be honest, I was afraid to quit social media because I thought I would miss out on so many fun things like sharing photos or video links with my friends. However, some great things happened. I began to sleep better and I was able to prepare well for my exams without taking breaks to check my phone. It was a great feeling! Once my exams were over, I went back on social media, but, now, I control it much better. I only check my phone twice a day.

Name: ....

Class: ....

UNIT 9: SKILLS TEST B

DICTATION

You are going to listen to a recording about using social media. Listen to the whole recording once. Then you will hear the recording again with pauses for you to write down what you hear. Make sure you spell the words correctly.

....

....

....

....

....

....

....

....

....

....

....

....

/ 10

LISTENING

Task 1

You are going to listen to a talk about an event to raise money for charity. Complete the notes. Write the correct answer in each gap.

Offline – log off and have fun!

Offline is an event that raises money for **(1)** ....

Smartphones first became popular in the early **(2)** .... and we now use them for everything.

Offline takes place on two days and ends on June **(3)** ....

Sponsors give money for **(4)** .... that someone doesn't go online.

If you take part in Offline, as well as the internet, you mustn't use the **(5)** .... or television.

There will be activities at the school on Saturday in the **(6)** ....

/ 18

Task 2

Are the sentences true (T) or false (F)?

7 The Offline event ends at 12 o'clock at night. ....

8 There is something to be won by a school. ....

/ 2

Name: ______________________

Class: ______________________

READING

Task 1

Read the article and choose the answer (A, B, C or D) which you think fits best according to the text.

9 Sally left social media because some companies

- **A** aren't honest with users.
- **B** don't help us to communicate.
- **C** have made lots of money.
- **D** didn't look after her private information.

10 After she deleted the apps, Sally

- **A** realised they were silly.
- **B** checked her phone without thinking.
- **C** received some notifications.
- **D** decided she wanted to get them back again.

11 Why did Sally join social media?

- **A** She liked to appear popular.
- **B** She wanted to do the same as other people.
- **C** She hoped people would like her.
- **D** She enjoyed writing updates.

12 Max was worried about his exams because he

- **A** didn't spend enough time studying.
- **B** couldn't stop using social media.
- **C** didn't find the apps on his phone useful.
- **D** wasn't able to remember information.

13 What happened when Max stopped using social media?

- **A** He was able to rest and study well.
- **B** He no longer wanted to use his phone.
- **C** He didn't communicate with his friends.
- **D** He became afraid of how it controlled his life.

14 What would be a good introduction to this article?

- **A** Giving up social media is much easier then you think. Two teenagers explain how they did it and how their lives have improved as a result.
- **B** Teenagers depend on social media to communicate. Sally and Max tell us why it's so important for them to be online.
- **C** Do young people realise how social media affects their lives? Meet two teens who found out and acted to do something about it.
- **D** Are the effects of social media on young people's lives good or bad? Sally and Max give us their opinions on this important question.

	18

Task 2

Read the article again and answer the question in your own words.

15 What do Sally and Max think about using social media now?

....

	2

Total:		50

TEEN TIME OUT

Sally, 14

I read about social media companies that were selling the information of their users. It made me angry because I hadn't agreed to that! These huge companies say their purpose is to bring people together and make communication easier, but actually, we – the users – are just products that they sell to make lots of money. So I deleted my accounts and never went back.

It wasn't easy though. For the first few days, I kept looking at my phone for notifications. It was silly because I no longer had the apps! That's when I realised it had become a bad habit. I asked myself why I used social media. At first, it was because most of my friends were on Facebook. Then, as time passed, I wanted to be liked. I wrote and rewrote my updates and posts many times, hoping I seemed clever or funny to get more attention. The truth is, we care what people think about us and want them to like us. Social media makes those feelings stronger. When social media starts to control your life like that, it's time to leave!

Max, 15

My exams were a few weeks away and it was important for me to work hard. I had started to panic because although I was studying every night, I forgot so much. It was really strange! Then my mum suggested something that I didn't like: to remove the social media apps from my phone. Why? Because I was always looking at my phone. I just couldn't pay attention to anything else.

I promised my mum I would stop until my exams finished. To be honest, I was afraid to quit social media because I thought I would miss out on so many fun things like sharing photos or video links with my friends. However, some great things happened. I began to sleep better and I was able to prepare well for my exams without taking breaks to check my phone. It was a great feeling! Once my exams were over, I went back on social media, but, now, I control it much better. I only check my phone twice a day.

Name: ______________________

Class: ______________________

GRAMMAR

Task 1

Choose the correct answer (A, B or C).

1 I love this book. I think .... story is really exciting.
A the
B a
C -

2 My dad gave me .... advice.
A a few
B a lot
C a little

3 There aren't .... clothes that I like in this shop.
A much
B some
C any

4 I have .... good news. I passed all of my exams!
A any
B some
C many

5 Nick is very busy these days and we .... ever see him.
A rarely
B hardly
C occasionally

6 **A:** Where .... ?
B: To school. See you later.
A were you going
B do you go
C are you going

7 I found some money under my bed when I .... for my football boots.
A was looking
B looked
C am looking

8 It was a fantastic party – .... had a great time.
A anyone
B everyone
C someone

	8

Task 2

Complete the sentences with one word.

9 Holly has .... unusual hobby – she collects spoons.
10 How .... time will it take to drive to London?
11 A: .... you seeing your friends tonight?
B: No, I'm tired.
12 A: What .... she do?
B: She's a doctor.
13 A: .... did they go for their holiday?
B: They went to Greece.
14 Alex and Mike .... working hard when I saw them.
15 A: .... you send Alice an email?
B: No, I forgot.
16 A: Is there anything in the box?
B: No, there's .... It's empty.

	8

Task 3

Complete the sentences with the correct form of the words in brackets.

17 .... (you / read) while Mia was studying?
18 He .... (rarely / buy) a newspaper – he prefers to read the news online.
19 Anna .... (not know) the answer so she asked me.
20 It .... (not rain) now – let's go to the park.
21 A: I saw a UFO last night.
B: I .... (not believe) you.
22 .... (your friends / live) in this street or is their house near the school?
23 While I .... (walk) to the shops I saw my teacher.
24 .... (try) to fix your computer? Let me look – maybe I can help.
25 I found the information that I needed online and I .... (send) it to my friend.

	9

Name: ______________________

Class: ______________________

VOCABULARY

Task 1

Choose the correct words to complete the sentences.

26 We waited at the **crossing** / **path** for the cars to stop.

27 The town where I live is **by** / **in** the sea.

28 **I'd like** / **I like** to go shopping for trainers tomorrow.

29 There are many **ordinary** / **valuable** paintings in this museum – it's famous for them.

30 We found a **pavement** / **seat** in the park and stopped there to have our lunch.

31 Mobile phones are so **special** / **useful** – you can call anyone from anywhere.

32 When I got my exam results, I was **delighted** / **exhausted** – all As!

33 Put on a coat before you go out – it's **freezing** / **starving** today.

	8

Task 2

Match 34–40 with A–G to complete the conversations.

34 Tell me about your painting lessons. Are you improving? ....

35 I'd like to start playing squash. Where can I do that? ....

36 I enjoyed the film. What about you? ....

37 Do you have plans for the summer holidays? ....

38 Elena is the best student in the class. ....

39 I'm terrible at rock climbing. How can I improve? ....

40 What's that in the sky? Is it a plane? ....

A Actually, I thought it was very dull.

B I agree – she's very clever.

C Yes, I'm making a lot of progress.

D Maybe, but it's tiny and I can't see it well.

E Not yet, but I'd like to stay in a cottage on the coast.

F Try the new sports centre.

G Practise and you'll get it right.

	/

Task 3

Choose the correct answer (A, B or C).

Hi. My name's Carlo. I'm from Milan – it's a city **(41)** .... the north of Italy. I'm fourteen **(42)** .... I go to my local high school. When I'm not studying, I **(43)** .... a lot of time with my friends. We sometimes go to a skate **(44)** .... in our neighbourhood. My friends **(45)** .... part in skateboarding competitions there. I can skate too, **(46)** .... I'm not very good at it yet. I need to practise more to **(47)** .... better. I actually prefer basketball **(48)** .... I really enjoy team sports and I'm a good player, too. I live in a nice **(49)** .... block, on the fourth floor. My best friend lives in the same building on the third floor, **(50)** .... we see each other every day.

	A	B	C
41	**A** in	**B** from	**C** to
42	**A** because	**B** but	**C** and
43	**A** give	**B** make	**C** spend
44	**A** place	**B** park	**C** stop
45	**A** take	**B** have	**C** do
46	**A** so	**B** but	**C** and
47	**A** go	**B** make	**C** get
48	**A** but	**B** so	**C** because
49	**A** department	**B** apartment	**C** pavement
50	**A** because	**B** so	**C** but

	10

Total:		50

Name: ____________________

Class: ____________________

GRAMMAR

Task 1

Choose the correct answer (A, B or C).

1 I have .... old video games. Do you want them?
- **A** a few
- **B** a lot
- **C** a little

2 In general, ... young people enjoy going out with their friends.
- **A** A
- **B** –
- **C** The

3 I don't have .... free time these days because I'm studying.
- **A** many
- **B** some
- **C** much

4 Do you need .... help?
- **A** any
- **B** little
- **C** many

5 I hardly .... go to the cinema.
- **A** often
- **B** never
- **C** ever

6 **A:** Who .... to when I saw you at the bus stop yesterday?
B: My friend Julie.
- **A** were you talking
- **B** did you talk
- **C** are you talking

7 We can't go swimming now because ....
- **A** it rains
- **B** it's raining
- **C** it was raining

8 .... sent me a text message, but I don't know the person.
- **A** Anyone
- **B** Everyone
- **C** Someone

| | 8 |

Task 2

Complete the sentences with one word.

9 Where is .... shop that you went to yesterday?

10 How .... students are in your class?

11 A: .... they enjoy going to the beach?
B: Yes, they said it was great.

12 A: It costs a lot to buy a good tennis racket.
B: Yes, it ....

13 A: .... do you like playing chess?
B: Because it's interesting and challenging.

14 The girls .... walking to the park when I saw them.

15 A .... people from my class are members of the same youth club I go to.

16 A: Did you get .... that we needed from the supermarket?
B: Yes, it's all here.

| | 8 |

Task 3

Complete the sentences with the correct form of the words in brackets.

17 There's a problem with my phone – it .... (not work) at the moment.

18 A: What .... (you / look for)?
B: My glasses. I can't find them.

19 She .... (occasionally / listen to) podcasts.

20 While we .... (ride) our bikes, Sam's phone fell out of his pocket.

21 .... (Max / study) while you were at the shops?

22 Is it expensive to use the gym? .... (students / pay) less?

23 We bought our tickets in the morning and .... (go) to the concert later that day.

24 A: I think it's better if school starts at eleven o'clock in the morning.
B: I'm sorry, but I .... (not agree).

25 Julie .... (not study) at the library on Saturdays.

| | 9 |

Name: ____________________

Class: ____________________

VOCABULARY

Task 1

Choose the correct words to complete the sentences.

26 Stella was walking to school when she dropped her phone on the **pavement** / **station** and it broke.

27 I didn't have breakfast this morning and now I'm **terrible** / **starving**.

28 That writer's books are about **ordinary** / **ancient** people like you and me.

29 It's a **special** / **scary** day today – it's Nick's eighteenth birthday.

30 **I'd like** / **I like** spending time with my best friend.

31 At the end of the long race, the runners were **confident** / **exhausted**.

32 There are some very nice villages **on** / **in** the coast.

33 We walked along a **crossing** / **path** in the forest.

	8

Task 2

Match 34–40 with A–G to complete the conversations.

34 Where can I put this empty bottle? ....

35 Everyone likes your friend Lucy. ....

36 My parents bought a holiday house. ....

37 Why don't you play video games? ....

38 I love the paintings in your living room. ....

39 Why are you wearing a scarf? ....

40 Where do you live? ....

A Thanks, we got them at an art gallery.

B Great! Is it by the sea?

C In an apartment block near the school.

D That's because she's friendly and polite.

E Because it's freezing in here!

F I don't like to waste time.

G There's a rubbish bin over there.

	7

Task 3

Choose the correct answer (A, B or C).

Hello. My name's Inez **(41)** .... I'm from Spain. I live **(42)** .... the south of the country, near the sea. I'm a high school student. When I'm not studying, I spend **(43)** .... with my best friends, Marta and Elsa. We sometimes go to a sports **(44)** .... after school. We go there **(45)** .... the facilities are very good. There are tennis courts, as well as two swimming **(46)** .... One is outside and the other is inside, **(47)** .... we can go swimming in the winter months too. I want to **(48)** .... well at school and **(49)** .... good results. I study hard, **(50)** .... I also like to have fun!

	A	B	C
41	but	so	and
42	in	on	at
43	it	time	hour
44	area	centre	place
45	but	so	because
46	pools	blocks	parks
47	but	so	because
48	be	get	do
49	give	get	take
50	but	because	so

	10

Total:		50

Name: ______________________

Class: ______________________

Task 1

Listen to the questions from your teacher and answer them.

Task 2

Your friend is having a birthday. You and your partner want to buy him a present. Here are some ideas for gifts. Talk together about the items and say which would be the best one.

Name: ______________________

Class: ______________________

Task 1

Say good morning/afternoon to both students and then follow the script below:

(*Student A*) What's your name?

Thank you.

(*Student B*) What's your name?

Thank you.

(*Student A*) What's your surname? How do you spell it?

Thank you.

(*Student B*) What's your surname? How do you spell it?

Thank you.

(*Student A*) Where do you live?

(*Student B*) How old are you?

Ask three questions to each student from the list below:

- Do you have any hobbies?
- What do you want to do when you grow up?
- What do you usually do at the weekend?
- What do you enjoy reading?
- Who do you like to spend time with?

Allow about 2 minutes.

Thank the students and move on to Task 2.

Name: ____________________

Class: ____________________

Task 2

Tell students that they will do Task 2 together and that they need to discuss the items in the picture. Say to both students:

I'm going to describe a situation to you. Your friend is having a birthday. You and your partner want to **buy him a present**. Talk together about different gifts you could give him and say which would be the best one. Here is a picture with some ideas to help you.

Ask both students to look at the picture and repeat the information about the task, above.

All right? Talk together.

Allow students enough time to complete the task without intervention (3–4 minutes). Prompt only if necessary.

Thank you. That is the end of the test.

Name: ____________________

Class: ____________________

REVIEW (UNITS 1–3): WRITING

Read the exam task below. Write **100** words in an appropriate style. Write your answer on **a separate answer sheet**.
Your English teacher has asked you to write a story.
Your story must begin with this sentence:

I went to the window and looked outside.

Write your **story** in about **100 words**.

....

....

....

....

....

....

....

Name: ____________________

Class: ____________________

GRAMMAR

Task 1

Choose the correct answer (A, B or C).

What **(1)** .... the world be like in the future? You **(2)** .... be a scientist to predict some things. For example, it will probably be much **(3)** .... That's because we **(4)** .... climate change right now. Are we being **(5)** .... about it? There are many things that we can do to help. However, we **(6)** .... do them now because we don't have **(7)** .... much time as we think. **(8)** .... thing we can do is to wait and hope that something terrible **(9)** .... happen!

	A	B	C
1	**A** will	**B** does	**C** can
2	**A** mustn't	**B** can't	**C** don't have to
3	**A** hot	**B** hotter	**C** hottest
4	**A** will experience	**B** experienced	**C** are experiencing
5	**A** enough serious	**B** serious enough	**C** quite serious
6	**A** must	**B** can	**C** need
7	**A** quite	**B** too	**C** as
8	**A** A bad	**B** The worst	**C** The worse
9	**A** didn't	**B** won't	**C** doesn't have to

___ / 9

Task 2

Complete the second sentence so that it means the same as the first sentence, using the word in brackets.

10 Do you have any plans for the weekend?
What .... do at the weekend? (going)

11 Tanya is more polite than Nick.
Nick .... Tanya. (as)

12 It isn't necessary for us to leave now.
We .... now. (have)

13 Thanks, but I don't need any help to do this.
Thanks, but I can do this
.... (by)

14 I don't have much free time today.
I only have .... free time today. (a)

15 Anna is too young to drive a car.
Anna .... to drive a car. (old)

16 I think he's staying at home tonight, but I'm not sure.
He .... at home tonight. (may)

17 Luisa and Jim are tall, but Tom is taller.
Tom is .... of all. (the)

___ / 8

Task 3

Complete the text with one word in each gap.

Are you a fashion victim?

Fashion victims are people who think that being trendy is **(18)** .... important than looking nice. They always have **(19)** .... wear the newest designs. They don't understand that the **(20)** .... fashionable styles aren't always attractive. To look good it's a **(21)** .... better to wear clothes that suit you and fit you well. But fashion victims wear silly hats or clothes that are one or two sizes **(22)** .... big for them. The next time you want to buy clothes, the **(23)** .... thing to do is to ask someone that you trust for an honest opinion – it could be a friend or, yes, even your parents! Your mum and dad may not be quite as boring **(24)** .... you think! So, what are you **(25)** .... to do the next time you go shopping for clothes – buy something trendy or something that looks great?

___ / 8

Name: ______________________

Class: ______________________

VOCABULARY

Task 1

Choose the correct answer (A, B or C).

26 His favourite subject at school is .... because he wants to be an actor.
- **A** dance
- **B** music
- **C** drama

27 He wants to create an app and .... a lot of money.
- **A** make
- **B** take
- **C** do

28 When you wear bright colours, you really ....
- **A** dress up
- **B** stand out
- **C** check out

29 Don't be afraid to .... a go and try something new and exciting.
- **A** give
- **B** get
- **C** have

30 **A:** Why don't we go to the countryside?

B: OK, that .... good.
- **A** sounds
- **B** feels
- **C** looks

31 Koalas have cute faces and grey ....
- **A** skin
- **B** fur
- **C** feathers

32 Some birds can .... the sea to catch fish.
- **A** dive into
- **B** climb up
- **C** jump from

33 My parents are tall, but I'm of .... height.
- **A** tiny
- **B** ordinary
- **C** average

	8

Task 2

Complete the sentences with the correct form of these verbs.

cross fancy get give hand note open start tell

34 Are you going to .... a business?

35 I think rock climbing might be fun. Why don't we .... it a try?

36 She's working hard because she wants to .... good grades.

37 My aunt wants to .... a shoe shop in the town centre.

38 I .... down everything she said because I didn't want to forget it.

39 We must be quiet in class or our teacher will .... us off.

40 This answer is wrong. Please .... it out and write it correctly.

41 Do you .... playing tennis later today?

42 At the start of the lesson, we always .... in our homework.

	9

Task 3

Complete the words in the sentences.

43 Did you know that bats can't see? They're **b** _ _ _ _ .

44 Alice is a **f** _ _ _ _ _ _ _ girl – she always stops to have a chat when she sees me.

45 Sharks and crocodiles are scary because they have very **s** _ _ _ _ teeth.

46 My hair is short and straight, but my sister's is long and **c** _ _ _ _ .

47 His teeth aren't straight, so he has to wear **b** _ _ _ _ _ .

48 Oh no! I can't find my **w** _ _ _ _ _ and all of my money is in it.

49 My favourite subject is **g** _ _ _ _ _ _ _ _ because I'm interested in mountains and rivers.

50 Although a **p** _ _ _ _ _ _ can swim very well, it isn't a fish – it's actually a bird.

	8

Total:		50

Name: ______________________

Class: ______________________

GRAMMAR

Task 1

Choose the correct answer (A, B or C).

Do you wonder what **(1)** .... to our planet in the future? People are **(2)** .... more worried about climate change. They **(3)** .... that we will have huge problems because we aren't being **(4)** .... now. We **(5)** .... wait for governments to do something. **(6)** .... many things that we can do **(7)** .... For example, whenever possible, walking or riding a bike is **(8)** .... than asking your parents to drive you. Go online and you **(9)** .... good information about what you can do.

	A	B	C
1	happens	will happen	is happening
2	much	lot	quite
3	believe	are believing	will believe
4	too careful	careful enough	enough careful
5	don't	may not	mustn't
6	It's	There is	There are
7	yourself	ourselves	itself
8	good	best	better
9	will find	find	are going to find

[ ] 9

Task 2

Complete the second sentence so that it means the same as the first sentence, using the word in brackets.

10 Does he have any plans for Saturday?
What .... do on Saturday? (going)

11 Books are more interesting than comics.
Comics .... books. (as)

12 It isn't necessary for him to stay after school.
He .... after school. (have)

13 Max doesn't need help to fix his bike.
Max can fix his bike .... (by)

14 These shoes are too small for my feet.
These shoes .... for my feet. (big)

15 I think it's going to rain tomorrow, but I'm not sure.
It .... tomorrow. (might)

16 The red trainers and the blue trainers are nice, but the black trainers are nicer.
The black trainers are .... of all. (the)

17 I have a few more exams than you.
You .... many exams as me. (quite)

[ ] 8

Task 3

Complete the text with one word in each gap.

Are you a fashion victim?

Fashion victims are people who think that looking nice isn't **(18)** .... important as being trendy. They only want to wear **(19)** .... newest styles. Unfortunately, those styles aren't always the **(20)** .... attractive. If you want to look good, you **(21)** .... to wear clothes that suit you and fit you well. You **(22)** .... not wear anything that is silly and don't buy clothes that are much bigger **(23)** .... your size. Also, think about colours – some are probably **(24)** .... attractive on you than others, so try to choose them. When you go shopping, be confident **(25)** .... to ask the assistants for advice, they are there to help you!

[ ] 8

Name: ________________

Class: ________________

VOCABULARY

Task 1

Choose the correct answer (A, B or C).

26 Before you start a business, you need to .... a business plan.
- **A** open
- **B** develop
- **C** run

27 Listen to your parents and .... their advice.
- **A** give
- **B** take
- **C** have

28 You should .... this great app. It shows you different styles for your hair.
- **A** check out
- **B** try on
- **C** get up

29 He's carrying a very big .... – all of his books are in it.
- **A** baseball cap
- **B** wallet
- **C** backpack

30 **A:** What do birds eat?
B: I think they .... insects.
- **A** hunt for
- **B** land on
- **C** jump from

31 Bees and butterflies both have ....
- **A** tails
- **B** wings
- **C** feathers

32 Don't sleep all day – .... and do something fun.
- **A** settle down
- **B** take out
- **C** get up

33 I'm so happy! We're going to spend the day .... the sea!
- **A** by
- **B** to
- **C** on

	8

Task 2

Complete the sentences with the correct form of these verbs.

dress have lie make manage run save take throw

34 These shoes are very old. I'm going to .... them out.

35 Don't be scared. You should .... a chance and see what you can do.

36 Are you going to .... up for the party?

37 Last year, I .... up my money and bought some great boots.

38 You have to .... up your mind about what you're going to do.

39 Harry is .... his new business very well.

40 My sister .... freckles on her face, but I don't.

41 If you're tired, you should .... down.

42 The woman who owns that company knows how to .... people.

	9

Task 3

Complete the words in the sentences.

43 I taught my dog to do tricks – he's very **c** _ _ _ _ _ .

44 Animals that can run fast have very **p** _ _ _ _ _ _ _ legs.

45 My brother's hair is curly, but mine is **s** _ _ _ _ _ _ _ .

46 I love holding my kitten because it has very **s** _ _ _ fur.

47 I can't see very well without my **g** _ _ _ _ _ _ .

48 My grandma's gold **j** _ _ _ _ _ _ _ _ is very valuable, especially her necklace.

49 At the moment, we are studying the ancient **h** _ _ _ _ _ _ of Egypt at school.

50 **D** _ _ _ _ _ _ _ are beautiful. They swim so well and they always look like they're smiling.

	8

Total:		50

Name: ______________________

Class: ______________________

Task 1

Look at the photo and describe what you can see.

Name: ____________________

Class: ____________________

REVIEW (UNITS 4–6): SPEAKING STUDENT B

Task 1

Look at the photo and describe what you can see.

Name: ____________________

Class: ____________________

Task 2

Your friends live in another city. They are coming to visit you in the summer holidays. You want to do something fun together. Here are some ideas for activities. Talk together about the activities and say which would be the best one.

Name: ______________________

Class: ______________________

Task 1

Say good morning/afternoon to both students and then follow the script below: Tell students that first they will each talk about a photograph for about one minute. Say to both students:

I'd like each of you to talk on your own about something. I'm going to give each of you a photograph of young people doing activities. Student A, here is your photograph. (*Ask Student A to look at their photo.*) Please show it to Student B, but I'd like you to talk about it. Student B, you just listen. I'll give you your photograph in a moment. Student A, please tell us what you can see in the photograph.

Allow approximately one minute. If there is a need to intervene, prompts rather than direct questions should be used.

What do you think the girl enjoys about her activity?

Retrieve the photo.

Thank you.

Now, Student B, here is your photograph. It shows some young people doing an activity. (*Ask Student B to look at their photo.*) Please show it to Student A and tell us what you can see in the photograph.

Allow approximately one minute.

What do you think the young people enjoy about their activity?

Retrieve the photo.

Thank the students and move on to Task 2.

Name: ______________________

Class: ______________________

Task 2

Tell students that they will do Task 2 together and that they need to discuss the items in the picture. Say to both students:

I'm going to describe a situation to you. Your friends live in another city. They are coming to visit you in the summer holidays. You want to **do something fun together**. Talk together about the different activities and say which would be the best one.

Ask both students to look at the picture and repeat the information about the task, above.

All right? Talk together.

Allow the students enough time to talk about the task without intervention (3–4 minutes). Prompt only if necessary.

Thank you. That is the end of the test.

Name: ______________________

Class: ______________________

REVIEW (UNITS 4–6): WRITING

Read the exam task below. Write **100** words in an appropriate style. Write your answer on **a separate answer sheet**.

Articles wanted!

Why do you enjoy going to school? How important is it for you to do well at school?

Tell us what you think!

Write an article answering these questions and we will publish the most interesting articles on our website.

Write your **article** in about **100 words**.

....

....

....

....

....

....

....

Name: ____________________

Class: ____________________

GRAMMAR

Task 1

Choose the correct words to complete the sentences.

1 Kathy hasn't **had** / **have** a holiday this year.
2 We looked online for a hotel **who** / **which** was nice, but not expensive.
3 I've **ever** / **never** travelled to another country, but I'd like to.
4 The cake is cooking – it's been in the oven **for** / **since** thirty minutes.
5 He's **just** / **yet** found a good summer camp to go to in July.
6 Cristina cooks very **good** / **well** and she wants to become a chef.
7 Where have you decided **to go** / **going** for your holiday?
8 If we go to Egypt this year, we **visit** / **will visit** the pyramids, of course.
9 The boys are studying **quiet** / **quietly** in their room.

	9

Task 2

Complete the conversations with the correct form of the verbs in brackets.

10 A: What are you going to do tonight?
B: If my friend .... (call) me, we'll go to the cinema.
11 A: Is Elena your sister's best friend?
B: Yes, she is. She .... (know) her since they were five years old.
12 A: Come with us to the new burger café.
B: No, thanks. I .... (already eat) there and I didn't like the food.
13 A: Oh no! I forgot to buy milk.
B: Don't worry. If I go to the shops later, I .... (get) some.
14 A: It's difficult .... (find) cool clothes here.
B: I know! The shops in this town are terrible.
15 A: Have you finished .... (plan) your holiday?
B: Not yet. There's so much to do!
16 A: Do you know about this great new music app?
B: Yes, it looks cool, but I .... (not download) it yet.
17 A: I'm not sure Jim likes going to the theatre.
B: Well, if he .... (not enjoy) it, we won't ask him to come with us.

	8

Task 3

Complete the text with one word in each gap.

Why travel?

Many people agree that **(18)** .... best thing about travelling is that it gives you the chance to have new experiences. One of those experiences is trying unusual food. For example, octopus. Have you **(19)** .... eaten it? It's certainly unusual! People **(20)** .... have tried it say it's delicious! It's a food **(21)** .... is very popular in Asia. **(22)** .... are many different ways to eat it. In Korea, they have it raw. **(23)** .... you go to Japan, you will see that they put it on pizzas! It's fun and exciting **(24)** .... discover different foods, so don't be afraid to give them a try. If you do, you **(25)** .... be amazed!

	8

Name: ____________________

Class: ____________________

VOCABULARY

Task 1

Match 26–34 with A–I to complete the sentences.

26 Toast is usually ....
27 Most fries are ....
28 Pineapples are ....
29 Marshmallows are ....
30 A tourist goes on ....
31 Guests stay in ....
32 Passengers wait on ....
33 A phone needs ....
34 You can delete ....

A soft.
B a charger.
C salty.
D a photo.
E a hotel.
F dry.
G a platform.
H a trip.
I juicy.

/9

Task 2

Complete the words in the sentences.

35 Carrots, potatoes and onions are all **v** _ _ _ _ _ _ _ _ _.
36 A **t** _ _ _ _ _ _ _ is a flat round bread that is eaten in Mexico.
37 He put his **e** _ _ _ _ _ _ _ _ in and listened to some music.
38 We went through **c** _ _ _ _ _ _ at the airport without any problems.
39 Don't wait! Call your friends **i** _ _ _ _ _ _ _ _ _ _ and tell them your good news!
40 I can't go online because I don't have a good **c** _ _ _ _ _ _ _ _ _.
41 Carly is staying at her friend's house tonight – they are having a **s** _ _ _ _ _ _ _ _.
42 Can I borrow your **m** _ _ _ _ _ **p** _ _ _ _? I need to call my parents.

/8

Task 3

Choose the correct answer (A, B or C).

How to plan a holiday

Everyone looks forward to going on a holiday, but before you **(43)** .... your flight, there are so many things to do. **(44)** .... you have decided where and when you want to go, you need to arrange your travel and accommodation. It's easy to **(45)** .... accommodation online – just make sure the hotel you choose has good reviews. Also, **(46)** .... a search online for the best **(47)** .... before you buy your **(48)** .... ticket. And find out if you need **(49)** .... to enter the country you are going to – you have to pay for some, but others don't cost anything.When you're **(50)** .... on the plane, relax!

	A	B	C
43	make	catch	go
44	Then	While	After
45	make	book	have
46	do	make	get
47	journey	reservation	fare
48	tourist	double	return
49	a visa	an ID	a booking
50	suddenly	finally	afterwards

/8

Total: /50

GRAMMAR

Task 1

Choose the correct words to complete the sentences.

1 Sam is the boy **who** / **which** sits next to me in my maths class.
2 We're still working on our history project – we haven't finished it **just** / **yet**.
3 Emma's grandfather taught her French and she speaks it very **good** / **well**.
4 Did you remember **to close** / **closing** the windows before we left for the airport?
5 The girls have been at the sports centre **for** / **since** a few hours.
6 I don't mind **to spend** / **spending** my free time at home.
7 Stella won't help you if you **don't** / **won't** ask her.
8 Which computer game do you enjoy **to play** / **playing** the most?
9 If you **see** / **will see** Jake, tell him to call me.

| | 9 |

Task 2

Complete the conversations with the correct form of the verbs in brackets.

10 A: If Jason .... (decide) to go swimming, tell him to call me.
B: OK, I will.
11 A: What does your brother plan to do after university?
B: If he doesn't find a job, he .... (travel) for a few months.
12 A: How's your friend Gina?
B: I don't know. I .... (not see) her for a few weeks because she's on holiday.
13 A: What's your favourite subject?
B: It's geography because I'm interested in .... (learn) about the world.
14 A: Let's go to the new amusement park tomorrow.
B: Sorry, but I .... (already be) there. I went last week.
15 A: Katya wants to stay at home tomorrow night.
B: That's OK. We'll go to her house if she .... (not feel like) going out.
16 A: Do you want to go to South America?
B: Yes, I would love .... (visit) Argentina and Brazil.
17 A: When are you leaving?
B: In a few minutes. If we don't leave soon, we .... (not catch) our train.

| | 8 |

Task 3

Complete the text with one word in each gap.

Why travel?

Everyone agrees that travelling is fun. It's one of **(18)** .... most exciting things you can do because you see new places and try different foods. Some foods can be very unusual! **(19)** .... you ever eaten a very strange food? How about a fried spider? **(20)** .... you go to Cambodia – a country in Asia – that's what you'll see. It's a snack **(21)** .... is popular there. The people **(22)** .... sell them say they are tasty. But for many of us, **(23)** .... are tastier snacks to eat than cooked insects. However, if we don't try them, how **(24)** .... we know? It's important **(25)** .... have new experiences, so have a go!

| | 8 |

Name: ____________________

Class: ____________________

REVIEW (UNITS 7–9): LANGUAGE TEST B

VOCABULARY

Task 1

Match 26–34 with A–I to complete the sentences.

26 Indian curries are ....
27 Cupcakes are ....
28 Sushi is fish that is ....
29 Lemons are ....
30 A hotel is a type of ....
31 Go online to do ....
32 A traveller goes on ....
33 You can delete ....
34 You must charge ....

A raw.
B a phone.
C a search.
D sweet.
E sour.
F a file.
G spicy.
H a journey.
I accommodation.

	9

Task 2

Complete the words in the sentences.

35 You need lots of milk to make creamy **y** _ _ _ _ _ _.
36 **P** _ _ _ _ _ is a well-known Spanish rice dish.
37 You can read about places to visit in a **g** _ _ _ _ _ _ _ _.
38 We went through **s** _ _ _ _ _ _ _ at the airport without any problems.
39 Everything was silent when **s**_ _ _ _ _ _ _ there was a loud noise!
40 Leo put on his **h** _ _ _ _ _ _ _ _ _ and listened to a podcast.
41 I can't use my phone because the **b**_ _ _ _ _ _ is dead.
42 He was thirsty, so he drank from his **w** _ _ _ _ **b** _ _ _ _ _.

	8

Task 3

Choose the correct answer (A, B or C).

How to plan a holiday

Is it time to plan your next holiday? Before you get into a taxi that will take you to the **(43)** ...., there are lots of things you need to do. The two most important are that you make a **(44)** .... at a hotel and buy your **(45)** .... ticket. You can do both of these online very **(46)** .... and easily. On the day of your **(47)** ...., make sure you have everything you need to travel, such as your **(48)** .... which is usually a passport. Also, make sure you aren't late to **(49)** .... your flight! When you're finally on the plane, relax and **(50)** .... a film – your holiday has just begun!

43	**A** customs	**B** reception	**C** airport
44	**A** reservation	**B** station	**C** connection
45	**A** flying	**B** journey	**C** return
46	**A** suddenly	**B** quickly	**C** immediately
47	**A** trip	**B** fare	**C** security
48	**A** visa	**B** ID	**C** guest
49	**A** catch	**B** hold	**C** go
50	**A** notice	**B** look	**C** watch

	8

Total:		50

Name: ____________________

Class: ____________________

Task 1

A group of classmates want to have a meal together to celebrate the end of the year. Here are some things they could do. Talk together about the different places and foods, and say which would be the best one.

It's the end of the year!

Task 2

Listen to your teacher and discuss the task.

Name: ____________________

Class: ____________________

Task 1

Say good morning/afternoon to both students and then follow the script below:

Tell students that they will work together and that they need to discuss the items in the picture. Say to both students:

I'm going to describe a situation to you. A group of classmates want to **have a meal together to celebrate the end of the year**. Here are some things they could do. Talk together about the different places and foods, and say which would be the best one.

Ask both students to look at the picture and repeat the information about the task, above.

All right? Talk together.

Allow the students enough time to talk about the task without intervention (3–4 minutes). Prompt only if necessary.

Thank the students and move on to Task 2.

Name: ______________________________

Class: ______________________________

Task 2

Now we are going to discuss something together. I would like you to talk together about the food you like and the places where you go to eat.

Repeat the information about the task.

All right? Talk together.

Back up prompts:

- What's your favourite food?
- Do you go out to eat with your friends? Where do you go?
- What events do you celebrate with food?

Allow 3–4 minutes.

Thank you. That is the end of the test.

It's the end of the year!

Name: ______________________________

Class: ______________________________

REVIEW (UNITS 7–9): WRITING

Write **100** words in an appropriate style. Write your answer on **a separate answer sheet**.
Read the **email** below from your English-speaking friend Jane, and the notes you have made.

From:	Jane
Subject:	Summer camp

Hi,

After we talked about going to a summer camp together, I did a search online and got lots of information. The best one is Teen Time, and I think that's where we should go. ← Great!

Would you like to go for two weeks or three weeks? ← Say for how long

There are lots of activities and also lessons in photography or drawing. Which would you prefer? ← Tell Jane. Explain why

Let's meet to discuss it and I can show you the information I found. When and where would you like to meet? ← Suggest

Write back soon,

Jane

Write your **email** to Jane, using **all** the **notes** in about **100 words**.

Name: ______________________

Class: ______________________

END OF YEAR TEST A

LISTENING

Task 1

You are going to listen to people talking in six situations. For each question, choose the correct answer (A, B or C).

1 What was the girl's mum most upset about?

A

B

C

2 What is the girl going to do now?

A

B

C

3 Where will the boy be on his birthday just before he goes home?

A

B

C

4 Which activity doesn't cost anything to do?

A

B

C

5 What did the girl and her sister do yesterday?

A

B

C

6 What does the boy enjoy doing the most?

A

B

C

	6

Task 2

Are the sentences true (T) or false (F)?

7 The boy can ski fast. ....

8 The girl and the boy go to the same judo school. ....

	2

Name: ______________________

Class: ______________________

Task 3

You are going to listen to a talk about a young tennis player. Complete the notes. Write one word in each gap.

Stefanos Tsitsipas

He was born in Greece in the year **(9)** ....

It's unusual that he plays tennis because the most popular sports in Greece are **(10)** .... and basketball.

His parents also play tennis. His mother, who is Russian, was a junior **(11)** .... and his father is a tennis coach.

Since he started to beat the most **(12)** .... tennis players, people have noticed him.

Stefanos' hobbies are photography and making **(13)** .... which he uploads to the internet.

On his YouTube channel, you can watch Stefanos as he's **(14)** .... to tournaments.

	6

Task 4

Is the sentence true (T) or false (F)?

15 Stefanos can speak three languages. ....

	1

Name: ____________________

Class: ____________________

END OF YEAR TEST A

LANGUAGE

Task 1

Complete the text. Write one word in each gap.

Travel Blog: Places to see

If you are lucky **(16)** .... to go to Egypt, you must visit the statue of the Great Sphinx at Giza. One thing **(17)** .... makes it amazing is its size – it's huge! It's a statue of a lion with the head of a human – a creature from mythology. Experts believe the ancient Egyptians built it around 4,500 years **(18)** .... when Khafre was the king and that it is his face on the lion. There are other statues of sphinxes, but this one is the **(19)** .... famous in the world. It has attracted visitors **(20)** .... thousands of years. The statue is close to the pyramids, so you can visit both on the same day. If you want to explore by **(21)** ...., you can download an app that has a **(22)** .... of useful information. But if you would **(23)** .... go with a guide or a tour group, there are many that you can choose from.

	8

Task 2

Read the text and decide which answer (A, B or C) best fits each gap.

Skateboarding

Skateboarding is a cool sport **(24)** .... probably started in the 1940s or 1950s. Surfers from California wanted an activity to do on the days when there weren't **(25)** .... waves for surfing. They had an idea to 'surf' on the streets, so they **(26)** .... a go and put small wheels on small boards. Skateboarding was born! It has been an important part of street culture **(27)** .... the late 1990s. These days, in **(28)** .... towns and cities around the world, there are skate **(29)** .... where teens can have fun and practise their skills. And, from 2020, the best skateboarders can even **(30)** .... part in the Olympic Games and win medals.

24 A who **B** has **C** which
25 A no **B** any **C** some
26 A had **B** did **C** gave
27 A in **B** then **C** since
28 A lots **B** many **C** much
29 A parks **B** places **C** centres
30 A get **B** have **C** take

	7

Name: ____________________

Class: ____________________

READING

Task 1

Five teenagers are looking for an activity to do in the summer. Read the article and decide which activity would be the most suitable for each teenager. Match the descriptions of the summer activities (A–G) with the people (31–35). There are two descriptions of activities which you do not need to use.

31 Alex enjoys being outdoors and learning about nature. He's a good photographer and likes to put his pictures online. He would prefer to do something with friends that doesn't cost too much. ....

32 Lisa has broken her leg and can't do any sports or go swimming for a while. She wants to do something at home that is interesting and will keep her busy. She enjoys reading and writing and doesn't mind being alone. ....

33 Tom likes to spend his free time with his friends. He prefers not to be indoors and is interested in trying an activity that isn't difficult to learn and can keep him fit. He enjoys competitions and likes winning. ....

34 Ellie is adventurous and she isn't afraid to try new activities. In winter, she goes skiing and she's very good at it. She would like to do a similar sport in the summer and she doesn't mind paying for lessons. ....

35 Andy is a fan of adventure sports. He has tried zip lining and he loved it. His parents want to give him an exciting experience for his birthday and he's looking for an activity that he'll never forget. ....

[ ] 5

Task 2

Read the article again and answer the questions in your own words.

36 Why are some animals in animal shelters?

....

....

[ ] 2

37 What reasons are there to have a blog?

....

....

[ ] 2

Name: ______________________

Class: ______________________

Summer holiday activities

A Surfing

Surfing may look easy, but it's quite difficult to stay on the board! If you enjoy challenging activities, this could be perfect for you. A teacher will show you how to stand up on the surfboard and how to stay on it in the water. There are lots of clubs that teach teenagers and they're not too expensive.

B Play games

If you can't go to the beach in the summer, don't worry. There are lots of other fun activities to keep you happy. Try doing quizzes and puzzles or playing board games. You can have a competition with your friends to find the best player and give small prizes to the winners. It's a lot of fun! It's even better when you make tasty snacks for everyone to enjoy.

C Explore a forest

This is an excellent activity for anyone who is interested in the environment. It doesn't cost anything and all you need is a notebook and pen, a camera and good walking shoes. Organise a day trip with your friends and be amazed by the beautiful plants and animals that live there. Don't forget to take plenty of water and some food, too.

D Volunteering

Become a volunteer at an animal shelter. Shelters always need people to help them take care of the animals. The animals don't have homes because they're lost or their owners can't look after them. Many of them feel lonely, scared or sad. You'll feel great about doing something important, and the animals will show you how much they love you.

E Beach volleyball

If you love team sports and being by the sea, you should try playing beach volleyball. It's the perfect summer sport and if you have played volleyball before, you already know the rules. Get your friends together, make two teams, and start playing. It's a fast game that will make you feel hot. At the end of the match, jump into the sea!

F Skydiving

If you're afraid of being up high, don't do this! Many people think it's too scary, but others love it. So, if you aren't afraid to jump out of a plane, give it a go. It isn't cheap though – each jump costs a lot of money, so it's best to do it as something special that you'll never forget.

G Blogging

Is there something you're very interested in, like a sport, fashion, TV or books? Why not share your interest with others? You can start a blog to write about your favourite hobby or free-time activity. Blogs are a great way to practise and improve your writing. You'll also have fun reading the comments other people leave on your blog.

Task 3

Read the article. Choose from the sentences (A–H) the one which fits each gap (38–42). There are three extra sentences which you do not need to use.

A The chess player moved the pieces on his own board.

B In the future, they will certainly be able to do more.

C During that time, chess wasn't a very popular game.

D On top of it there was a chess board.

E They were right and they finally discovered the secret.

F So it was difficult to move the desk to another place.

G They wondered how it was possible for a machine to play chess.

H It was a robot chess player that looked like and could move like a real person.

	5

Task 4

Read the article again and answer the questions in your own words.

43 How did the machine get its name?

....

....

44 Which famous people played chess against the machine?

....

....

45 What was the truth about the machine?

....

....

	6

Total:		50

The story of 'the Turk'

Robots can do many jobs that people do, especially boring jobs in factories. **(38)** .... But did you know that people have been excited by the idea of robots for hundreds of years? Nearly 250 years ago, in the 1770s, an inventor called Wolfgang von Kempelen presented his newest invention. **(39)** .... People called it 'the Turk' because it wore long clothes and a cap on its head, as people did in Turkey.

The machine sat behind a big wooden desk that was closed on all sides like a box. **(40)** .... The Turk played chess against anyone who thought they could beat it, but they usually lost. This included Napoleon Bonaparte and Benjamin Franklin – the scientist who was famous for his experiments with electricity.

When the Turk arrived in the USA in 1826, many people went to see it. Thousands of others read about its amazing skills in the newspapers. **(41)** .... They were also interested in the Turk because machines were starting to do work in factories.

However, there were people who thought it was a trick. None of them believed the Turk was a machine which could think. **(42)** .... The desk under the chess board was big enough to hide a man. Sitting inside, he had a way to control the arms of the Turk and move the pieces on the board. How did the Turk win so often? Its owner paid chess champions to work the machine.

Name: ______________________

Class: ______________________

END OF YEAR TEST B

LISTENING

Task 1

Listen to people talking in six situations. For each question, choose the correct answer (A, B or C).

1 What made the girls mum most unhappy?

A B C

2 What is the girl going to do the next day?

A B C

3 What will the boy do on his birthday just before he goes home?

A B C

4 Which activity does the club manager think people will be most excited about?

A B C

5 What are the girl and her sister finding difficult to do at the moment?

A B C

6 Which activity does the boy like best?

A B C

/6

Task 2

Are the sentences true (T) or false (F)?

7 The boy would like to go skiing again. ....

8 The girl and the boy have different teachers for judo. ....

/2

Name: ____________________

Class: ____________________

Task 3

You are going to listen to a talk about a young tennis player. Complete the notes. Write one word in each gap.

Stefanos Tsitsipas

His birthday is on the **(9)** .... of August.

In Greece, the most popular sports are football and **(10)** ...., so it's unusual that he plays tennis.

His parents also play tennis. His mother was an excellent junior player and Stefanos' father is his **(11)** ....

Since he started to win in important **(12)** ...., people have noticed him.

One of his hobbies is **(13)** .... and he also has a YouTube channel where he uploads the videos he makes.

On his channel, you can watch Stefanos when he's **(14)** .... hard to get ready for tournaments.

	6

Task 4

Is the sentence true (T) or false (F)?

15 Stefanos started playing tennis when he was three years old. ....

	1

Name: ____________________

Class: ____________________

END OF YEAR TEST B

LANGUAGE

Task 1

Complete the text. Write one word in each gap.

Travel Blog: Places to see

Have you **(16)** .... thought about visiting Egypt? If you go there, you must visit the Great Sphinx at Giza – a statue with the body of a lion and the head of a human. You'll be amazed by its size – it's huge! It's large **(17)** .... to see from far away. When **(18)** .... they build it? It was thousands of years ago. The man **(19)** .... was the king at the time was Khafre and it may be his face on the lion. There are other statues of sphinxes in the world, but none are as famous **(20)** .... this one. The statue is close to the pyramids, so you can visit both on the same day. If you want to explore it **(21)** .... yourself, it's quite easy to do. There are a **(22)** .... good apps you can download with lots of useful information. But if you **(23)** .... rather go with a guide or a tour group, there are many that you can choose from.

[ ] 8

Task 2

Read the text and decide which answer (A, B or C) best fits each gap.

Skateboarding

Surfers from California **(24)** .... wanted an activity to do on the days when the waves weren't big **(25)** .... for surfing probably started skateboarding in the 1940s or 1950s. They had an idea to 'surf' on the streets, so they **(26)** .... it a try and put small wheels on small boards. Skateboarding was born! It has been an important part of street culture **(27)** .... about twenty-five years, since the late 1990s. These days, in a **(28)** .... of towns and cities around the world, there are skate parks and sports **(29)** .... where teens can have fun and practise their skills. And, from 2020, skateboarders can even compete to be the best **(30)** .... the sport in the Olympic Games and win medals.

24 A who **B** which **C** have

25 A some **B** already **C** enough

26 A had **B** gave **C** did

27 A for **B** in **C** of

28 A much **B** lots **C** lot

29 A blocks **B** centres **C** accessories

30 A at **B** of **C** to

[ ] 7

Name: ____________________

Class: ____________________

READING

Task 1

Five teenagers are looking for an activity to do in the summer. Read the article and decide which activity would be the most suitable for each teenager. Match the descriptions of the summer activities (A–G) with the people (31–35). There are two descriptions of activities which you do not need to use.

31 Tim likes to spend his free time with his friends. He prefers not to be indoors and is interested in trying an activity that isn't difficult to learn and can keep him fit. He enjoys competitions and likes winning. ....

32 Jason is a fan of adventure sports. He has tried zip lining and he loved it. His parents want to give him an exciting experience for his birthday and he's looking for an activity that he'll never forget. ....

33 Kelly has broken her leg and can't do any sports or go swimming for a while. She wants to do something at home that is interesting and will keep her busy. She enjoys reading and writing and doesn't mind being alone. ....

34 David enjoys being outdoors and learning about nature. He's a good photographer and likes to put his pictures online. He would prefer to do something with friends that doesn't cost too much. ....

35 Cait is adventurous and she isn't afraid to try new activities. In winter, she goes skiing and she's very good at it. She would like to do a similar sport in the summer and she doesn't mind paying for lessons. ....

	5

Task 2

Read the article again and answer the questions in your own words.

36 How do many animals in shelters feel?

....

....

	2

37 What indoor activities can you do with your friends?

....

....

	2

Summer holiday activities

A Skydiving

If you're afraid of being up high, don't do this! Many people think it's too scary, but others love it. So, if you aren't afraid to jump out of a plane, give it a go. It isn't cheap though – each jump costs a lot of money, so it's best to do it as something special that you'll never forget.

B Explore a forest

This is an excellent activity for anyone who is interested in the environment. It doesn't cost anything and all you need is a notebook and pen, a camera and good walking shoes. Organise a day trip with your friends and be amazed by the beautiful plants and animals that live there. Don't forget to take plenty of water and some food, too.

C Volunteering

Become a volunteer at an animal shelter. Shelters always need people to help them take care of the animals. The animals don't have homes because they're lost or their owners can't look after them. Many of them feel lonely, scared or sad. You'll feel great about doing something important, and the animals will show you how much they love you.

D Beach volleyball

If you love team sports and being by the sea, you should try playing beach volleyball. It's the perfect summer sport and if you have played volleyball before, you already know the rules. Get your friends together, make two teams, and start playing. It's a fast game that will make you feel hot. At the end of the match, jump into the sea!

E Play games

If you can't go to the beach in the summer, don't worry. There are lots of other fun activities to keep you happy. Try doing quizzes and puzzles or playing board games. You can have a competition with your friends to find the best player and give small prizes to the winners. It's a lot of fun! It's even better when you make tasty snacks for everyone to enjoy.

F Blogging

Is there something you're very interested in, like a sport, fashion, TV or books? Why not share your interest with others? You can start a blog to write about your favourite hobby or free time activity. Blogs are a great way to practise and improve your writing. You'll also have fun reading the comments other people leave on your blog.

G Surfing

Surfing may look easy, but it's quite difficult to stay on the board! If you enjoy challenging activities, this could be perfect for you. A teacher will show you how to stand up on the surfboard and how to stay on it in the water. There are lots of clubs that teach teenagers and they're not too expensive.

Task 3

Read the article. Choose from the sentences (A–H) the one which fits each gap (38–42). There are three extra sentences which you do not need to use.

A Thousands of others read about its amazing skills in the newspapers.

B Is this a reason for us to worry about what could happen?

C But did you know that people have been excited by the idea of robots for hundreds of years?

D Next to it was another machine that was much smaller.

E None of them believed the Turk was a machine which could think.

F The Turk played chess against anyone who thought they could beat it, but they usually lost.

G Although it was quite difficult, they sometimes won the games.

H The desk under the chess board was big enough to hide a man.

	5

Task 4

Read the article again and answer the questions in your own words.

43 Where did the Turk sit?

....

44 What was happening in factories when the Turk went to the USA?

....

45 Why was the Turk good at chess?

....

	6

Total:		50

Name: ____________________

Class: ____________________

The story of 'the Turk'

Robots can do many jobs that people do, especially boring jobs in factories. In the future, they will certainly be able to do more. **(38)** .... Nearly 250 years ago, in the 1770s, an inventor called Wolfgang von Kempelen presented his newest invention. It was a robot chess player that looked like and could move like a real person. People called it 'the Turk' because it wore long clothes and a cap on its head, as people did in Turkey.

The machine sat behind a big wooden desk that was closed on all sides like a box. On top of it there was a chessboard. **(39)** .... This included Napoleon Bonaparte and Benjamin Franklin – the scientist who was famous for his experiments with electricity.

When the Turk arrived in the USA in 1826, many people went to see it. **(40)** .... They wondered how it was possible for a machine to play chess. They were also interested in the Turk because machines were starting to do work in factories.

However, there were people who thought it was a trick. **(41)** .... They were right and they finally discovered the secret. **(42)** .... Sitting inside, he had a way to control the arms of the Turk and move the pieces on the board. How did the Turk win so often? Its owner paid chess champions to work the machine!

Name: ______________________

Class: ______________________

END OF YEAR TEST: SPEAKING STUDENT A

Task 1

Your teacher will ask you some questions. Remember to give full answers.

Task 2

Look at the photo and describe what you can see.

Name: ______________________

Class: ______________________

END OF YEAR TEST: SPEAKING STUDENT B

Task 1

Your teacher will ask you some questions. Remember to give full answers.

Task 2

Look at the photo and describe what you can see.

Name: ______________________

Class: ______________________

Task 3

Your friend wants to take up a new hobby. Here are some ideas for hobbies. Talk together about the hobbies and say which would be the best one.

Task 4

Listen to your teacher and discuss the task.

Name: ______________________

Class: ______________________

Task 1

Say good morning/afternoon to both students and then follow the script below:

(*Student A*) What's your name?

Thank you.

(*Student B*) What's your name?

Thank you.

(*Student A*) What's your surname? How do you spell it?

Thank you.

(*Student B*) What's your surname? How do you spell it?

Thank you.

(*Student A*) Where do you live?

(*Student B*) Do you study English at school?

Ask three questions to each student from the list below:

- Do you have any brothers or sisters?
- What do you usually do in the summer?
- Do you use social media?
- What kinds of films do you like?

Thank the students and move on to Task 2.

Task 2

Tell students that first they will each talk about a photograph for about one minute. Say to both students:

I'd like each of you to talk on your own about something. I'm going to give each of you a photograph. Student A, here is your photograph of **two students and a teacher**. (*Ask Student A to look at their photo.*) Please show it to Student B, but I'd like you to talk about it. Student B, you just listen. I'll give you your photograph in a moment. Student A, please tell us what you can see in the photograph.

Allow approximately one minute. If there is a need to intervene, prompts rather than direct questions should be used.

How are the students feeling and what do you think is going to happen next?

Retrieve the picture.

Thank you.

Now, Student B, here is your photograph. It shows **some friends**. (*Ask Student B to look at their photo.*) Please show it to Student A and tell us what you can see in the photograph.

Allow approximately one minute.

How are the friends feeling and what do you think is going to happen next?

Thank the students and move on to Task 3.

Name: ____________________

Class: ____________________

Task 3

Tell students that they will do Task 2 together and that they need to discuss the items in the picture. Say to both students:

I'm going to describe a situation to you. Your friend wants to take up **a new hobby**. Talk together about the different hobbies and say which would be the best one.

Ask students to look at the pictures and then repeat the task above.

All right? Talk together.

Allow the students enough time to talk about the task without intervention (3–4 minutes). Prompt only if necessary.

Thank the students and move on to Task 4.

Task 4

Now we are going to discuss something together. I would like you to talk together about your hobbies and favourite activities.

Repeat the information about the task.

All right? Talk together.

Back up prompts:

- Do you enjoy trying new activities and hobbies?
- Is there an activity you would like to try?
- Why is it important to have hobbies?

Allow 3–4 minutes.

Thank you. That is the end of the test.

Name: ____________________

Class: ____________________

END OF YEAR TEST: WRITING TEST

Choose <u>ONE</u> of the tasks below. Write your answer in approximately 100 words in an appropriate style. Write your answer on a separate answer sheet.

Task 1

Read the email from your English-speaking friend Tom, and the notes you have made.

From:	Tom
Subject:	Cinema

Hi,

Guess what? My aunt works at a cinema and she gave me two free passes to see a film. Do you want to come with me? ← Of course!

We can go any day this week. When would you like to go? ← Say which day

There's a new action film. Would you like to see that? ← No, because …

Let's get something to eat after the film. Where should we go? ← Suggest

Write back soon,

Tom

Write an **email** to Tom, using **all** the **notes**. Write your answer in approximately **100 words**.

Task 2

Your English teacher has asked you to write a story. Your story must begin with this sentence:

I felt nervous when I held the envelope.

Write your **story** in approximately **100 words**.

Diagnostic Test A

No	Key	Language Area
1	D	Adverbs of frequency
2	A	Adverbs of frequency
3	C	Collocations (lexis)
4	C	Present continuous
5	B	Technology (lexis)
6	A	Collocations (lexis)
7	A	Past simple
8	D	Past simple
9	B	Education (lexis)
10	C	Comparative adjectives
11	A	Superlative adjectives
12	D	Shopping (lexis)
13	D	Shopping (lexis)
14	C	Past continuous
15	B	Adjectives (lexis)
16	A	*Be going to*
17	A	Collocations (lexis)
18	B	Modals of ability
19	B	Modals of obligation
20	A	Collocations (lexis)
21	D	Present perfect
22	D	Present perfect
23	B	Nature (lexis)
24	C	First conditional
25	D	Advice: *should*
26	D	Articles
27	D	Quantifiers
28	C	Adjectives (lexis)
29	A	Prepositional phrases (lexis)
30	B	Present simple
31	C	Present continuous
32	A	Subject and object questions
33	B	Phrases (lexis)
34	D	Adjectives (lexis)
35	C	Past simple
36	D	Past continuous
37	B	Indefinite pronouns
38	C	Adjectives (lexis)
39	D	Strong adjectives (lexis)
40	B	*Be going to*
41	C	Future simple: predictions
42	A	Modals of possibility
43	C	Sports (lexis)
44	B	Education (lexis)
45	A	Collocations (lexis)
46	D	Making comparisons
47	B	Making comparisons
48	A	Making comparisons
49	C	Making comparisons
50	A	Making comparisons
51	D	Appearance (lexis)
52	C	Phrasal verbs (lexis)
53	D	Modals for rules
54	B	Modals for rules
55	B	Reflexive pronouns
56	C	*There is/are*
57	C	Animals (lexis)
58	A	Adjectives (lexis)
59	B	Animals (lexis)
60	C	Food (lexis)
61	D	Food (lexis)
62	D	Present perfect
63	A	Present perfect with *never*
64	B	Present perfect with *yet*
65	C	Present perfect with *for* and *since*
66	B	Present perfect with *for* and *since*
67	D	Travel (lexis)
68	C	Travel (lexis)
69	B	Collocations (lexis)
70	A	Zero conditional
71	A	First conditional
72	B	Verb patterns: *-ing* and *infinitive*
73	B	Verb patterns: *-ing* and *infinitive*
74	D	Verb patterns: infinitive without *to*
75	C	Technology (lexis)
76	C	Adjective + preposition
77	D	Verb patterns: *-ing* form
78	B	Verb patterns: *-ing* form
79	A	Language (lexis)
80	A	Future simple
81	D	*Be going to*
82	C	Making suggestions
83	B	Phrasal verbs (lexis)
84	D	Technology (lexis)
85	C	Present perfect
86	A	Sports (lexis)
87	C	Sports (lexis)
88	B	Second conditional
89	B	*Unless*
90	B	Entertainment (lexis)
91	C	The passive
92	D	The passive
93	A	*Have/Get sth done*
94	C	Defining relative clauses
95	C	Travel (lexis)
96	B	Indirect questions
97	D	Adjectives (lexis)
98	D	Past perfect
99	A	*Used to*
100	B	Phrasal verbs (lexis)

Placement Guidance:

- If students score fewer than 10 correct answers, consider starting in the level below.
- If students score between 10 and 40, start at the expected level and assess scores to check whether remediation is required.
- If students score between 50 to 75, assess scores and consider an additional oral interview to decide whether the expected level or the upper level with some remediation would be more appropriate.
- Students who scored 75+ should be started at an upper level.

Diagnostic Test B

No	Key	Language Area
1	C	Adverbs of frequency
2	B	Adverbs of frequency
3	D	Collocations (lexis)
4	A	Present continuous
5	A	Technology (lexis)
6	C	Collocations (lexis)
7	D	Past simple
8	B	Past simple
9	A	Education (lexis)
10	C	Comparative adjectives
11	D	Superlative adjectives
12	A	Shopping (lexis)
13	C	Shopping (lexis)
14	A	Past continuous
15	D	Adjectives (lexis)
16	C	*Be going to*
17	B	Collocations (lexis)
18	D	Modals of ability
19	C	Modals of obligation
20	C	Collocations (lexis)
21	B	Present perfect
22	A	Present perfect
23	D	Nature (lexis)
24	A	First conditional
25	B	Advice: *should*
26	C	Articles
27	A	Quantifiers
28	A	Adjectives (lexis)
29	B	Prepositional phrases (lexis)
30	A	Present simple
31	D	Present continuous
32	B	Subject and object questions
33	C	Phrases (lexis)
34	D	Adjectives (lexis)
35	A	Past simple
36	C	Past continuous
37	D	Indefinite pronouns
38	A	Adjectives (lexis)
39	C	Strong adjectives (lexis)
40	B	*Be going to*
41	C	Future simple: predictions
42	A	Modals of possibility
43	B	Ways of learning (lexis)
44	D	Education (lexis)
45	C	Collocations (lexis)
46	B	Making comparisons
47	D	Making comparisons
48	C	Making comparisons
49	A	Making comparisons
50	B	Making comparisons
51	C	Appearance (lexis)
52	B	Phrasal verbs (lexis)
53	B	Modals for rules
54	A	Modals for rules
55	C	Reflexive pronouns
56	B	*It's*
57	A	Animals (lexis)
58	C	Adjectives (lexis)
59	D	Animals (lexis)
60	D	Food (lexis)
61	B	Food (lexis)
62	A	Present perfect
63	D	Present perfect with *ever*
64	B	Present perfect with *yet*
65	A	Present perfect with *for* and *since*
66	C	Present perfect with *for* and *since*
67	A	Travel (lexis)
68	B	Travel (lexis)
69	A	Collocations (lexis)
70	B	Zero conditional
71	C	First conditional
72	D	Verb patterns: *-ing* and *infinitive*
73	A	Verb patterns: *-ing* and *infinitive*
74	C	Verb patterns: infinitive without *to*
75	D	Technology (lexis)
76	A	Adjective + preposition
77	C	Verb patterns: *-ing* form
78	B	Verb patterns: *-ing* form
79	D	Language (lexis)
80	C	Future simple
81	D	*Be going to*
82	B	Making suggestions
83	B	Phrasal verbs (lexis)
84	C	Technology (lexis)
85	C	Present perfect)
86	D	Sport (lexis)
87	A	Sports (lexis)
88	B	Second conditional
89	D	*Unless*
90	B	Entertainment (lexis)
91	A	The passive
92	B	The passive
93	D	*Have/Get sth done*
94	C	Defining relative clauses
95	D	Travel (lexis)
96	B	Indirect questions
97	C	Adjectives (lexis)
98	C	Past perfect
99	A	*Used to*
100	D	Phrasal verbs (lexis)

Placement Guidance:

- If students score fewer than 10 correct answers, consider starting in the level below.
- If students score between 10 and 40, start at the expected level and assess scores to check whether remediation is required.
- If students score between 50 to 75, assess scores and consider an additional oral interview to decide whether the expected level or the upper level with some remediation would be more appropriate.
- Students who scored 75+ should be started at an upper level.

UNIT 1

LANGUAGE TEST A

Grammar

TASK 1

1 – **2** the **3** a **4** the **5** an **6** an **7** – **8** –

For revision, go to Student's Book: p12

TASK 2

9 little **10** any **11** lot **12** many **13** All **14** few
15 much **16** any

For revision, go to Student's Book: p14

TASK 3

17 C **18** A **19** B **20** C **21** B **22** C **23** A **24** A **25** B

For revision, go to Student's Book: p12, p14

Vocabulary

TASK 1

26 gallery **27** bin **28** rack **29** centre **30** apartment
31 stop **32** park **33** department **34** lift **35** crossing
36 seat

For revision, go to Student's Book: p13

TASK 2

37 between **38** behind **39** but **40** in **41** on **42** near
43 out **44** on

For revision, go to Student's Book: p15, p17

TASK 3

45 D **46** B **47** F **48** A **49** E **50** C

For revision, go to Student's Book: p15, p17

LANGUAGE TEST B

Grammar

TASK 1

1 – **2** – **3** – **4** an **5** the **6** the **7** a **8** the

For revision, go to Student's Book: p12

TASK 2

9 any **10** lot **11** many **12** little **13** any **14** All
15 few **16** much

For revision, go to Student's Book: p14

TASK 3

17 B **18** C **19** A **20** B **21** A **22** A **23** B **24** C **25** C

For revision, go to Student's Book: p12, p14

Vocabulary

TASK 1

26 block **27** lift **28** park **29** bin **30** seat **31** gallery
32 stop **33** rack **34** centre **35** crossing **36** store

For revision, go to Student's Book: p13

TASK 2

37 and **38** in **39** at **40** because **41** between **42** near
43 on **44** under

For revision, go to Student's Book: p15, p17

TASK 3

45 B **46** F **47** D **48** C **49** A **50** E

For revision, go to Student's Book: p15, p17

SKILLS TEST A

Dictation

Why are Dutch teens so happy at school? It's because there isn't a lot of pressure from parents and teachers, and students feel very close to their school community.

Listening

TASK 1

1 B **2** C **3** A **4** B **5** C **6** C

TASK 2

7 F **8** T

Reading

TASK 1

9 F **10** DS **11** T **12** DS **13** T **14** T **15** DS **16** T

TASK 2

17 It's important for young people to spend time with their friends because this helps them to learn how to be around other people.

18 Exams make young people unhappy because they worry that exams will be difficult and they will get bad marks.

SKILLS TEST B

Dictation

Why are Dutch teens so happy at school? It's because there isn't a lot of pressure from parents and teachers, and students feel very close to their school community.

Listening

TASK 1

1 C **2** B **3** C **4** A **5** B **6** A

TASK 2

7 T **8** F

Reading

TASK 1

9 T **10** DS **11** F **12** DS **13** DS **14** T **15** DS **16** T

TASK 2

17 They ask a lot of questions and send too many text messages. However, they are happy to have their parents' support.

18 It's good because it helps them to learn how to be around other people, for example, to be kind and polite.

UNIT 2

LANGUAGE TEST A

Grammar

TASK 1

1 Do you like **2** Are you looking for **3** seems **4** go **5** climb **6** aren't going up **7** are trying **8** love

For revision, go to Student's Book: p24

TASK 2

9 are playing **10** don't believe **11** isn't going **12** needs **13** spend **14** Do, think **15** listen **16** hates **17** Am, walking **18** doesn't like

For revision, go to Student's Book: p24

TASK 3

19 B **20** C **21** A **22** B **23** C **24** A **25** C

For revision, go to Student's Book: p24, p26

Vocabulary

TASK 1

26 F **27** C **28** H **29** A **30** E **31** D **32** B **33** G

For revision, go to Student's Book: p25

TASK 2

34 honest **35** polite **36** careful **37** friendly **38** clever **39** quiet **40** serious **41** confident

For revision, go to Student's Book: p28

TASK 3

42 site **43** share **44** follow **45** program **46** He'd like **47** press **48** get **49** waste **50** work

For revision, go to Student's Book: p22, p29

LANGUAGE TEST B

Grammar

TASK 1

1 do you usually spend **2** Are you looking for **3** use **4** rains **5** don't fall **6** am starting **7** are looking forward to **8** looks

For revision, go to Student's Book: p24

TASK 2

9 agree **10** isn't running **11** don't understand **12** watches **13** Does, know **14** Are, learning **15** love **16** doesn't do **17** Do, want **18** Is, raining

For revision, go to Student's Book: p24

TASK 3

19 C **20** A **21** B **22** C **23** A **24** B **25** A

For revision, go to Student's Book: p24, p26

Vocabulary

TASK 1

26 D **27** G **28** E **29** H **30** B **31** F **32** A **33** C

For revision, go to Student's Book: p25

TASK 2

34 quiet **35** friendly **36** confident **37** clever **38** serious
39 polite **40** careful **41** honest

For revision, go to Student's Book: p28

TASK 3

42 follow **43** getting **44** work **45** program **46** site
47 press **48** waste **49** share **50** I'd like

For revision, go to Student's Book: p22, p29

SKILLS TEST A

Dictation

To get better at any skill, you need to practise. By working hard and spending some time on it you can make progress and have fun at the same time.

Listening

TASK 1

1 activities **2** every day **3** five/5 **4** hours **5** lunch **6** clothes

TASK 2

7 T **8** F

Reading

TASK 1

9 A **10** B **11** C

TASK 2

12 M **13** J **14** B **15** J **16** B

TASK 3

17 something you enjoy
18 at home or somewhere in your town

SKILLS TEST B

Dictation

To get better at any skill, you need to practise. By working hard and spending some time on it you can make progress and have fun at the same time.

Listening

TASK 1

1 trips **2** costs **3** eight/8 **4** two/2 **5** town **6** shoes

TASK 2

7 F **8** T

Reading

TASK 1

9 B **10** C **11** A

TASK 2

12 B **13** M **14** J **15** J **16** M

TASK 3

17 it's fantastic exercise for hands, arms and shoulders
18 how to start a blog

UNIT 3

LANGUAGE TEST A

Grammar

TASK 1

1 were sitting, started **2** was chatting, were waiting
3 was reading, called **4** were playing, broke **5** kicked, scored
6 was Pat sitting, were listening **7** didn't meet, was studying
8 was raining, was blowing

For revision, go to Student's Book: p36

TASK 2

9 wasn't watching **10** Did you buy **11** was doing **12** paid
13 Was she driving **14** went out **15** opened **16** wasn't going

For revision, go to Student's Book: p36

TASK 3

17 anything **18** no one **19** everything **20** Someone
21 anything **22** nothing **23** everyone **24** something
25 anyone

For revision, go to Student's Book: p38

Vocabulary

TASK 1

26 F **27** H **28** A **29** G **30** B **31** C **32** E **33** D

For revision, go to Student's Book: p41

TASK 2

34 dark, light **35** exciting, dull **36** modern, ancient
37 ordinary, special **38** tiny, huge

For revision, go to Student's Book: p37

TASK 3

39 valuable Italian painting **40** brilliant young writer
41 beautiful gold ring **42** fantastic German sports car
43 scary black and white film **44** strange old man
45 long wooden spoon

For revision, go to Student's Book: p37

LANGUAGE TEST B

Grammar

TASK 1

1 was showing, dropped **2** found, was looking
3 was going, called **4** was skiing, fell **5** didn't invite, forgot
6 Were you sitting, were reading **7** didn't cycle, was raining
8 was shining, were singing

For revision, go to Student's Book: p36

TASK 2

9 wasn't listening **10** Did you take **11** was doing **12** visited
13 Were you having **14** came **15** went **16** wasn't snowing

For revision, go to Student's Book: p36

TASK 3

17 someone **18** everyone **19** anything **20** no one
21 everything **22** anything **23** anyone **24** nothing
25 something

For revision, go to Student's Book: p38

Vocabulary

TASK 1

26 H **27** E **28** F **29** B **30** C **31** G **32** D **33** A

For revision, go to Student's Book: p41

TASK 2

34 Ancient, modern **35** light, dark **36** huge, tiny
37 dull, exciting **38** special, ordinary

For revision, go to Student's Book: p37

TASK 3

39 funny American film **40** uncomfortable wooden chair
41 valuable gold jewellery **42** favourite young tennis player
43 strange blue bottle **44** incredible Greek island
45 brilliant opera singer

For revision, go to Student's Book: p37

SKILLS TEST A

Dictation

When I travel I make sure that I have an exciting story with me. If I have to wait for a bus or train I pass the time reading it.

Listening

TASK 1

1 C **2** B **3** A **4** C **5** C **6** A

TASK 2

7 T **8** F

Reading

TASK 1

9 C **10** H **11** J **12** A **13** E **14** D

TASK 2

15 by plane, taxi, train and bus

SKILLS TEST B

Dictation

When I travel, I make sure that I have an exciting story with me. If I have to wait for a bus or train, I pass the time reading it.

Listening

TASK 1

1 A **2** C **3** B **4** A **5** B **6** C

TASK 2

7 F **8** T

Reading

TASK 1

9 E **10** J **11** B **12** C **13** G **14** F

TASK 2

15 her dad's pockets, their bags and suitcases

UNIT 4

LANGUAGE TEST A

Grammar

TASK 1

1 B **2** C **3** A **4** B **5** A **6** C **7** B **8** A

For revision, go to Student's Book: p48

TASK 2

9 will **10** may **11** won't **12** might **13** will **14** might **15** will **16** may not **17** will **18** may

For revision, go to Student's Book: p50

TASK 3

19 Are you going to make **20** will be **21** are going **22** do you start **23** will help **24** are having **25** ends

For revision, go to Student's Book: p48

Vocabulary

TASK 1

26 C **27** B **28** A **29** C **30** B **31** C **32** A **33** B

For revision, go to Student's Book: p49

TASK 2

34 F **35** C **36** H **37** B **38** G **39** D **40** A **41** E

For revision, go to Student's Book: p46, p49

TASK 3

42 make **43** open **44** out **45** take **46** run **47** down **48** around **49** make **50** sounds

For revision, go to Student's Book: p46, p49

LANGUAGE TEST B

Grammar

TASK 1

1 A **2** A **3** B **4** C **5** C **6** B **7** B **8** A

For revision, go to Student's Book: p48

TASK 2

9 might **10** won't **11** might **12** will **13** may **14** will **15** won't **16** might **17** will **18** may

For revision, go to Student's Book: p50

TASK 3

19 Is Andy going to walk **20** will love **21** are looking **22** does it open **23** will tidy **24** are coming **25** comes

For revision, go to Student's Book: p48

Vocabulary

TASK 1

26 A **27** C **28** B **29** A **30** B **31** A **32** C **33** A

For revision, go to Student's Book: p49

TASK 2

34 H **35** E **36** B **37** D **38** A **39** F **40** C **41** G

For revision, go to Student's Book: p46, p49

TASK 3

42 fancy **43** make **44** off **45** open **46** have **47** around **48** take **49** up **50** runs

For revision, go to Student's Book: p46, p49

SKILLS TEST A

Dictation

It isn't easy to decide about your future when you're young. Before you make up your mind about school or work, take advice from people who can help you.

Listening

TASK 1

1 C **2** A **3** B **4** A **5** C **6** B

TASK 2

7 She leaves five minutes before the end to go over her answers.

Reading

TASK 1

8 C **9** B **10** D **11** A **12** B **13** C

TASK 2

14 They became best friends. They shared Charlie's bedroom and they often talked for ages before they fell asleep.

SKILLS TEST B

Dictation

It isn't easy to decide about your future when you're young. Before you make up your mind about school or work, take advice from people who can help you.

Listening

TASK 1

1 B **2** A **3** C **4** B **5** A **6** C

TASK 2

7 Because she isn't great at maths.

Reading

TASK 1

8 D **9** C **10** A **11** B **12** D **13** A

TASK 2

14 Young people like to look fashionable all the time and it makes some students feel bad because they don't have nice clothes.

UNIT 5

LANGUAGE TEST A

Grammar

TASK 1

1 C **2** B **3** C **4** B **5** A **6** B **7** A **8** A

For revision, go to Student's Book: p60, p62

TASK 2

9 C **10** F **11** H **12** A **13** G **14** B **15** D **16** E

For revision, go to Student's Book: p60, p62

TASK 3

17 too curly **18** isn't hot enough **19** too big
20 talented enough **21** comfortable enough
22 aren't fashionable enough **23** too angry
24 fast enough **25** too tired

For revision, go to Student's Book: p62

Vocabulary

TASK 1

26 check **27** save **28** try **29** slogan **30** fancy
31 dark **32** average **33** glasses

For revision, go to Student's Book: p58, p61

TASK 2

34 like, personality **35** look, freckles **36** Who, curly
37 What, might **38** How, probably

For revision, go to Student's Book: p61, p63

TASK 3

39 A **40** A **41** B **42** C **43** A **44** B **45** C

For revision, go to Student's Book: p58, p61

LANGUAGE TEST B

Grammar

TASK 1

1 A **2** C **3** C **4** A **5** A **6** B **7** B **8** A

For revision, go to Student's Book: p60, p62

TASK 2

9 F **10** C **11** E **12** A **13** D **14** H **15** G **16** B

For revision, go to Student's Book: p60, p62

TASK 3

17 confident enough **18** cheap enough **19** too young
20 too loud **21** isn't good enough **22** too old
23 aren't big enough **24** too excited **25** tall enough

For revision, go to Student's Book: p62

Vocabulary

TASK 1

26 dress **27** slim **28** stand **29** freckles **30** try
31 braces **32** make-up **33** pattern

For revision, go to Student's Book: p58, p61

TASK 2

34 Who, tall **35** like, friendly **36** look, average
37 How, Maybe **38** What, probably

For revision, go to Student's Book: p61, p63

TASK 3

39 C **40** C **41** C **42** B **43** A **44** B **45** A

For revision, go to Student's Book: p58, p61

SKILLS TEST A

Dictation

The internet has made shopping much easier. You can check out as many different shops as you like without leaving your home. It's great for finding what you need.

Listening

TASK 1

1 2005 **2** fill in **3** personality **4** work **5** 8/eight
6 (free) gifts/presents

TASK 2

7 T **8** F

Reading

TASK 1

9 E **10** G **11** H **12** C **13** B **14** A

TASK 2

15 Good quality items last longer than cheap ones. They make you stand out and feel special.

SKILLS TEST B

Dictation

The internet has made shopping much easier. You can check out as many different shops as you like without leaving your home. It's great for finding what you need.

Listening

TASK 1

1 2010 **2** online **3** interested in **4** filming **5** 16/sixteen
6 latest fashions

TASK 2

7 F **8** T

Reading

TASK 1

9 D **10** C **11** F **12** B **13** H **14** E

TASK 2

15 You can keep a good item for a long time, but you only wear the cheap ones a few times.

UNIT 6

LANGUAGE TEST A

Grammar

TASK 1

1 C **2** A **3** A **4** B **5** A **6** B **7** C **8** B

For revision, go to Student's Book: p72, p74

TASK 2

9 yourselves **10** myself **11** yourself **12** itself **13** herself
14 themselves **15** himself **16** ourselves

For revision, go to Student's Book: p72

TASK 3

17 has to/must **18** There are **19** ourselves **20** mustn't
21 it's **22** myself **23** There is **24** can **25** have to

For revision, go to Student's Book: p72, p74

Vocabulary

TASK 1

26 powerful **27** clear **28** blind **29** empty **30** clever
31 colourful **32** loud **33** sharp

For revision, go to Student's Book: p73, p76

TASK 2

34 D **35** G **36** B **37** E **38** H **39** C **40** F **41** A

For revision, go to Student's Book: p73, p77

TASK 3

42 C **43** B **44** A **45** B **46** C **47** A **48** C **49** B **50** A

For revision, go to Student's Book: p73, p76, p77

LANGUAGE TEST B

Grammar

TASK 1

1 C **2** A **3** B **4** B **5** A **6** B **7** C **8** A

For revision, go to Student's Book: p72, p74

TASK 2

9 herself **10** ourselves **11** themselves **12** yourselves
13 yourself **14** myself **15** itself **16** himself

For revision, go to Student's Book: p72

TASK 3

17 It's **18** mustn't **19** there's/there is **20** have to
21 has to/must **22** herself **23** There are
24 themselves **25** Can

For revision, go to Student's Book: p72, p74

Vocabulary

TASK 1

26 clever **27** sharp **28** powerful **29** empty **30** clear
31 loud **32** colourful **33** blind

For revision, go to Student's Book: p73, p76

TASK 2

34 E **35** H **36** C **37** F **38** A **39** D **40** G **41** B

For revision, go to Student's Book: p73, p77

TASK 3

42 B **43** A **44** B **45** A **46** B **47** C **48** B **49** A **50** C

For revision, go to Student's Book: p73, p76, p77

SKILLS TEST A

Dictation

Every city needs to have green spaces. They make life better for the people who live there. These are places where we can relax, forget our problems and enjoy nature.

Listening

TASK 1

1 A **2** C **3** B **4** C **5** B **6** A

TASK 2

7 F **8** T

Reading

TASK 1

9 C **10** B **11** D **12** A **13** B **14** D

TASK 2

15 They can go to amusement parks, shopping malls and museums.

SKILLS TEST B

Dictation

Every city needs to have green spaces. They make life better for the people who live there. These are places where we can relax, forget our problems and enjoy nature.

Listening

TASK 1

1 A **2** A **3** C **4** B **5** A **6** B

TASK 2

7 F **8** F

Reading

TASK 1

9 B **10** A **11** C **12** B **13** A **14** C

TASK 2

15 They can meet their friends, have a coffee or a meal, shop at an open market or see a concert.

UNIT 7

LANGUAGE TEST A

Grammar

TASK 1

1 who **2** which **3** which **4** who **5** which **6** who
7 who **8** which **9** who **10** which

For revision, go to Student's Book: p84

TASK 2

11 which **12** who **13** which **14** which **15** which
16 who **17** who **18** who

For revision, go to Student's Book: p84

TASK 3

19 carefully **20** easily **21** well **22** hard **23** quickly
24 rudely **25** beautifully

For revision, go to Student's Book: p86

Vocabulary

TASK 1

26 crispy **27** juicy **28** soft **29** dry **30** sweet **31** salty
32 tasty **33** sour

For revision, go to Student's Book: p85

TASK 2

34 paella **35** tortillas **36** curry **37** yoghurt **38** pasta
39 sushi **40** toast **41** popcorn

For revision, go to Student's Book: p84, p85, p88

TASK 3

42 vegetarian, fish, chicken **43** burgers, fries
44 expensive, fortune **45** short, promotion

For revision, go to Student's Book: p82, p84, p85

LANGUAGE TEST B

Grammar

TASK 1

1 which **2** who **3** who **4** which **5** who **6** which
7 which **8** who **9** which **10** who

For revision, go to Student's Book: p84

TASK 2

11 who **12** which **13** who **14** which **15** which
16 who **17** who **18** which

For revision, go to Student's Book: p84

TASK 3

19 slowly **20** politely **21** comfortably **22** noisily
23 fast **24** carefully **25** well

For revision, go to Student's Book: p86

Vocabulary

TASK 1

26 cooked **27** hard **28** spicy **29** burned **30** raw
31 roast **32** soft **33** fried

For revision, go to Student's Book: p85

TASK 2

34 Pineapples **35** steak **36** burger **37** kebabs
38 marshmallows **39** sushi **40** scones **41** chilli

For revision, go to Student's Book: p82, p85, p88, p91

TASK 3

42 pop-up, cupcake **43** cost, chain, promotion
44 toast, butter **45** expensive, money

For revision, go to Student's Book: p82, p85

SKILLS TEST A

Dictation

Television cooking competitions have become very popular recently. Millions of people watch these shows because they are exciting, but few viewers actually try to make the recipes at home.

Listening

TASK 1

1 A **2** C **3** B **4** A **5** C **6** B

TASK 2

7 F **8** T

Reading

TASK 1

9 D **10** H **11** B **12** F **13** A **14** J

TASK 2

15 They would rather eat something tastier like pizza.

SKILLS TEST B

Dictation

Television cooking competitions have become very popular recently. Millions of people watch these shows because they are exciting, but few viewers actually try to make the recipes at home.

Listening

TASK 1

1 B **2** A **3** C **4** B **5** C **6** A

TASK 2

7 T **8** F

Reading

TASK 1

9 B **10** I **11** G **12** E **13** C **14** A

TASK 2

15 It's important because an unpleasant smell tells us that something is bad and shouldn't be eaten.

UNIT 8

LANGUAGE TEST A

Grammar

TASK 1

1 have bought **2** has decided **3** haven't tried
4 Has Tom gone **5** have found **6** has delayed
7 haven't spoken **8** Have they seen

For revision, go to Student's Book: p96

TASK 2

9 never **10** just **11** ever **12** already **13** yet **14** since
15 for **16** yet

For revision, go to Student's Book: p96, p98

TASK 3

17 have already seen **18** have never swum **19** has shone
20 have spent **21** hasn't rained **22** Have you ever eaten
23 hasn't stopped **24** has just had **25** Have you made

For revision, go to Student's Book: p96

Vocabulary

TASK 1

26 tourists **27** ticket **28** booked **29** diary **30** suddenly
31 take **32** go through **33** caught

For revision, go to Student's Book: p97, p99, p101

TASK 2

34 D **35** G **36** A **37** F **38** C **39** E **40** B

For revision, go to Student's Book: p94, p97

TASK 3

41 passengers **42** guidebook **43** customs officer **44** visa
45 choice **46** platform **47** challenging **48** single
49 sunglasses **50** booking

For revision, go to Student's Book: p94, p97, p99

LANGUAGE TEST B

Grammar

TASK 1

1 has read **2** have lost **3** haven't met **4** Has Lou taken
5 Has she kept **6** haven't slept **7** have you done
8 has delayed

For revision, go to Student's Book: p96

TASK 2

9 for **10** already **11** never **12** yet **13** just **14** yet
15 since **16** ever

For revision, go to Student's Book: p96, p98

TASK 3

17 have already explored **18** have never seen **19** has been
20 haven't stayed **21** have visited **22** Have you ever had
23 has eaten **24** hasn't rained **25** Have you taken

For revision, go to Student's Book: p96

Vocabulary

TASK 1

26 passengers **27** fare **28** make **29** guidebook **30** finally
31 went on **32** go to **33** catch

For revision, go to Student's Book: p97, p99, p101

TASK 2

34 E **35** A **36** B **37** G **38** D **39** F **40** C

For revision, go to Student's Book: p94, p97

TASK 3

41 tourists **42** platform **43** flip flops **44** diary
45 booking **46** accommodation **47** customs **48** double
49 visa **50** choice

For revision, go to Student's Book: p94, p97, p99

SKILLS TEST A

Dictation

Have you ever thought about travelling to the stars? Companies are developing special planes right now, so you may get the chance to be a space tourist in the future.

Listening

TASK 1

1 C **2** B **3** A **4** C **5** A **6** B

TASK 2

7 T **8** F

Reading

TASK 1

9 C **10** H **11** E **12** A **13** F **14** B

TASK 2

15 The best activity for people who enjoy adventure is zip lining (club D) because it's fast and exciting.

SKILLS TEST B

Dictation

Have you ever thought about travelling to the stars? Companies are developing special planes right now, so you may get the chance to be a space tourist in the future.

Listening

TASK 1

1 A **2** C **3** B **4** A **5** B **6** C

TASK 2

7 F **8** T

Reading

TASK 1

9 E **10** A **11** F **12** B **13** G **14** C

TASK 2

15 Club C (Green Team). It cleans up local beaches and collects glass, paper and aluminium for recycling.

UNIT 9

LANGUAGE TEST A

Grammar

TASK 1

1 play, hurt **2** want, ask **3** will come, invite
4 decide, will call **5** rains, won't go out **6** mix, get
7 calls, tell **8** arrive, will send

For revision, go to Student's Book: p108

TASK 2

9 to play **10** winning **11** missing **12** to go **13** to speak
14 to drive **15** getting up **16** watching

For revision, go to Student's Book: p110

TASK 3

17 need to pay **18** if I don't use **19** we go **20** will give
21 tried to fix **22** won't wait **23** don't eat **24** at writing
25 if you don't study

For revision, go to Student's Book: p108, p110

Vocabulary

TASK 1

26 B **27** C **28** A **29** C **30** B **31** A **32** B **33** C

For revision, go to Student's Book: p107, p109

TASK 2

34 F **35** C **36** E **37** B **38** H **39** A **40** I **41** G **42** D

For revision, go to Student's Book: p107, p109

TASK 3

43 play **44** have **45** do **46** run out of **47** leave **48** forget
49 download **50** listen to

For revision, go to Student's Book: p107, p109

LANGUAGE TEST B

Grammar

TASK 1

1 is, will go **2** put, melts **3** want, will order
4 won't finish, plays **5** cries, gets **6** don't know, check
7 hurts, see **8** will visit, travel

For revision, go to Student's Book: p108

TASK 2

9 playing **10** watching **11** to buy **12** to take **13** cooking
14 listening **15** to relax **16** to start

For revision, go to Student's Book: p110

TASK 3

17 plans to become **18** don't forget to call **19** you rather play
20 doesn't arrive **21** hope to improve **22** if you eat
23 won't find **24** interested in travelling
25 don't have a charger

For revision, go to Student's Book: p108, p110

Vocabulary

TASK 1

26 A **27** B **28** C **29** B **30** A **31** C **32** C **33** B

For revision, go to Student's Book: p107, p109

TASK 2

34 G **35** D **36** F **37** C **38** I **39** B **40** A **41** H **42** E

For revision, go to Student's Book: p107, p109

TASK 3

43 do **44** have **45** get **46** delete **47** forget **48** leave
49 watch **50** play

For revision, go to Student's Book: p107, p109

SKILLS TEST A

Dictation

The main reasons teenagers use social media are to talk to their friends, join group conversations, share photos and videos, and to have something to do whenever they feel bored.

Listening

TASK 1

1 24/twenty-four **2** break **3** June **4** 12/twelve
5 computers **6** businesses

TASK 2

7 T **8** F

Reading

TASK 1

9 D **10** A **11** B **12** C **13** D **14** B

TASK 2

15 Max doesn't use it because he has deleted all of his apps. Sally controls how she uses social media, checking her phone only twice a day.

SKILLS TEST B

Dictation

The main reasons teenagers use social media are to talk to their friends, join group conversations, share photos and videos, and to have something to do whenever they feel bored.

Listening

TASK 1

1 charity **2** 2010s/twenty tens **3** 25/25th **4** every hour
5 radio **6** afternoon

TASK 2

7 F **8** T

Reading

TASK 1

9 A **10** B **11** C **12** D **13** A **14** C

TASK 2

15 Sally doesn't use it at all because she doesn't like the way it controls people's lives. Max is careful about using it and checks his phone only twice a day.

REVIEW (UNITS 1–3)

LANGUAGE TEST A

Grammar

TASK 1

1 A **2** C **3** C **4** B **5** B **6** C **7** A **8** B

TASK 2

9 an **10** much **11** Are **12** does **13** Where **14** were
15 Did **16** nothing

TASK 3

17 Were you reading **18** rarely buys **19** didn't know
20 isn't raining **21** don't believe **22** Do your friends live
23 was walking **24** Are you trying **25** sent

Vocabulary

TASK 1

26 crossing **27** by **28** I'd like **29** valuable **30** seat
31 useful **32** delighted **33** freezing

TASK 2

34 C **35** F **36** A **37** E **38** B **39** G **40** D

TASK 3

41 A **42** C **43** C **44** B **45** A **46** B **47** C **48** C
49 B **50** B

LANGUAGE TEST B

Grammar

TASK 1

1 A **2** B **3** C **4** A **5** C **6** A **7** B **8** C

TASK 2

9 the **10** many **11** Did **12** does **13** Why **14** were
15 few **16** everything

TASK 3

17 isn't working **18** are you looking for
19 occasionally listens to **20** were riding
21 Was Max studying **22** Do students pay
23 went **24** don't agree **25** doesn't study

Vocabulary

TASK 1

26 pavement **27** starving **28** ordinary **29** special
30 I like **31** exhausted **32** on **33** path

TASK 2

34 G **35** D **36** B **37** F **38** A **39** E **40** C

TASK 3

41 C **42** A **43** B **44** B **45** C **46** A **47** B **48** C
49 B **50** A

SPEAKING

Sample answers

TASK 1

What's your name?

My name is Maria.

What's your surname? How do you spell it?

Conti. C…O…N…T…I

Where do you live?

I live in a city called Genoa, in Italy.

How old are you?

I am fourteen years old.

Do you have any hobbies?

Yes, I do. I go swimming every week at a sports centre. I'm also learning to play the guitar and I have two lessons a week.

What do you want to do when you grow up?

I'm not sure. At school, I like art and history very much, so maybe I can be a teacher.

What do you usually do at the weekend?

I usually have homework, but when I'm not studying, I meet my friends and we go to the shops or we play sports. Sometimes we go to parties.

What do you enjoy reading?

I love comics and sometimes I read adventure stories. There are some sports blogs that I read too.

Who do you like to spend time with?

I like to spend time with my best friend, and also my family. My sister and I do a lot of things together.

TASK 2

A: Shall I start? What do you think about the bike helmet? I'm sure he would like it.

B: Yes, I think that's a good idea. He likes to ride his bike every day and maybe he needs a new helmet. Now, what about the game controller? He has some video games.

A: That's good too. It's a nice present for him. He plays games and I don't think it costs a lot. He also loves music, but is he interested in playing music – on the guitar?

B: I'm not sure, but I think he prefers to listen to music and go to concerts. But look at the T-shirt. It's really cool and he likes to wear dark colours. I'm sure he would love that.

A: Yes, I agree. That's a really good idea because he likes to wear cool clothes.

B: So what the boogie board? That's a fun activity to do.

A: It is, yes, but when could he use it? I don't think he goes to the beach a lot. What about the bracelets? He wears jewellery sometimes.

B: Yes, you're right, and these ones look really cool, too.

A: We've talked about all of the ideas now. Shall we decide on the best one?

B: OK. I would choose the T-shirt. I think that's the best idea because it's very fashionable and he will enjoy wearing it.

A: I agree that's the best idea. Let's choose that one.

WRITING

Sample answer

I went to the window and looked outside. It was snowing! Everywhere was white. I was delighted because I wanted to play in the snow. First, I put on some warm clothes. Then I opened the door and went outside. While I was walking in my garden, someone called my name. It was my neighbour Tom. He was outside too. There was something in his hand. He raised his arm and threw some snow at me! It hit me on my leg and Tom started laughing. So I threw some at him. Soon, we were having a snow fight. It was a lot of fun!

REVIEW (UNITS 4–6)

LANGUAGE TEST A

Grammar

TASK 1

1 A **2** C **3** B **4** C **5** B **6** A **7** C **8** B **9** B

TASK 2

10 are you going to **11** isn't as polite as **12** don't have to leave
13 by myself **14** a little **15** isn't old enough **16** may stay
17 the tallest

TASK 3

18 more **19** to **20** most **21** lot **22** too **23** best
24 as **25** going

Vocabulary

TASK 1

26 C **27** A **28** B **29** C **30** A **31** B **32** A **33** C

TASK 2

34 start **35** give **36** get **37** open **38** noted
39 tell **40** cross **41** fancy **42** hand

TASK 3

43 blind **44** friendly **45** sharp **46** curly **47** braces
48 wallet **49** geography **50** penguin

LANGUAGE TEST B

Grammar

TASK 1

1 B **2** A **3** A **4** B **5** C **6** C **7** B **8** C **9** A

TASK 2

10 is he going to **11** aren't as interesting as
12 doesn't have to stay **13** by himself **14** aren't big enough
15 might rain **16** the nicest **17** don't have quite as

TASK 3

18 as **19** the **20** most **21** have/need **22** must/should
23 than **24** more **25** enough

Vocabulary

TASK 1

26 B **27** B **28** A **29** C **30** A **31** B **32** C **33** A

TASK 2

34 throw **35** take **36** dress **37** saved **38** make
39 running **40** has **41** lie **42** manage

TASK 3

43 clever **44** powerful **45** straight **46** soft **47** glasses
48 jewellery **49** history **50** Dolphins

SPEAKING

Sample answers

TASK 1

A: This photo shows a young girl and a horse. Maybe it's her horse or maybe she goes to a club to ride horses. I don't think she's at home, in her garden. I think she's at a club. The girl is wearing a helmet and clothes that you wear for horse riding, so I think she was riding the horse and now the horse is hot. That's why it needs the water. It looks like a sunny day so I think she enjoys being outside in good weather with the horse.

B: The photo shows a boy with a violin. I think the woman is a music teacher and he is learning to play the violin. There are other people in the photo and they are playing different instruments. Maybe they are all having a music lesson at school. The boy is listening carefully to the teacher. He looks very serious. I think they enjoy playing music together and creating something nice to listen to.

TASK 2

A: Would you like to start?

B: Yes, OK. I think the beach is a good idea because it's summer and it could be hot in the city. It would be nice to go swimming.

A: That's true, and everyone likes to go to the beach. Now, what about the cinema? I love the cinema but I don't think it's a good idea to be inside in the summer.

B: I agree. It's nicer to be outdoors when the weather is good. How about the museum?

A: I think that's OK. There are lots of interesting things to see in a museum, so it might be fun.

B: I'm not sure about that. Maybe it's a boring thing to do in a big, exciting city. I think sightseeing would be fun, especially if it's their first time in the city. And on a bus like that, you can see a lot.

A: Yes, you're right. They can see lots of sights, but also people and shops. So, the last one is shopping. I think shopping is fun, but they can go shopping in their own city.

B: I agree. I think it's better to see new places and have new experiences. So which one do you think is the best?

A: In my opinion, they should see the city and visit the important places.

B: Yes, I agree. I think that's the best activity to do when you visit a city.

A: Great, so we both think it's the best activity.

WRITING

Sample answer

I enjoy going to school for a couple of reasons. First, I see my friends there and we have fun during the break! But that's not the most important reason, of course. At school, I learn useful things that will help me in life and make me a better person. For me, it's very important to do well at school because I hope to go to university and become a science teacher. It's a job that I think is difficult, but also very interesting. Also, I'd like to teach young people and help them to learn about the world. Who knows? Maybe it will happen!

REVIEW (UNITS 7–9)

LANGUAGE TEST A

Grammar

TASK 1

1 had **2** which **3** never **4** for **5** just **6** well **7** to go **8** will visit **9** quietly

TASK 2

10 calls **11** has known **12** have already eaten **13** will get **14** to find **15** planning **16** haven't downloaded **17** doesn't enjoy

TASK 3

18 the **19** ever **20** who **21** which/that **22** There **23** If **24** to **25** will

Vocabulary

TASK 1

26 F **27** C **28** I **29** A **30** H **31** E **32** G **33** B **34** D

TASK 2

35 vegetables **36** tortilla **37** earphones **38** customs **39** immediately **40** connection **41** sleepover **42** mobile phone

TASK 3

43 B **44** C **45** B **46** A **47** C **48** C **49** A **50** B

LANGUAGE TEST B

Grammar

TASK 1

1 who **2** yet **3** well **4** to close **5** for **6** spending **7** don't **8** playing **9** see

TASK 2

10 decides **11** will travel **12** haven't seen **13** learning **14** have already been **15** doesn't feel like **16** to visit **17** won't catch

TASK 3

18 the **19** Have **20** If **21** which/that **22** who **23** there **24** will **25** to

Vocabulary

TASK 1

26 G **27** D **28** A **29** E **30** I **31** C **32** H **33** F **34** B

TASK 2

35 yoghurt **36** Paella **37** guidebook **38** security
39 suddenly **40** headphones **41** battery **42** water bottle

TASK 3

43 C **44** A **45** C **46** B **47** A **48** B **49** A **50** C

SPEAKING

Sample answers

TASK 1

A: OK, shall I start?

B: Yes, please.

A: I don't think a barbecue is a good idea because they will have to buy meat and cook it. It isn't easy to do.

B: Yes, I agree. They should do something more relaxing. I think the picnic is a good idea though. They have to bring their own food, but they don't have to make it if they don't want to – they can buy food and share it.

A: I agree. It's also nice to eat outdoors, in a park or even by the sea. What about the café with the burger and fries? I think they would like that. Teenagers love eating fast food.

B: That's true, they do. And it isn't expensive food. But maybe they should do something 'special' to celebrate. I mean, they can have fast food any day. How about sushi? That's quite different. Maybe they would like to do something unusual that they will remember.

A: I see what you mean, but I'm not sure many teenagers want to eat raw fish.

B: Yes, you're right. Some people think it's disgusting!

A: Well, that leaves the last one – a vegetarian café. Salads are nice, but, I don't know – they seem a bit boring to me.

B: I don't agree. I think some salads are very tasty, but not everyone is a vegetarian, so maybe not that one.

A: OK, so let's decide. I think the picnic is the best idea. They can have a fun day outdoors.

B: Yes, that's my choice too.

TASK 2

T: What are your favourite foods, Student A?

A: I like my mum's food the best because she cooks very well, especially pasta. But pizza is my favourite food.

T: What about you, Student B?

B: Yes, I love the food my parents cook, and I also love pizza! And I can make it myself. My favourite food is Mexican food. It's very tasty!

T: Do you go out to eat with your friends, Student B? Where do you go?

B: Yes, I often go to a café with my friends. We order a drink and a sandwich or a burger, and have fun chatting.

T: What about you, Student A?

A: The same. We go to cafes because there's usually cool music and lots of other teens go there too. The food is tasty and it isn't expensive.

T: What events do you celebrate with food, Student A?

A: We always celebrate birthdays with lots of food. I have a party and my mum orders a big birthday cake, of course, and we have nice snacks.

T: How about you, Student B?

B: Yes, my family celebrates birthdays with food, but also the New Year. We have some traditional foods that we eat then.

WRITING

Sample answer

Hi Jane,

That's great! Thanks for finding the information. I can't wait to go! It's going to be really fun.

I'd rather go for three weeks. I want to spend as much time there as possible. I hope you do too.

I'd prefer to have photography lessons. You see, I've got a new phone and it has a very good camera, but the photos I take are terrible! I really need to learn how to use it well!

How about meeting on Saturday when you finish work? I'll wait for you outside the shop at two o'clock. Is that OK?

See you soon,

Bella

END OF YEAR

LANGUAGE TEST A

Listening

TASK 1

1 B **2** A **3** B **4** C **5** A **6** C

TASK 2

7 F **8** T

TASK 3

9 1998 **10** football **11** champion **12** famous **13** videos **14** travelling

TASK 4

15 T

LANGUAGE

TASK 1

16 enough **17** which **18** ago **19** most **20** for **21** yourself **22** lot **23** rather

TASK 2

24 C **25** B **26** A **27** C **28** B **29** A **30** C

Reading

TASK 1

31 C **32** G **33** E **34** A **35** F

TASK 2

36 They are in shelters because they're lost or their owners can't look after them.

37 You can write about something you are interested in and improve your writing.

TASK 3

38 B **39** H **40** D **41** G **42** E

TASK 4

43 The named it the Turk because it wore long clothes and a cap on its head, as people did in Turkey.

44 Napoleon Bonaparte and Benjamin Franklin played chess against the machine.

45 A man sat inside the desk and he had a way to control the arms of the Turk and move the pieces on the board.

LANGUAGE TEST B

Listening

TASK 1

1 C **2** A **3** A **4** A **5** B **6** A

TASK 2

7 T **8** F

TASK 3

9 12th/12/twelfth **10** basketball **11** teacher **12** competitions **13** photography **14** training

TASK 4

15 T

LANGUAGE

TASK 1

16 ever **17** enough **18** did **19** who **20** as **21** by **22** few **23** would

TASK 2

24 A **25** C **26** B **27** A **28** C **29** B **30** A

Reading

TASK 1

31 D **32** A **33** F **34** B **35** G

TASK 2

36 They feel lonely, scared or sad.

37 You can do quizzes and puzzles or play board games.

TASK 3

38 C **39** F **40** A **41** E **42** H

TASK 4

43 It sat behind a big wooden desk that was closed on all sides like a box.

44 Machines were starting to do work in factories then.

45 Chess champions worked the machine.

SPEAKING

Sample answers

TASK 1

Teacher: *What's your name?*
Student: My name is Nicholas.
Teacher: *What's your surname? How do you spell it?*
Student: Pappas. P…A…P…P…A…S
Teacher: *Where do you live?*
Student: I live in Athens, in Greece.
Teacher: *Do you study English at school?*
Student: Yes, I do, and I also have lessons at a language school.
Teacher: *Do you have any brothers or sisters?*
Student: Yes, I have a brother. His name is George and he's two years younger than me.
Teacher: *What do you usually do in the summer?*
Student: I spend a lot of time with my friends and I go to the beach. Sometimes my family goes to an island for a week.
Teacher: *Do you use social media?*
Student: Yes, I use it all the time. I share videos and photos with my friends. It's fun.
Teacher: *What kinds of films do you like?*
Student: I like comedies because they're funny and action films because they're exciting.

TASK 2

Student A

I can see a girl and a boy who are both students and a teacher. The girl has long fair hair and the boy has red hair which is long on the top. The teacher is showing them something on a tablet or maybe in a book, I'm not sure. She has long curly hair. There are the things you use in science for making small things look big so you can see them properly on the table, so I think they are having a science lesson at school.

Maybe the students are trying to understand something that the teacher is explaining to them. Next, they might look at something or write about what they can see.

Student B

I can see five teenagers. There are three girls and two boys. I think they're about 12 or 13 years old. They're sitting on a long seat and are somewhere in a city or a town. It's funny because they're all together, but they're all looking at their mobile phones and aren't talking.

They look happy and they're having a good time. Maybe they're all watching funny videos. Next, they might buy something to drink or some fast food.

TASK 3

A: Would you like to start?
B: OK, thanks. Let me see … I think going to a gym is a good hobby to have because it can keep her fit and healthy. What do you think?
A: Yes, I agree. It's a good habit to have because it's important to be healthy. What about playing football? That's good for keeping fit too.
B: Yes, you're right about that, but you can't play football if you don't have people to play it with. Swimming is also fun and you don't need to join a team.
A: Swimming is good for your body, but I think it can be a bit boring.
B: Hmm. I don't think it's boring. OK, so how about learning to play the guitar? I think that would be fun and it's also creative.
A: That's true, it looks like fun, and she could make a band with her friends. Do you think chess is a good hobby for her? I'm not sure it is.
B: Well, it seems good to me. It's a hobby that makes you think and maybe it could help her to do better at school.
A: Oh, I see, yes, you could be right about that. And I guess she could join a club and meet other young people too.
B: You're right, I think she could. OK, well there's one more … cooking. What do you think about that for a hobby?
A: It's good if you want to do something at home, but it's not a good way to keep fit or meet other people.
B: Yes, I agree, but I think it could be fun when you have nothing to do at home. So, shall we make a decision? Which do you think is the best hobby?
A: In my opinion, playing football is the best because it's a sport so it will keep her fit and she'll have fun playing with other people.
B: Yes, I agree with you. I think it's the best hobby, too.

TASK 4

Student A: I love drawing and painting. I do it at home when I have free time and at school in art. And I also like going to museums because I can look at nice art there. How about you?

Student B: My favourite hobby is cycling because I love being outdoors. I usually ride with my best friend and we go to the countryside or by the sea.

Teacher: Do you enjoy trying new things, Student B?

Student B: Yes, I do. I think it's interesting and fun to try something new and see if I'm good at it. Do you like trying new things?

Student A: Yes, I do, too. It's great because if you try different things, you can find something you really love.

Teacher: Is there an activity you would like to try, Student A?

Student A: Yes, I'd like to make videos and start a vlog, but I don't have much time these days because I'm studying. What do you want to try?

Student B: I'd like to try something challenging, like skydiving. I think adventure sports are great!

Student A: Me too. I want to try that!

Teacher: And why do you think it's important to have hobbies, Student A?

Student A: Because they help you to learn new skills maybe, or to have fun when you have free time. I think it's important for young people to do something outdoors too, and not play video games or look at social media all the time.

Teacher: And you, Student B? What do you think?

Student B: I agree with Student A. Hobbies make you happy and you can use your time in a good way.

WRITING

Sample answer

TASK 1

Hi Tom,

That's fantastic news. Of course I'll go to the cinema with you! I haven't been in a really long time, so I'm looking forward to it.

I'm not busy at the weekend, so how about Saturday? We could go in the afternoon or the evening.

Actually I don't want to watch an action film because I'm not very interested in them. What about a comedy? Is that OK with you?

Maybe we could go to the new burger café for something to eat. What do you think? I've heard that the burgers there are quite good.

Write soon.

Ben

Sample answer

TASK 2

I felt nervous when I held the envelope. My English results were inside! My mum could see that I was anxious. 'Do you want me to open it?' she asked. I thought about it for a second, but I decided to be brave and open it myself. Slowly I tore the envelope and took out the paper. My parents were waiting to hear the results. I could see that they were also nervous. Then, I read the grade. 'Yes!' I shouted. 'What is it? What grade did you get?' asked my dad. 'Look!' I said and gave him the paper. It was an A. It was one of the happiest days of my life!

SPEAKING MARK SCHEME

25 score points in total. Responses are scored according to how well students perform against the following criteria:

	Task achievement	Spoken production and fluency	Spoken interaction	Range	Accuracy
Band 5	Very good attempt at the task. All elements of the task are communicated.	Conveys meaning for the task well. Constructs many longer (connected) utterances. Almost no hesitation.	Works well with the other candidate and offers appropriate support. Shows appropriate turn taking.	There is a very good range of structures and vocabulary for the tasks. At times it reaches above level.	There are no mistakes at the level at which they are speaking. Where errors are made this is in reaching beyond level.
Band 4	Good attempt at the task. Nearly all elements of the task are communicated.	Mainly conveys meaning for the task well. Constructs some longer (connected) utterances. Little hesitation.	Works with the other candidate and offers support. Shows mainly appropriate turn taking.	There is a good range of structures and vocabulary for the tasks. Occasionally reaches above level.	There are few mistakes at the level at which they are speaking. Errors are made in reaching beyond level.
Band 3	Satisfactory attempt at the task. Most elements of the task are communicated.	Generally conveys meaning for the task. Constructs occasional longer (connected) utterances. Some hesitation.	Works satisfactorily with the other candidate. Shows some appropriate turn taking.	There is an adequate range of structures and vocabulary for the tasks according to the level.	There are some mistakes at the level at which they are speaking, but they do not interfere with the conveyance of meaning.
Band 2	Inadequate attempt at the task. Only some elements of the task are communicated.	Conveys little meaning for the task. No longer (connected) utterances. A lot of hesitation.	Doesn't work very well with the other candidate. Little appropriate turn taking.	There is an inadequate range of structures and vocabulary for the tasks.	There are many mistakes at the level at which they are speaking which impair understanding of meaning in places.
Band 1	Poor attempt at the task. Most elements of the task are not communicated.	Conveys almost no meaning for the task. Hesitation is very intrusive.	Almost no communication with the other candidate. Turn taking not appropriate.	There is almost no range of structures and vocabulary for the tasks.	There are so many mistakes at the level at which they are speaking that it is difficult to understand.
Band 0	Incomprehensible, silent or only speaking first language.				

WRITING MARK SCHEME

25 score points in total. Responses are scored according to how well students perform against the following criteria:

Marks	Content	Task achievement	Organisation and structure	Range	Accuracy
5	All content points covered with exemplary depth and scope. The text would have a positive effect on the intended reader throughout due to good lexical and/or grammatical accuracy and/or sufficient control of register.	Control of language is clearly sufficient to respond to simple and more complex tasks. There is demonstrable achievement of all parts of the task, and perhaps even evidence of writing beyond the demands of the task.	Text organised and sequenced logically and effectively throughout. Linking between sentences throughout. Paragraphs used appropriately for the purpose and genre of the writing throughout the text.	Uses an excellent range of level-appropriate vocabulary and grammar structures with excellent accuracy, including some complex and compound sentences. May even use lexis and structure that is beyond the level.	Very occasional lexical and grammatical errors do not impede the communication of ideas in any way.
4	All content points covered with sufficient depth and scope. The text would largely have a positive effect on the intended reader due to good lexical and/ or grammatical accuracy and/or sufficient control of register.	Control of language is clearly sufficient to respond to simple and working towards more complex tasks. There is demonstrable achievement of all parts of the task.	Text organised and sequenced simply but logically throughout. Linking between sentences throughout. Paragraphs used appropriately for the purpose and genre of the writing throughout most of the text.	Uses a good range of level-appropriate vocabulary and grammar structures. Largely used accurately. Possibly some complex as well as compound sentences attempted.	Occasional lexical and grammatical errors probably evident but not in sufficient quantity or severity to impede the communication of ideas.
3	All points may have been covered, but some in insufficient depth. Sections of the content would probably have a positive effect on the intended reader.	Control is sufficient to respond to all simple tasks and to complete some more complex ones. The majority of the response would achieve its intended purpose.	Text organised largely at sentence level. Some simple and logically sequenced sections with linking between sentences. There may be evidence of paragraphing, but this may not always be inappropriate.	Writing limited to fairly basic vocabulary for the level, largely used accurately. Uses basic grammar structures, perhaps with a few errors. Possibly no complex sentences attempted, but some compound sentences used.	A number of lexical and grammatical errors probably evident but not in sufficient quantity to greatly impede communication of ideas.
2	May omit one or two content points, or cover them in insufficient depth. Content would probably have a negative effect on the intended reader due to lexical and/or grammatical inaccuracies and/or poor control of register.	Lexical and grammatical inaccuracies impede task achievement. Control may be sufficient for very simple tasks but generally not more complex ones.	Little text organisation according to genre. Text organised partly at phrase level but with some sentence-level language attempted too. Occasional linking between sentences.	Uses only very basic vocabulary and grammar structures for the level, perhaps with a lot of errors. No complex but maybe one or two compound sentences attempted.	Frequent lexical and grammatical errors, even in basic language, may impede the effective communication of ideas.
1	Two or more content points may be omitted completely, or covered in insufficient depth and/or scope. Content would have a negative effect on the intended reader due to lexical and/ or grammatical inaccuracies and/or poor control of register.	Lexical and grammatical inaccuracies impede task achievement, severely at times. Control may be sufficient for very simple tasks but not more complex ones. Stretches of text may be unintelligible or require a lot of effort by the reader to decode.	Little or no text organisation according to genre. Text organised largely at phrase level, perhaps with some complete sentences evident. Little or no linking between phrases or sentences.	Uses only very basic vocabulary and grammar structures with a lot of errors evident. No attempt at complex or compound sentences.	Many lexical and grammatical errors, even in basic language, which severely impede communication of ideas.
0	Award 0 marks only if there is no written response to assess or if what is written is unintelligible or is an obviously rehearsed response bearing little or no relation to the task.				

Unit 1 Skills Test Dictation

Why are Dutch teens so happy at school? It's because there isn't a lot of pressure from parents and teachers, and students feel very close to their school community.

Unit 1 Skills Test Listening

N = Narrator

N: One.

A: I've got a new video game. Do you want to play?

B: Maybe later. I need to finish my homework first.

A: So why are you relaxing in the garden if you have to study?

B: I'm just taking a short break. I've been at my desk for hours. Anyway, what's your new game?

A: It's a football game and I can't wait to play it!

N: Two.

Listen carefully, please. This is about what to take on your school trip. Write it down in your notebooks. You're going to spend a lot of time walking, so you don't want to carry a heavy backpack. Keep it light with just a few things in it. You'll need an umbrella or a raincoat, and, of course, your phones to take photos.

N: Three.

A: There's a new photography club after school. I'd like to try that.

B: I take terrible photos! Maybe I should join and get some good advice.

A: The classes are on Monday, Wednesday and Friday.

B: Oh, I can't go three times a week.

A: No, no, you only go once depending on your level. On Mondays, it's for beginners. Wednesday is for intermediate and Friday is for advanced.

B: Great! I'll go to the beginners' class.

N: Four.

A: How was your weekend?

B: Busy! My cousins visited me and we saw the city.

A: Cool. Did you go to the castle?

B: No, they went there last year. This time we passed it on the bus and took photos.

A: So what did you do?

B: We went to a concert and it was great. We also went to the theme park. They loved the rollercoaster, but it looked so scary that I stayed on the ground!

N: Five.

It's easy to keep fit and I think more teenagers should do some exercise. Ice skating is my favourite, but I only do it in the winter and not very often. Luckily, there's a gym near my house. I go there three times a week and use the running machine, so it doesn't matter what the weather is like – I just get on it and run for 30 minutes.

N: Six.

A: Thanks for inviting me to the cinema. I really enjoyed the film.

B: Me too. And thanks for buying the popcorn.

A: No problem. But I think I had too much!

B: Really? I was thinking maybe we could get a pizza.

A: Oh, I'm too full! But what about an ice cream? A small one!

B: Sure. I know a shop near here that sells the best ice cream. Let's go.

Unit 2 Skills Test Dictation

To get better at any skill, you need to practise. By working hard and spending some time on it, you can make progress and have fun at the same time.

Unit 2 Skills Test Listening

Hi everyone. Well, as you all know, we asked you to give us some ideas about fun activities we can do and day trips we can go on with the youth club. Thanks for your suggestions! The most popular ideas were a day at the beach, go-karting, circus skills – that's unusual! – and paintballing. The good news is, we'll do all of them over the summer break, and we'll start with paintballing.

The paintballing centre is open every day, but we pay less on Mondays and Tuesdays. It normally costs eight pounds, but we only pay five on those days. If you'd prefer to go sometime between Wednesday and Sunday, let me know. We can stay on the paintballing course for two hours. So, if we leave here at nine o'clock and get there an hour later, we can play until twelve o'clock. After that, we can come back here, or go into the town for lunch. Again, let me know what you'd like to do.

Oh, and you'll need to bring some old clothes, of course, and some old trainers! We can change at the centre when we get there – they've got changing rooms.

Unit 3 Skills Test Dictation

When I travel, I make sure that I have an exciting story with me. If I have to wait for a bus or train, I pass the time reading it.

Unit 3 Skills Test Listening

I = Interviewer, M = Molly

I: Today, we're talking to Molly, a teenager who started an online book club. Why did you start it, Molly?

M: A while ago, I had to do a project on a book we were studying in school. I wanted to talk about it with other students, but there was no online forum for us. I could only find reviews that people left on different sites. We needed a place where students could chat about books, get different opinions and maybe understand a book better.

I: So, at the club you only discuss books that people are studying?

M: Well, that's how it started. But, of course, we also read for enjoyment, and teenagers started visiting the site to talk about other things they loved reading like comics or blogs, and for suggestions about new writers or books.

I: Were you surprised by the success of the online book club?

M: Yes and no. The incredible thing I discovered was that so many teenagers read in their free time, in addition to doing other activities. I thought I was one of a few, but reading is quite popular with young people, despite some thinking it's boring. I wasn't surprised that students joined the club – it's really useful for them and helps them to do better with their projects.

I: Can you tell us why you like to read?

M: When I read a story, I imagine that I'm the main character. It's so enjoyable to experience a different life. Reading improves my vocabulary too and I sound clever when I talk! Um, what else? I can read when there's nothing else to do, and sometimes when there <u>are</u> other things to do!

I: What do you think about audio books?

M: I prefer paper books myself. I love holding them and turning the pages, but I can understand why others like them. You just put on your headphones, close your eyes and imagine the story as you listen. It's a great way to relax, but you can learn something, too, like how to pronounce new words. I don't think it helps with spelling though – you can't see the words!

I: How many members are in the club? And how can someone join?

M: There are about 1,000 now and growing! Just go to the website and sign up. You need to give your name, age and which school you go to. Oh, and it's free to join!

I: Thanks very much for talking to us, Molly.

Unit 4 Skills Test Dictation

It isn't easy to decide about your future when you're young. Before you make up your mind about school or work, take advice from people who can help you.

Unit 4 Skills Test Listening

N = Narrator

N: One. You will hear a girl telling her friend about a problem with a school project.

A: Are you working on your geography project?

B: Yes, I've nearly finished it. I think it's pretty good. Maybe I'll get a good grade! What about you?

A: Um … I haven't started mine yet.

B: What? We have to hand it in next week.

A: I don't think I'll be able to. I just don't have enough time to work on it. I joined a dance school and, right now, we're preparing for a competition. We practise every night and it's a lot of hard work.

B: Hmm … Why don't you talk with our teacher and explain what's happening?

A: That's a good idea.

N: Two. You will hear a boy, Tom, talking to his teacher about his homework.

A: I'm sorry, I don't have my homework today, Mrs Smith.

B: You usually hand in your work on time, Tom. What happened?

A: I wasn't well. I had bad headaches and I went to see the doctor.

B: Oh, I hope you're alright now.

A: Yes, it's nothing really, I just need glasses and I'm getting them tomorrow.

B: Well, I'm glad you're OK. Why don't you sit at the front of the class today so that you can see the board? You can bring me your homework in a few days.

A: Thank you, Mrs Smith. I promise you'll have it on Friday.

N: Three. You will hear a brother and sister talking about cooking.

A: Are you watching a cooking show? When did you become interested in cooking?

B: I didn't, but I like this TV show. The food is difficult to make, but it's amazing. I want to eat it all!

A: You know, cooking is fun and it isn't hard. Why don't you give it a try? I've got lots of cookbooks. Just do what they say but start with an easy dish first.

B: Like a sandwich?

A: Making a sandwich isn't cooking! How about an omelette with cheese?

B: That's OK, I'm not hungry now, but I'll have one later if you make it.

N: Four. You will hear two friends preparing for an exam.

A: There are so many facts we need to remember for this exam. Let's test each other again. I'll ask you first. OK?

B: I can't – I'm too tired. Let's stop for a while.

A: OK, but only for ten minutes. Do you want to drink something?

B: No, thanks, I'm not thirsty. I think I just want to move around.

A: Why don't we go for a walk or kick a football about?

B: Sure. Anything to forget about science for a little while!

A: I'll just note down where we are in the book and then we can go for a walk.

N: Five. You will hear two friends talking about their lessons.

A: Our lessons are really great this year!

B: Do you mean because we all have computers? Yeah, it's amazing that we do everything on our laptops. Not like last year!

A: Do you remember how heavy our school bags were? They were full of books. Now I just bring my computer, a notebook and a few pens.

B: Me too, and I think I'm learning more now. I'm definitely getting better grades.

A: I like that I can read my notes or study anywhere. Yesterday when the bus was late, I took out my laptop and did some homework! Computers really do make life easier.

N: Six. You will hear two friends talking about a maths test.

A: Look at the mistakes I made in my maths test. I can't believe I passed it!

B: Don't be too upset. Everyone says it was a difficult test. I got more than a few answers wrong too.

A: That's not why I'm upset. Sure, the test was hard, but my mistakes were really silly. And because I didn't check my work, I didn't see them. I'll definitely be more careful next time!

B: Well, I'm not great at maths, and that's why I always leave five minutes before the end to go over my answers carefully. You should do the same.

Unit 5 Skills Test Dictation

The internet has made shopping much easier. You can check out as many different shops as you like without leaving your home. It's great for finding what you need.

Unit 5 Skills Test Listening

How many TV advertisements do you see a day? Lots, for sure. Every day, thousands of ads are shown around the country. Have you ever wondered how you can be in a TV ad? If you're interested, call us. We're the Kidz Model Agency, that's K–I–D–Z, Kidz. We're experts in child and teen actors. We started in 2005 and, just five years later, in 2010, our agency won an award. And don't worry … you don't need to be a great actor to appear in a TV ad.

The first step is to contact us. Ask a parent to fill in the form online or call us. We'll arrange for an interview after school so we can get to know you and find out a little about your personality and what you're interested in doing. When you meet us, your mum or dad must be with you and give their permission for you to work. If we find a job for you, they also have to be present at the filming.

You probably think that you aren't tall enough or your hair is too curly, or because you wear braces, you won't get work. You're wrong! The companies we work with are looking for children aged 8 to 16, of all shapes and sizes. You can be short, tall or of average height. The companies that use our models are looking for REAL kids to advertise their products, the kind of kids you see every day at school, at the shops or out playing sport. Kids with freckles, glasses or both! Kids like you.

We can't promise you work, but we will do our best. It doesn't cost anything to join the agency, but when you get a job, we'll keep 10% of your payment and give the rest to your parents. They'll help you decide what to do with it. And you'll be pleased to know that TV advertising pays quite well, plus you can get free gifts like the latest fashions, video games and toys.

But apart from the money and the presents, imagine how you'll feel when you see yourself on TV!

Unit 6 Skills Test Dictation

Every city needs to have green spaces. They make life better for the people who live there. These are places where we can relax, forget our problems and enjoy nature.

Unit 6 Skills Test Listening

N = Narrator

N: One.

And now, the weather. The news isn't very good, I'm afraid, especially if you have plans for any outdoor activities. While last weekend we had perfect sunny weather for picnics or a day at the beach, this weekend will be a real disappointment. It's going to be cloudy on Saturday with rain to follow on Sunday.

N: Two.

A: Are you ready for our camping trip?

B: I've got my tent and everything I need is in my backpack.

A: Great! I can't wait to get away from the noise and pollution here. Just think … no cars, buses or people for five days.

B: I'm looking forward to sleeping under the stars and cooking over a fire.

A: Me too! We'll find a good place to camp, far away from everyone and everything with just the birds in the trees for company!

N: Three.

A: It's a lovely day. Why don't we go to the countryside?

B: Good idea. It's still early and if we leave soon, we can spend the whole day there.

A: According to this timetable, there's a bus at half-past nine, and we can be in the countryside by ten o'clock. The next one after that is at 10:38am. That's not too bad. What do you think?

B: I'd rather spend more time in the countryside, so let's take the first bus.

N: Four.

A: What are you going to do in the summer?

B: We're going to visit my cousins in America.

A: Wow. Summer in America! Are you going to swim in the sea?

B: Oh, they don't live near the beach, but there's a swimming pool in their town. Oh, and there's a lake too. We go swimming and fishing there.

A: What's it like?

B: It's scary at first because the water's dark and you can't see the bottom!

N: Five.

I love being out in nature and breathing in the clean, fresh air. That's why I really like riding my bike in the countryside. Sometimes I stop at a farm and pick some apples. They're so sweet – they're the best snack! I take my paints and brushes with me too. Painting is my favourite hobby. My friend says I'm quite good at it, but I think she's just being polite!

N: Six.

I looked everywhere in my tent for it, even in my sleeping bag and my jacket. I couldn't call my mum to ask if it was at home because we weren't allowed to have out phones with us on the trip. So I was pretty thirsty by the time we hiked to the next village where I could buy a new one.

Unit 7 Skills Test Dictation

Television cooking competitions have become very popular recently. Millions of people watch these shows because they are exciting, but few viewers actually try to make the recipes at home.

Unit 7 Skills Test Listening

N = Narrator

N: One. You will hear a girl and her father talking about a restaurant.

A: We're leaving now, Kelly. Are you ready?

B: Yes, Dad, and I'm really hungry. I hope the food at the restaurant is good.

A: Well, I've heard the paella is excellent.

B: It isn't vegetarian though, is it?

A: Do you mean the restaurant?

B: No, I mean the paella. It's rice with vegetables, chicken, sausages and fish.

A: That's right. But I'm sure there'll be something you can eat that doesn't have meat in it.

B: Hopefully it's something tasty too!

N: Two. You will hear a woman explaining a recipe for a cake.

Have you got five minutes? That's all you need to make a delicious chocolate cake. And you won't make a mess because you don't need a pan or a plate – you can make it in a coffee cup and eat it from it too. You probably already have the ingredients in your kitchen – some butter, flour, sugar and cocoa powder. No eggs needed! Mix everything in a cup and cook for a minute and a half in a microwave oven. It's so easy!

N: Three. You will hear a girl ordering food at a fast food restaurant.

A: Hello. What would you like?

B: Can I have a burger and fries, please?

A: Sure. What size fries would you like? There's small, regular and large.

B: Oh, small fries.

A: Would you like a drink with that?

B: Just the food, thanks. Actually, can I change that to large fries, please?

A: Of course. That's four pounds fifty.

B: Here you are.

N: Four. You will hear a boy talking to his sister.

A: You don't look very well. What's wrong?

B: My stomach hurts.

A: Why don't you go to the doctor? I can call and make an appointment for you if you like.

B: Well, there's nothing seriously wrong with me. It's just that I had a big pizza for dinner.

A: ... and you ate it all yourself?

B: Um ... yes ... it was delicious. And vanilla ice cream afterwards.

A: Oh! I'm not surprised you feel bad. Drink a little water and you'll feel better.

N: Five. You will hear a woman and a man talking about what to eat.

A: We've got a packet of pasta and a jar of sauce. If you go to the shop for some cheese, I'll cook.

B: Don't worry about cooking. Let's order something and watch a film. There's a good one on Channel 7 tonight.

A: No, not takeaway again. We had curry last night.

B: OK, OK. Do you feel like going out to eat? How about Japanese?

A: You know sushi is my favourite, but we've been spending too much money lately. Please, just go to the shop and I'll cook.

B: OK.

N: Six. You will hear a girl and boy talking about some biscuits he cooked.

A: Phew! What smells in here?

B: I was making biscuits. After I put them in the oven, Maddy called to ask me something about our homework, and then we started talking about her party next week ...

A: I see ...

B: Yes, well, when I remembered, the biscuits were black. There was no way we could eat any of them so I had to throw them out.

A: I'm going to open all of the windows to get rid of the smell.

Unit 8 Skills Test Dictation

Have you ever thought about travelling to the stars? Companies are developing special planes right now, so you may get the chance to be a space tourist in the future.

Unit 8 Skills Test Listening

I = Interviewer, A = Adam

I: Today, we're talking to Adam, a teenager who travelled around the world with his family last year. How was it, Adam?

A: It was incredible! The holiday of a lifetime.

I: How did you do it?

A: We got special 'round-the-world' tickets. The thing is, we were planning an overseas holiday, but it was difficult as we wanted to visit different places. My sister and I wanted to see Australia. As for my parents, it's always been their dream to drive across the USA.

I: So your round the world ticket allowed you to visit both places?

A: Well, that's what eventually happened, but we did more than that. After my mum did some research online, looking at fares, you know, she found out that instead of flying only to Australia or the USA on a return ticket, we could pay a bit more for a round-the-world fare and visit more countries.

I: So you left London, flew all the way around the world, then back to London. I believe you stopped in Japan first.

A: Yes, we flew there for a week. I was surprised because Japan is like two different countries. Tokyo – the capital – is very modern, as you can imagine, but life in the countryside is very traditional – you can see it in the style of the buildings and the clothes people wear.

I: From there you went to Australia?

A: Yes, we were in Australia for two weeks. It's huge and the distances between cities are very long, so you need more time to explore. The beaches are amazing and I went surfing, something I've always wanted to do.

I: I see. And then you flew to the USA?

A: Actually, we decided to see South America first. I mean, it's sort of between Australia and the USA, so we thought 'why not'? There are daily flights from Australia to Chile, so it was very easy.

I: What did you do in Chile?

A: We went to the Atacama desert – it's the driest place in the world. It rains once every five to seven years, but when it does, the area fills with white, yellow and purple flowers. We were lucky because we went just after the rainfall and it was so beautiful and colourful.

I: Amazing! And then what did you do? Did you go to the USA next?

A: That's right. We flew to Los Angeles on the west coast of the USA. That's where our road trip began. We rented a car and drove across the country to New York. It was 4,500 km, it took three weeks and we loved it!

I: How lucky you were, Adam. What a wonderful trip.

A: It really was. We saw more in one trip than we ever thought would be possible.

Unit 9 Skills Test Dictation

The main reasons teenagers use social media are to talk to their friends, join group conversations, share photos and videos, and to have something to do when they feel bored.

Unit 9 Skills Test Listening

Hi everyone. I'm here to tell you about a great event called Offline. As you may have guessed, it's the opposite of 'online'. Basically, you spend a whole day – that's 24 hours – without internet, and raise money for charity.

Now, I know, this might seem difficult. We use the internet for everything nowadays, don't we? Whether it's for work, school, shopping or just having fun, we can't live without it. And since the early 2010s when smartphones became popular, it's been possible to have the internet with you at all times. But think about it. When was the last time you didn't use your phone for two hours? Offline gives you the chance to take a break from technology and discover other fun things to do.

If you want to take part in Offline, just fill in the forms I'll hand out at the end of this talk. We've chosen Saturday the 24th and Sunday the 25th of June for the event. So, this is how it works, and it's really simple: On Saturday at midday, you stop using the internet and you can only go back online 24 hours later on Sunday at 12 o'clock midday. And to give you a good reason to do this, it's to help a charity that gives computers to schools in Africa. You'll need to find sponsors who will agree to donate money for every hour that you spend offline. So, the longer you can stay off your phones, the more money you'll be able to raise.

Every school in the area will be taking part and there'll be a special prize for the school that raises the most money. You can ask your friends, family and local businesses to support and sponsor you.

Now, this year, to make it a bit more interesting, we've decided that radios and TV, along with the internet, also can't be used in the 24-hour period. Hopefully, this will make you think of fun things to do outdoors or some creative activities.

So I'll now hand over to your head teacher who will tell you about some great activities that the school has organised for the Saturday afternoon of the event.

End of Year Test Listening Task 1

N = Narrator
N: One.

A: I'm sorry about last night, Mum.

B: You should be! How is it possible for you and your friend to make such a mess? Empty drinks cans and packets all over the floor!

A: Um ... er ... yes, well, I've cleaned it up.

B: Well, I'm happy about that. I certainly wasn't going to clean it. Honestly, Lucy, I don't mind you having sleepovers and I'm happy to make you pizzas, but please be more careful. And the music you were listening to was much too loud. That was the worst thing of all. I couldn't sleep!

A: OK, Mum. Maybe next time I'll go to Fiona's for a sleepover.

N: Two.

A: I'm going out now, Dad. I'll be back later.

B: OK, what time does the concert finish? Will you be late? Do you want me to pick you up?

A: Dad, my favourite band is playing tomorrow. Remember?

B: Oh, that's right! Sorry, I forgot. So where are you going?

A: Grandma gave me money and I want to check out the shops. I need some new things anyway.

B: Alright then, but come back soon and we'll watch the match together.

N: Three.

A: It's your birthday in a few weeks. I'm sure you're very excited about it!

B: I am! I always look forward to celebrating it with my friends.

A: So will you invite me to your party?

B: Of course! But it's going to be different this year, not just a party or a going for a burger. We're going to start with something really fun ... paintballing! I've always wanted to do it. Afterwards, we'll go somewhere to eat.

A: Sounds great. I can't wait!

B: That's not all! We have to have a birthday cake, so we'll go home for that.

N: Four.

Welcome to our new youth club! It's great to see so many people here! I'm sure you're going to enjoy the activities we have for you. So, let me tell you about them. There are the usual sports as well as art and photography, but I think you're going to be excited about the video classes where you'll learn to edit your own films on a computer! As you know, most activities are free, but you will need to pay for the materials you'll use in art and robotics. But don't worry! It isn't much.

N: Five.

A: How's your project coming along? Are you making progress?

B: Well, that's difficult right now because my parents are decorating the house and it's too noisy for me and my sister to study there.

A: Why don't you go to the library? It's very quiet there and you can do a lot of work.

B: I know, but I wanted a break from homework yesterday, so I decided to spend some time outdoors with my sister and do some exercise.

A: That's a good idea. I should do it too!

B: I'll call you next time I go out.

N: Six.

A: How was your holiday? Did you learn how to ski?

B: Well, I learnt a few things, but I'm not very good and I can't go fast. But I had a good time and I'm looking forward to doing it again. Anyway, where are you going?

A: To my judo class. I love it! It's my favourite sport.

B: Yes, mine too. The teacher's really great.

A: I agree. Thanks for telling about the judo school you go to.

B: No problem. Hey, I've got a new table tennis set at home. Do you want to play tomorrow?

A: Sure, why not!

End of Year Test Listening Task 3

My name is Jack Williams and I've been invited to talk to you today because I've just won a tennis championship for junior players aged fourteen and under. But I'm not going to talk about myself, I'm going to tell you about my favourite tennis player at the moment, Stefanos Tsitsipas. Have you heard of him? He's been in the news a lot lately.

So, let me tell you a bit about him. Stefanos was born on the 12th of August, 1998 and he's from Greece. He first picked up a tennis racket when he was only three.

Well, as I said, he's Greek, and it's unusual that he's a tennis player because it isn't a very popular sport in Greece where most people follow football and basketball. But he chose to play tennis because both of his parents played. His mum was a junior champion in Russia – that's where she's from. That's why he speaks Russian, as well as Greek, of course, and English. His dad was a tennis teacher, but now he only teaches Stefanos.

People began to notice Stefanos when he started winning matches against the most famous players in important competitions.

I like him because of the way he plays. He's amazing – really fast and he never gives up, he fights for every point. He's also a really cool person too. He's interested in photography and making videos for his YouTube channel. They're great hobbies. I love the videos because they show him when he's travelling to tournaments, training hard to prepare for his next tournament and going on holiday with his family. I really hope to be as successful as him one day.

I think that would be really great!

1A THE MISSING ARTICLE

0 *I have ....a.... friend who is very honest.*

1 She has never studied in .... UK before.

2 Being .... adult can be really dull.

3 Life in .... capital can be hard if you are .... student from the countryside.

4 I don't have .... brother or .... sister, I'm .... only child.

5 .... mobile phones must be on silent when I am in class.

6 I read .... interesting blog yesterday.
In .... blog it talked about my favourite programme.

1B FIND MY PLACE

Grid A

	A	B	C	D	E
1					
2					
3					
4					
5					

Grid B

	A	B	C	D	E
1					
2					
3					
4					
5					

1C DESCRIBE AND DRAW

Worksheet A

1

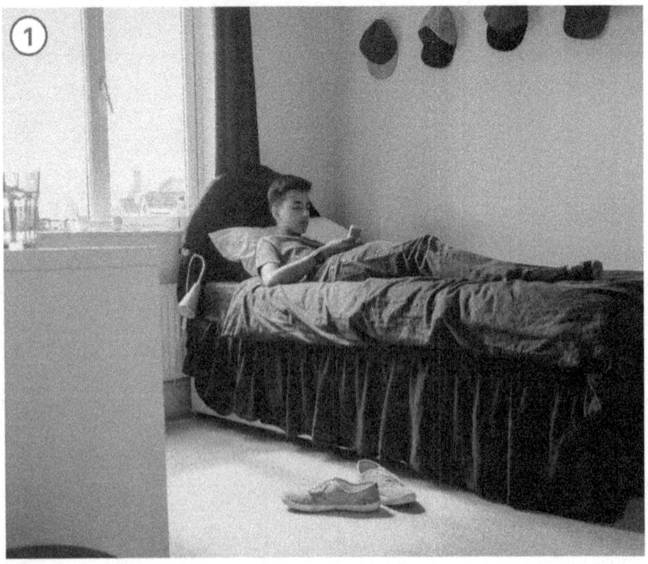

2

Worksheet B

1

2

2A MY FREE TIME

Student A

A The activity you do most often in your free time.
B A new hobby you are thinking of starting soon.
C A sport you never play because you don't like it.
D An activity you always do when you are on holiday.
E An activity your parents make you do most weekends.
F An activity you don't mind doing in the house.

1	**2**
3	**4**
5	**6**

Student B

A A sport you often watch on TV, but you don't play.
B An activity you are getting better at right now.
C An activity you do at the weekend, but you don't do on school days.
D A sport you are playing at school in your PE class at the moment.
E A club you belong to (or want to belong to).
F An activity you do at home that you hate.

1	**2**
3	**4**
5	**6**

2B TWO HALVES

Cards A

I really want to do … 1	On school nights, I spend … 2	I don't take my mobile to school because I waste … 3	I usually get good … 4
When my exams don't go … 5	I am more organised now and I am getting … 6	I always make more … 7	I enjoy taking … 8
Doing extra sports practice doesn't always … 9	I find it easier … 10	I prefer doing activities which I am good … 11	If I don't get it … 12

Cards B

… well this year at school, so I can choose go to university. B	… most of my time doing homework. D	… time playing on Facebook! G	… results if I study hard. J
… well, my parents don't let me go out at the weekends. H	… better at doing my homework on time. F	… progress in class when I don't sit next to my friends. C	… part in school activities, like drama groups, orchestra, or extra music classes. L
… work and sometimes I don't improve. K	… to exercise when I listen to music. I	… at. A	… right the first time, I make more effort! E

2C MY FAVOURITE TEAM SPORT

Part A

Team Sports:	**Team Sports:**	**Team Sports:**
Name: ______________	*Name:* ______________	*Name:* ______________
• My friend loves playing [1]	• My friend loves playing [1]	• My friend loves playing [1] ....
• S/he plays every [2]	• S/he plays every [2]	• S/he plays every [2] ....
• [3] .... play(s) this sport with him/her.	• [3] .... play(s) this sport with him/her.	• [3] .... play(s) this sport with him/her.
• There are [4] .... people that play this sport with him/her.	• There are [4] .... people that play this sport with him/her.	• There are [4] .... people that play this sport with him/her.
• S/he plays this sport at/in [5]	• S/he plays this sport at/in [5]	• S/he plays this sport at/in [5] ....
• My friend feels [6] .... when playing this sport.	• My friend feels [6] .... when playing this sport.	• My friend feels [6] .... when playing this sport.

Fold here

Part B

Think about a team sport you enjoy playing. You are going to talk about it with your group.
You must include this information (you can make some notes here):

1 What sport you play.

....

2 When you play.

....

3 Who you play the sport with (if you give a specific name, you will need to spell it).

....

4 How many people you play with in your team.

....

5 Where you play.

....

6 How it makes you feel when you play the sport.

....

3A CORRECT MY PAST

1 I **was going** to New York last summer. **(WENT)**	2 My mum walked in when I **was doing** my homework. **(✓)**
3 I **was waking** up very early this morning. **(WOKE UP)**	4 The train **was moved** very fast. **(WAS MOVING)**
5 At 6pm on Saturday morning, I **was travelling** to the airport. **(✓)**	6 I **played** in the park when it started to rain. **(WAS PLAYING)**
7 The family **broke** the window to escape. **(✓)**	8 While I **ran**, the bus arrived. **(WAS RUNNING)**
9 She **was having fun** when she was staying at her friend's house. **(HAD)**	10 A girl **was jumping** into the river to find her smartphone. **(JUMPED)**
11 I **was watching** TV when I saw the fire across the street. **(✓)**	12 He **was arriving** when I was sleeping, so I didn't hear him! **(ARRIVED)**

3B SENTENCE SCRAMBLE

Worksheet A

1

I found an .... (*age*) book I read when I was young in my grandmother's house!

2

She bought a .... , ... (*size, colour*) jacket last week, but she took it home to try it on and it wasn't her size.

3

For my birthday, I asked for a holiday to a .... country, but I got a .... , ... (*size, material*) plane instead.

4

It was an .... day yesterday, because I passed the exam! I didn't get any answers .... !

5

There is a .... , ... , ... house next to mine. Everyone wants to live there.

Worksheet B

dull	dark	exciting	modern	scary
useful	old	important	big	expensive
black	wrong	wooden	tiny	ordinary
light	right	gold	young	cheap
small	beautiful	difficult	foreign	huge

3C SCAN THE STORY

Worksheet A

RESCUE!

A cat was stuck in a tree in for four hours last week. Finally, someone called the police and the hero policeofficer saved the scared cat.

SAFE AT LAST

A family are finally back together after one week. The mum and daughter went walking on a remote road and didn't know the way to their accommodation where the dad and son were.

FIRE ON THE RAILWAY LINE

The police stopped all trains from London to Manchester on Thursday because of a fire. The trains started again after seven hours. Train staff said sorry.

HELICOPTER HELP

A man parked his car in a dark forest to walk his dog on Tuesday night. The man lost his car and called the police for help. It was so cold that night, they sent a helicopter to find him.

Worksheet B

1 Which story happened on Tuesday?

....

2 How long was the cat in the tree for?

....

3 What did the train staff do?

....

4 Why did the man go to the forest?

....

5 How long were the mum and daughter lost?

....

4A STUDENT COMMITTEE

What we have already organised for the next academic year:

1 *New support teachers in literature, maths, and science classes to start: Monday 18th September.*

2 *New homework club to open: Friday 22nd September. Intention is once a week, every Friday.*

What we have planned for the next academic year, but not organised yet:

1 *Give all students a one-to-one tutorial with their teacher every term.*

2 *Start a buddy system: create pairs of students – one older, one younger – so the older student can help.*

Other possibilities:

1 *Have an online chat system on the school website?*

2 *Give extra homework? Give less homework?*

3 *Have longer lessons? Have shorter lessons?*

4 *Have more breaktimes?*

4B TELL ME ABOUT …

LEARN TRY GOT DO FIND EASY HAD MADE GOT GIVE USING MADE

1 **START**	2 A time you were nervous about doing something, but you.............................. a go anyway.	3 How you .... best.	4 **GO FORWARD ONE SPACE**
8 A time you .... bad grades in a test and how you felt.	7 The best advice you can .... to a new person starting at your school.	6 **GO BACK ONE SPACE**	5 A subject you .... difficult to understand at school and why.
9 If you have .... up your mind what job you want in the future.	10 **GO FORWARD TWO SPACES**	11 A time you .... a big mistake at school.	12 A skill you would like to ....
16 **GO BACK TWO SPACES**	15 If you prefer learning by listening, watching or .... your hands.	14 A subject at school you find	13 **GO FORWARD TWO SPACES**
17 Something you want to learn how to	18 Something you .... interested in when you started school.	19 **GO BACK ONE SPACE**	20 **FINISH**

4C JIGSAW EMAILS

Part A

Email 1:

Dear Angie,

How are you? I can't believe that you are coming to visit me next week! We have organised the spare bedroom for you and my teacher is excited about you spending a day at my school!

(1) Thanks!

My mum wants to make your favourite meal for the day you arrive. What kind of food do you like? Is there a special dish you love?

(2) Suggest

There are lots of activities to do in my town. Is there anything you would really love to see? Any ideas? I want to plan the weekend before you get here.

(3) Tell Angie

I hope I can visit you too this year! What dates are good for you and your family?

(4) give a time of year

Bye for now,

Marie.

Email 2:

Hi there,

I hope you are well! I am going on a school exchange to France next month and I want some advice.

(5) of course!

I know that you did an exchange in Spain two years ago. Did you enjoy it? What was the best part?

(6) Yes! Tell Tim

I would like to take a present for my host family – maybe some typical food from here. Can you suggest something?

(7) Suggest

My parents told me that you and your sister are going to visit us in the summer. That's so exciting! What date do you arrive?

(8) give dates

Write back soon,

Tim.

Part B

A We are really excited about coming to see you again. I have to go to summer school for the whole month of July, so we are travelling at the beginning of August. Can't wait!	**B** That's so kind! Well, I love all types of food, but my favourite is Italian. How about some pasta with tomato sauce? It's delicious!
C We are going on holiday to Germany at the beginning of the summer, so around the end of August or September is best. I need to ask my mum and I'll tell you next week.	**D** I'm so jealous about your trip abroad! And of course, I'm always happy to help.
E Why don't you get some of those wonderful chocolates from the shop next to your school? They were really incredible! I'm sure your host family would like them too.	**F** Please tell your mum and dad thank you from me. I'm sure I am going to feel at home!
G I really want to visit the famous parks in your city. I have seen many pictures and they look beautiful. Maybe we can make a picnic one day and go for a walk.	**H** It was such an amazing experience! I enjoyed meeting lots of new people and practising the language every day. It was interesting to go to a different school for a week too.
Email 1: BEGINNING Hi there! Thanks so much for your email!	Email 1: ENDING See you soon, Rebecca
Email 2: BEGINNING Dear Tim, How are you? It was so nice to hear from you.	Email 2: ENDING Bye for now, Laura.

5A WHAT'S BETTER, WHAT'S BEST?

Cards A

shopping online vs. shopping in a shop	having a lot of money vs. being very happy	being a model vs. being a teacher	designer brands vs. high street clothes
dressing up for a party vs. dressing casually	a filter on a photo vs. no filter	taking a selfie vs. someone taking your photo	being tall vs. being short
buying expensive things vs. buying cheap things	blogging vs. vlogging	spending money vs. saving money	trying on clothes in the shop vs. trying on clothes at home

Cards B

good	important	bad	funny
confident	popular	expensive	friendly
adventurous	happy	big	crazy
tall	cheap	practical	interesting

5B PEN FRIEND

Dear pen friend,

My name is .... and I'm .... years old.

Today, I'm going to tell you what I look like.

I am .... (height) and I am .... for my age.

I have .... (hair) and I have .... (face).

I usually wear .... (clothes/style) and .... (clothes/style).

I often have .... (accessories) with me.

Some people say I look like .... (family/famous person), but I think I look like .... (family/famous person).

My personality is very .... (what you are like) and sometimes .... (what you are like).

In my free time, I like .... and .... (hobbies).

Please write back to me and tell me what you look like :-)

Bye!

5C WHISPERS RELAY

Worksheet A

1

It's also good for the environment!

2

If you don't like spending a lot of money on clothes, you can find nice, cheap clothes too.

3

If you have experience with different styles, or just love to shop, it could be the perfect hobby for you!

4

Your new style will give you a more interesting wardrobe!

Worksheet B

To blog – or vlog?

Checking out blogs or vlogs is a good way to get the latest fashion tips on accessories and new styles.

On many blogs, you can see pictures of fashionable looks, celebrity style, videos with advice and sometimes you can even submit your own blog post. Not a writer? It doesn't matter. ☐ Some blogs have style advisors that can help you choose a style you feel confident in or can help you if you feel you dress too ordinary. It might be a new hairstyle, a nice suit or just clothes that are the best colour for you. ☐

If you don't like to stand out in a crowd, you can wear colours like black or white. ☐ Blogs sometimes even recommend clothes exchanges for people who prefer to save money. This means people give you clothes they don't want, and you give them clothes you don't want. ☐

6A TRIP TO THE NATIONAL PARK

Modal verbs

Use these to help create your set of rules for the trip.

must have to can can't mustn't don't/doesn't have to

Camping in the national park

General Rules
(E.g. times for activities, phone calls/communication, precautions)

What you need to bring	What you don't need to/mustn't bring
(clothes, food, camping and cooking equipment, money, etc.)	*(clothes, food, camping and cooking equipment, money, etc.)*

Activities allowed	Activities not allowed
(things you can do alone/in a group, types of activities, etc.)	*(things you can do alone/in a group, types of activities, etc.)*

6B OUR WORLD

Part A

Write these places/animals in your 'world' below.

1 Your favourite type of pet.
2 A place you both really like going to in your town.
3 A place you both like going on holiday.
4 A wild animal you both like.
5 A farm animal you both like.
6 A place in your country that you would both like to visit.

Part B

Prepare your clues. Write at least three per category.

1	2	3
4	5	6

6C HOLIDAY PARK

Part A

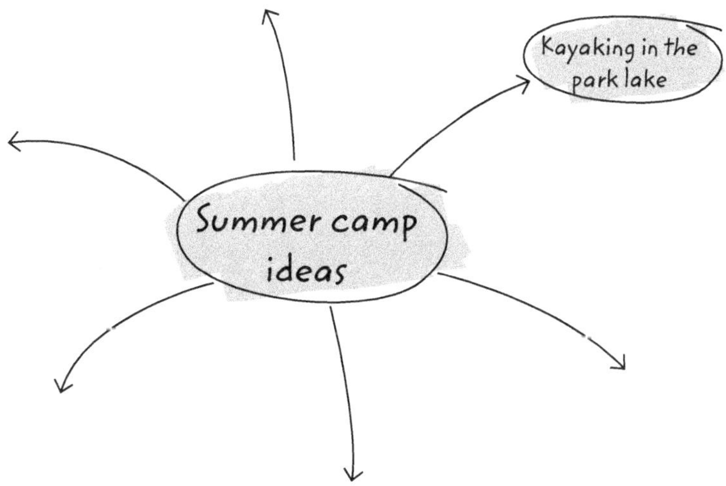

Part B

Yes, you're right.	Yes, I agree with you because …	No, I disagree because …
I'm not sure about that because …	I think .... it better because …	I think that's the best idea too because …
I think .... is the worst idea because …	What do you think about .... ?	How about .... ?
.... could be a good idea because …	That's a good point.	I think so, too.

7A FIND MY OPINIONS

Worksheet A

FOOD	DRINKS	PLACES
1 I love …………… because ……………	1 …………… ……………	1 …………… ……………
2 I like …………… because ……………	2 …………… ……………	2 …………… ……………
3 I dislike …………… because ……………	3 …………… ……………	3 …………… ……………

Worksheet B

WHO SAID IT?

FOOD

1 ……………

2 ……………

3 ……………

DRINKS

1 ……………

2 ……………

3 ……………

PLACES

1 ……………

2 ……………

3 ……………

7B HOW'S MY FOOD?

Worksheet A

1 'I had to drink so much water after I finished it. My mouth hurt. It was like drinking lots of water from the sea!'
2 'They didn't cook the food correctly – it almost broke my teeth!'
3 'It is a cool café, but they only sell cakes and food with lots of sugar.'
4 'I really love eating fruit like limes or lemons in the morning. They give me energy and really wake me up!'
5 'The food was so horrible. It was cooked too much and was black …'
6 'It wasn't juicy – it was the opposite. I needed to drink so much water!'
7 'My mum is a chef and owns a chain of restaurants. It is popular because she cooks with a lot of chillies …'
8 'Bread here is not the same in my country. Here, it is very hard and sometimes difficult to eat …'

Worksheet B

salty	hot	spicy	soft
dry	cold	hard	sweet
sour	crispy	burned	juicy

7C WHAT AM I?

Worksheet A

recipe	onion	lunchtime
crispy	takeaway	snack
banana	juicy	sweet
soft	chef	hungry
cafe	raw	burned

Worksheet B

butter	popcorn	restaurant
expensive	vegetarian	dry
spicy	pineapple	curry
sour	tasty	salty
meal	presentation	summer

8A HOW WELL DO YOU KNOW ME?

Make guesses and complete these sentences for your partner.

1 You have lived in this city/town/village for/since .... (*a period of time / a specific date or time*)

2 You have travelled on holiday to .... in the past. (*a place, country, city*)

3 You haven't been to .... yet, but you would like to go in the future. (*a place, country, city*)

4 You have just started .... (*an activity, hobby*)

5 You have never eaten .... (*a food*)

6 You have never been/done/played ...., but you would love to. (*an activity*)

7 You have studied English for/since .... (*a period of time / a specific date or time*)

8 You have travelled by .... many times. (*a mode of transport*)

Verdict:

1–3 correct answers:
You are almost strangers! You need to get to know you partner better. Take time to ask about his/her weekend at the beginning of class or go to the cinema together one day. We are always happier with more friends!

4–6 correct answers:
You are friends, but not best friends! You know your partner quite well; maybe you have seen each other outside of class a few times. Why don't you get together more? It's always nice to have more friends.

7–8 correct answers:
You are like two peas in a pod! You are excellent friends and obviously spend a lot of time together. It must be nice to study in the same class, but why don't you try to work with other people too and make even more friends?

Make guesses and complete these sentences for your partner.

1 You have lived in this city/town/village for/since .... (*a period of time / a specific date or time*)

2 You have travelled on holiday to .... in the past. (*a place, country, city*)

3 You haven't been to .... yet, but you would like to go in the future. (*a place, country, city*)

4 You have just started .... (*an activity, hobby*)

5 You have never eaten .... (*a food*)

6 You have never been/done/played ...., but you would love to. (*an activity*)

7 You have studied English for/since .... (*a period of time / a specific date or time*)

8 You have travelled by .... many times. (*a mode of transport*)

Verdict:

1–3 correct answers:
You are almost strangers! You need to get to know you partner better. Take time to ask about his/her weekend at the beginning of class or go to the cinema together one day. We are always happier with more friends!

4–6 correct answers:
You are friends, but not best friends! You know your partner quite well; maybe you have seen each other outside of class a few times. Why don't you get together more? It's always nice to have more friends.

7–8 correct answers:
You are like two peas in a pod! You are excellent friends and obviously spend a lot of time together. It must be nice to study in the same class, but why don't you try to work with other people too and make even more friends?

8B TRANSPORT DOMINOES

… on the platform. C	I went to New York last year and bought all of my friends … **START HERE**	… souvenirs – a magnet of the Statue of Liberty! E	Did Sarah catch …
… the last train or do you think she'll be late? H	I always travel by …	… train and usually buy a return ticket because it's cheaper. F	On the city tram, you don't buy tickets in advance. You pay …
… the fare when you're on it. K	I really hate going on …	… long journeys, especially by car. A	You have to show …
… your passport many times at the airport. J	Did you make …	… a reservation for the theatre tonight? There aren't many tickets left. L	We went to Venice last year and booked …
… a beautiful hotel in the centre. B	Going through …	… security at the airport is stressful. You have to take everything out of your bag! I	When they make an announcement, you must go to …
… your gate to catch the flight. G	Did you have to get …	… a travel visa when you went to Thailand? D	I always arrive early to catch my train and wait …

8C EDUCAMPS

Part A

Student Cards

A Tina/Tom

You can only go to a camp in the winter because of your parents' jobs, but you love hot weather. Your hobby is windsurfing and you adore being by the sea. You don't like camping because you hate insects.

B Louise/Lewis

You finish school for two months at the end of July and want to go to a camp during your holidays. You want to help others and would prefer to go to a non-English-speaking country. You would like to learn a new skill that you can add to your application for vet school next year. You don't like very hot weather.

C Jean/John

You can only travel in August and would like to practise your Spanish while at camp. You don't have a lot of money, so would prefer to do some charity work in exchange for accommodation. You adore most animals, but you're afraid of cows, sheep and horses!

D Beth/Ben

You don't like hot weather, but only have one week free in August. You don't speak other languages, so would prefer to go somewhere where people will understand you. You love any extreme activities. You don't like sharing with other people.

E Rebecca/Robert

You want to go to a camp somewhere warm, but not too hot. You love nature and being near water. Your hobbies are orienteering and hiking, and you like discovering wild environments. You can't spend more than $1000.

F Carly/Carl

You want to learn something completely new and would like to return home with a certificate. You love doing any kind of physical exercise. You have a maximum of $1500 to spend.

Camp Cards

1 EduCamp: Help at our animal refuge and learn something new!

Camp dates: August 15th – August 29th

Temperature: Around 18 degrees.

Activities: Horse riding, farming.

Accommodation: Single rooms in a large farm house.

Cost: free

What you'll learn: Spanish classes, planting and picking fresh food, caring for abandoned farm animals.

2 EduCamp: Learn to fly in the north of Canada.

Camp dates: August 1st – August 7th

Temperature: Around 15 degrees

Activities: Flying.

Accommodation: Single rooms in a hotel.

Cost: $2000

What you'll learn: how to fly a plane, reading monitors in planes.

3 Learn to parachute in the paradise island of Hawaii, USA.

Camp dates: August 8st – August 15th

Temperature: Around 28 degrees

Activities: Parachuting, hiking.

Accommodation: 2 students per hotel room.

Cost: $1400

What you'll learn: how to use a parachute, first aid certificate.

4 EduCamp: Into the desert in Australia's outback.

Camp dates: February 20th – March 1st

Temperature: Around 24 degrees.

Activities: Desert trekking, canoeing on a lake.

Accommodation: Camping: 2 students per tent.

Cost: $900

What you'll learn: survival guide, map reading.

5 EduCamp: Enjoy being by one of Australia's most famous beaches!

Camp dates: January 16th – February 8th

Temperature: Around 29 degrees.

Activities: Watersports.

Accommodation: Hostel: 3 students per room.

Cost: $1750

What you'll learn: lifeguard certification, an introduction to surfing.

6 EduCamp: Help us to look after elderly people in Spain!

Camp dates: August 10th – August 20th

Temperature: Around 30 degrees.

Activities: Dog walking, cooking.

Accommodation: Private room in a house.

Cost: free

What you'll learn: cooking for people, first aid.

8C EDUCAMPS

Part B

Note Card

Name of person/Camp	Information given
E.g. Fred	*Wants hot country, spend $500 or less, doesn't like animals, etc.*
E.g. EduCamp: Brazil carnival	*Costs $1400, costume making, in October … etc.*

9A THROUGH THE GRID

Student A

START

When/feel bored …	If/weather/good/ weekend …	If/pass/exam …	When/sad …
If/hungry …	If/free time …	When/do sport …	If/travel/tomorrow …
When/meet/ new people …	When/don't have/ my phone …	When/rains …	If/sleep too long …
If/win something …	When/play a game …	If/friend/sad …	If/don't do/ homework …

FINISH

Student B

START

When/feel brave …	If/weather/bad/ weekend …	If/fail/exam …	When/feel/happy …
If/tired …	When/ have time …	When/listen/music …	If/do/something tomorrow …
When/friends want to see me …	When/watch/film …	When/sunny …	When/go to school …
If/don't see my friends today …	When/learn/ something …	If/watch TV/tonight …	If/go/holiday/next month …

FINISH

9B COLLOCATION COLLECTOR

Part A

download	have	watch	do
play	forget	search for	make
delete	listen to	go to	eat

Part B

music	a good time	a film	a quiz
piano	a password	an answer	a cake
an app	a podcast	the cinema	dinner

9C PAIRS AND PREFERENCES

Worksheet A

Playing piano	Watching a film at home	Listening to music online	Playing computer games inside	Chatting with friends on social media
Playing guitar	Watching a film at the cinema	Going to a concert	Doing sports outside	Chatting with friends face to face

Worksheet B

Downloading music to your phone	Going to a costume party	Reading a comic	Going camping	Having a sleepover with one friend
Listening to music online	Going to a party without costumes	Reading a book	Going on a beach holiday	Having a sleepover with ten friends

1A The missing article

AIM
To practise the use of articles

EXAM LINK
Reading Part 6

ACTIVITY TYPE
A competitive group activity where students fill the gaps for points

CLASSROOM DYNAMICS
Pairwork

TIME TAKEN
10–12 minutes

WHEN TO USE
After Grammar: Exercise 4, page 12

PREPARATION
You will need one copy of the activity for each pair, folded, with the example showing

PROCEDURE
1 Divide the students into pairs and distribute the handout. Tell the students not to unfold the piece of paper.

2 Tell students to look at the example. Explain that there are six sentences in total – one under each fold with a missing article. Explain they will have one minute to read the sentence and to write which article they think is missing. The options are *a, an, the* or *nothing*. If students think the space should be empty, tell them to put a – on it. Once the time is up, go through the answers as a class, awarding points to the teams that get the article correct. Answer any questions or correct errors during feedback.

3 Repeat the steps for the next questions, until all of the sentences have been completed.

4 The winning team is the pair with the most points at the end of the activity.

ADAPTATION AND EXTENSION
- For fast finishers, this could be made into a gap-fill worksheet activity.
- For a stronger group, each pair can write one or two sentences to read aloud to the class for other pairs to guess the correct missing word.

ANSWER KEY
1 the; 2 an; 3 the, a; 4 a, a, an; 5 –; 6 an, the

1B Find my place

AIM
To practise vocabulary of places around town

ACTIVITY TYPE
A competitive activity where students must find the places in the other students' towns

CLASSROOM DYNAMICS
Pairwork

TIME TAKEN
15 minutes

WHEN TO USE
After Vocabulary: Exercise 5, page 13

PREPARATION
One worksheet per student

PROCEDURE
1 Divide the students into pairs. Distribute the activity sheet to each student.

2 Before the class, prepare a sample grid to show to the class, with five places plotted onto the grid. Show students and tell students to plot five places from the vocabulary they have just learned onto their grid; this can be done by writing the word or drawing a picture. For example, *a bus stop*, or *a bike rack*. Each item must only take one square. Tell students they must keep this a secret from their partner. Set a time of three or four minutes for this stage.

3 Once completed, Student A asks Student B questions to find all of their plotted places before they swap turns. You may need to elicit present simple questions. Example: *Do you have anything in A5? Yes. Is it a bus stop? Yes.* If an item is found, the student must cross it off in Grid B. If they ask *Do you have anything in A5? Yes. Is it a bus stop?* and the answer is *No,* they must wait until the next turn to guess what the item in the square is. Monitor during the task to check for any errors.

4 The winner is the student who finds all of the items first. Ask for feedback after the task to see what places students included.

ADAPTATION AND EXTENSION
- To extend or add difficulty to the activity, ask students to draw a route in which they went to each place. Their partner asks questions to find the order of where they went. The first student to guess the route correctly, wins.
- For fast finishers, students can draw a map of their ideal town on the grid and label it, including the places from the unit.

1C Describe and draw

AIM
To practise describing a photo for Speaking Part 2

EXAM LINK
Speaking: Part 2

ACTIVITY TYPE
A speaking activity where students must describe a picture for their partner to draw

CLASSROOM DYNAMICS
Pairwork

TIME TAKEN
10–12 minutes

WHEN TO USE
After Speaking: Exercise 4, page 15

PREPARATION

You will need one copy of the activity for each pair, cut up into Student A/Student B worksheets. Students will need a separate blank piece of paper.

PROCEDURE

1 Divide the students into pairs and assign them as Student A or Student B. Distribute the corresponding activity sheet to each student.

2 Explain that Student A describes what they can see in their first photo to Student B. They have two minutes. Tell students they should use the vocabulary and phrases they have just learned to describe the positioning of each item in the photo. Student B must draw what Student A describes, but must not show them until the end.

3 Once finished, check the pictures to see if they described it correctly or what the differences might be. Then, it is Student B's turn to describe the first photo for two minutes. This continues until all of the pictures have been described.

4 Once the activity is completed, ask students for feedback. Ask them: *What did you find difficult? What did you find easy? Did your partner use the vocabulary and phrases to help you understand where everything was?*

ADAPTATION AND EXTENSION

- Could be done as a written activity where one picture is given to each student and they must write what they see in the picture.
- To add a competitive element, put students into small groups of three or four and give a different picture to each student. One person in the group describes their picture, and the others draw. The person who is describing chooses the winner as the student whose picture is most similar to the original one.

2A My free time

AIM

To practise using the present simple and continuous, as well as adverbs of frequency

EXAM LINK

Speaking: Part 1 (interview)

ACTIVITY TYPE

Making guesses about information and discussing in pairs

CLASSROOM DYNAMICS

Individual and pairwork

TIME TAKEN

15 minutes

WHEN TO USE

After Grammar: Exercise 6, page 24

PREPARATION

You will need one copy of the worksheet per pair, cut up as indicated

PROCEDURE

1 Divide the class into pairs and give out the corresponding part of the worksheet to each student (A & B). Tell students they are going to discuss activities and hobbies they do in their free time with their partner, but first they must prepare alone.

2 Ask students to write one/two-word responses to the list (a–f) at the top of their worksheet in the squares provided. They should not show these to their partner yet, nor discuss them. The notes should not be in numerical order, but rather written in the different squares at random.

3 Once completed, ask the students to exchange their worksheets with each other.

4 Now give the students around two or three minutes to look at the boxes and try to consider what the notes might refer to.

5 They are now ready to start the discussion. Student A starts by choosing one of the boxes on Student B's handout and explaining his/her guess in a full sentence. E.g. You are playing rugby at the moment in your PE class at school. Student B confirms if Student A is correct or incorrect. If correct, they put a tick in the box. If incorrect, Student A asks Student B two more questions, which Student B answers. Students take turns guessing and discussing the information in the boxes for around ten minutes. Monitor throughout and make notes.

6 At the end of the ten minutes, students count up how many ticks they have. The winner in the one with the most correct guesses.

7 Give some language and content feedback at the end of the activity.

EXTENSION TASK

- As an extension task, change the pairs and ask students to retell each other as much information as possible from memory about their original partner without looking at the handout.

2B Two halves

AIM

To practise using vocabulary of practising and improving

EXAM LINK

Reading: Part 1 (multiple-choice) and Part 5 (multiple-choice)

ACTIVITY TYPE

Matching two halves of sentences and discussing

CLASSROOM DYNAMICS

Pairwork

TIME TAKEN

20 minutes

WHEN TO USE

After Vocabulary: Exercise 4, page 25

PREPARATION

You will need one copy of the worksheet per pair, cut up into sets of cards

PROCEDURE

1 On the board, write this sentence with these two options and ask students which one is the second half: *My brother is a professional football player. He is really good ...* *a) spending time with friends. b) at keeping fit.* (The answer is b)

2 Tell students that they are going to get two sets of cards (two halves of the same sentence). They must try to match them.

3 Put the students into pairs and give them a set of Card As first. Tell them to place them face up on the desk in front of them. Now give them a set of Card Bs, which they should place face down in a pile.

4 The activity is as follows: Students turn over one of the Card Bs from the pile and together try to decide which Card A is its other half. Once decided, they should place the two halves alongside each other then talk for a minute about whether the sentence is true for them or not. (The numbers and letters on the cards are only for checking answers later.) This process continues until students have matched all the cards. Monitor closely throughout and make notes. Help where necessary.

5 Go through the answers as a whole class and give students some feedback.

EXTENSION TASK

- Tell students to put Card Bs aside and only look at the shaded Card As again. Give students five minutes to try to recall how the sentences are completed from memory and write these on a piece of paper. The pair with the most sentences is the winning group.

ANSWER KEY

1 B; 2 D; 3 G; 4 J; 5 H; 6 F; 7 C; 8 L; 9 K; 10 I; 11 A; 12 E

2C My favourite team sport

AIM

To practise listening for specific information and completing notes

EXAM LINK

Listening: Part 3 (sentence completion). Also useful for Speaking: Part 1 interview (*Tell me about* section)

ACTIVITY TYPE

Listening to a partner talking about their favourite hobby and completing information.

CLASSROOM DYNAMICS

Individual and pairwork

TIME TAKEN

15 minutes

WHEN TO USE

After Listening: Exercise 4, page 26

PREPARATION

You will need one copy of the worksheet per student

PROCEDURE

1 Tell the students that they are going to discuss their favourite team sports with their classmates and give them a minute or two to consider which sport they want to talk about.

2 Write this sentence on the board and elicit what type of information might be missing. *I play football once a* (the answer could be day/week/month – any time period).

3 Put the students into pairs and give each student a copy of the worksheet, folded in the middle as indicated. Tell students to look at Part A and guess what information might be missing from the gaps.

4 Get some feedback from the students and write these on the board.

5 Explain to the students that they are now going to prepare to talk about their favourite team sports for a few minutes. Let students look at Part B and make notes next to the numbered list.

6 Put students into groups of four (Student A, B, C, & D). They are now ready to start the listening activity. Student A starts by talking about their favourite team sport. Encourage students to talk for at least a minute, in full sentences, and include all the information in the numbered list in Part B. While Student A talks, the other students should listen and try to complete the first box in Part A. They should write the name of Student A next to where it says *Name*. This process is then repeated with Students B, C and D.

7 When all students have talked about their activities, students should compare the information completed in Part A and confirm if it is correct/incorrect.

EXTENSION TASK

- In their groups of four, ask students to discuss and vote on which of the four team sports is a) the most interesting, b) the hardest work, c) the most fun, d) the best exercise. Report these back to the whole class and compare the group decisions.

3A Correct my past

AIM

To practise using past simple and past continuous tenses

ACTIVITY TYPE

A card game where students identify and correct errors in sentences

CLASSROOM DYNAMICS

Pairwork

TIME TAKEN

10–12 minutes

WHEN TO USE

After Grammar: Exercise 5, page 36

PREPARATION

You will need one copy of the activity per pair, cut up into cards

PROCEDURE

1. Divide the students into pairs. Distribute a set of cards to each pair, face down in front of them.
2. Explain that this is a game where one student will need to pick up a card and read the sentence to their partner. Student B listens and identifies if the verb tense is correct. If it is incorrect, they must say why and try to correct the sentence. If Student B guesses correctly, they win the card. If the answer is not correct, Student A keeps the card.
3. The process is repeated until all of the cards have run out. Monitor understanding during the task. The student with the most cards at the end is the winner.
4. Afterwards, review the answers as a whole class. Answer any questions and correct any common errors.

ADAPTATION AND EXTENSION

- If you have a stronger group, each pair can write three of their own examples to read to another pair. If the other pair guess correctly, they keep the cards.
- This can be adapted to a competitive activity, where students are divided into two large groups. Read the sentences aloud to the students and one student from each team races to write the correct answer on the board first. If they think it is correct, they race to write a tick on the board. Points are awarded to the fastest team that is correct.

ANSWER KEY

1 went; 2 ✓; 3 woke up; 4 was moving; 5 ✓; 6 was playing; 7 ✓; 8 was running; 9 had; 10 jumped; 11 ✓; 12 arrived

3B Sentence scramble

AIM

To practise adjectives and their order in sentences

EXAM LINK

Reading: Part 5

ACTIVITY TYPE

A competitive team activity where students must find the missing adjectives to complete their sentences

CLASSROOM DYNAMICS

Small groups

TIME TAKEN

15 minutes

WHEN TO USE

After Vocabulary: Exercise 6, page 37

PREPARATION

You will need one copy of Worksheet A per group and a cut-up copy of Worksheet B per group, stuck around the room

PROCEDURE

1. Divide the students into small groups. Distribute a copy of Worksheet A to each group. A copy of Worksheet B per group will need to be copied and stuck onto the walls around the room.
2. Explain that this is a competitive activity where students will need to read their sentences and choose one student at a time to find the adjectives which fit correctly. Tell students their teammates can help but must remain seated. Students can only help by speaking to the person who is looking for the words. There are clues in the first three sentences to help students identify the correct adjective but explain that it becomes more difficult. Set a time of ten minutes to collect and write all of their adjectives into the sentences.
3. Award points for each correct adjective in its correct place. Feedback the answers as a whole class after the task to correct any errors. The team who has the most answers correct and in the right order is the winner.

ADAPTATION AND EXTENSION

- If you have a stronger group, the teams can write one or two of their own sentences and read them aloud for the other teams to complete with adjectives.
- For fast finishers, this can be done as a worksheet activity where students complete the sentences with suitable adjectives.

POSSIBLE ANSWERS:

1 exciting/old/important/expensive

2 big/tiny – dark/black/gold

3 foreign – big/tiny – wooden

4 exciting/important – wrong

5 Various answers possible according to adjective order

3C Scan the story

AIM

To practise scanning skills

EXAM LINK

Reading: Part 3

ACTIVITY TYPE

A competitive team game where students must scan four short texts to relay the information back to their team

CLASSROOM DYNAMICS

Groups of three or four

TIME TAKEN

10–12 minutes

WHEN TO USE

After Reading: Exercise 7, page 35

PREPARATION

One copy of the cut-up cards to stick on the wall and one copy of the question worksheet per group

PROCEDURE

1. Before the activity, cut up and stick the Worksheet A cards on four separate walls.
2. Divide the students into groups (three or four per group). Share Worksheet B sheets out – one per group.
3. For this activity, students will need to choose one member of their team to leave the room at a time, and to scan the information on the cards to bring specific information back to their group. They will need this information to answer the questions on their worksheet. Remind students of the meaning or technique for scanning, if necessary. Explain that it is a competitive activity, and the group that finds all of the correct information fastest and first is the winner. Tell students they will have a total time of five minutes to complete the activity, and that they must only look for the answer to the question they have been given.
4. Once the activity begins, monitor the students to ensure only one student is leaving at a time, and only bringing back the answer to one question at a time. Make a note of the order in which the teams finish.
5. When all of the groups have completed their worksheet, go through the answers and deal with any common errors or questions. Declare the winner, which is the group who has finished fastest and with the most correct answers.

ADAPTATION AND EXTENSION

- If you have a strong group, you could ask each group to write one or two more questions for the other groups to find.
- For fast finishers, this can be done as a worksheet activity, where students work in pairs to scan the texts to find the answers.
- To add a fun element, the activity could be done outside of the classroom in an outdoor area or around the school, where possible.

ANSWER KEY

1 Helicopter help; 2 Four hours; 3 They said sorry; 4 To walk his dog; 5 For one week

4A Student committee

AIM

To practise using future forms

EXAM LINK

Speaking: Part 4

ACTIVITY TYPE

Role-play: having a discussion and making decisions

CLASSROOM DYNAMICS

Small groups.

TIME TAKEN

20 minutes

WHEN TO USE

After Grammar: Exercise 7, page 48

PREPARATION

You will need one copy of the handout per group

PROCEDURE

1. Explain to students that they are going to roleplay being on a student committee at their school. The teachers have been discussing how to **improve learning** in the next academic year. They have some plans already organised, some things they intend to start and other ideas which are possibilities. The teachers would like you to discuss these with the other students on the committee.
2. Divide the class into small groups of around four students. Give them a worksheet and clarify any vocabulary they may not understand.
3. Tell students they have around ten minutes to discuss all the items on the teachers' notes. They should say what the plan/arrangement/possibility is, and then discuss if they think it is a good idea or not, and why.
4. By the end of the discussion, the students should have notes to help report back to the teachers. They should have comments on the organised/unorganised plans and arrangements and if they think they are good ideas or not. They should also choose two ideas from the possibility list which they think the teachers should implement and why.
5. Stop the discussion after ten minutes and ask students to present their ideas to the whole class. All group members should listen carefully to each other and take turns to talk.
6. Give some content and language feedback after the activity, focusing mainly on the use of future forms.

EXTENSION TASK

- Ask students to write a short email back to their teachers summarising their opinions.

4B Tell me about ...

AIM

To practise vocabulary of learning

EXAM LINK

Speaking: Part 1 (interview); Reading: Part 5 (multiple-choice)

ACTIVITY TYPE

Board game. Completing sentences with missing words and discussing.

CLASSROOM DYNAMICS

Small groups of three or four students

TIME TAKEN

15 minutes

WHEN TO USE

After Vocabulary: Exercise 7, page 49

PREPARATION

You will need one copy of the handout per group. You will also need dice and counters.

PROCEDURE

1. Divide the class into small groups of three or four students and give them a copy of the worksheet, a counter per student and a dice. Tell students to place their counters on the Start square.
2. All group members roll the dice and the student with the highest number goes first. The student moves their counter according to the number on the dice. They should then read the 'tell me about' sentence aloud, choosing one of the words from the box at the top of the board to complete the gap.
3. If all group members agree this is correct, the student then answers and discusses the statement for at least 30 seconds. If the group members believe it is incorrect, they should check with you before moving the student's counter back to the previous square on the board. Clockwise, the students take turns moving around the board, completing the sentences and discussing. Let this continue for up to ten minutes or until one member of the group reaches the Finish square.
4. Go through the answers to the gaps at the end of the activity and give some feedback on their discussions based on notes taken throughout.

ADAPTATION

- For weaker groups, get students to complete the gaps before playing the board game in pairs.

ANSWER KEY

2 had; 3 learn; 5 find; 7 give; 8 got; 9 made; 11 made; 12 learn; 14 easy; 15 using; 17 do; 18 got

4C Jigsaw emails

AIM

To analyse informal emails and tasks

EXAM LINK

Writing: Part 1 (an email)

ACTIVITY TYPE

Reading a task and matching answers to notes

CLASSROOM DYNAMICS

Pairwork

TIME TAKEN

10 minutes

WHEN TO USE

After Writing: Exercise 6, page 53

PREPARATION

You will need one copy of the worksheet per pair, cut into Part A and B as indicated. Part B should be cut into cards.

PROCEDURE

1. Divide the class into pairs and give them a copy of Part A of the worksheet. Ask students to read the two emails quickly and answer this question, which should be written on the board. *Who is going to visit their friend sooner – Tim or Angie?* The answer is *Angie* from email 1. Give students a couple of minutes to decide together before giving the answer to the whole class.
2. Now give each pair a set of Part B cards face down on the desk. Ask students to look through the cards very quickly (without reading them) and take out the four cards shaded in grey that say 'beginning' and 'ending'. Ask students to lay these, face up on the table, separating the cards for emails 1 and 2.
3. Tell students to divide the other cards equally between themselves (they should have four each).
4. Working together, the students should firstly try to match the cards to the notes written at the side of the emails in Part A and then put them in order to make a full response.
5. Once completed, ask students to compare their answers with another pair in the class before going through the answers as a whole class.

EXTENSION TASK

- Get students to choose one of the two emails and create their own response using their own ideas. These can then be passed to another pair, who can provide some peer feedback.

ANSWER KEY

1 F; 2 B; 3 G; 4 C; 5 D; 6 H; 7 E; 8 A

5A What's better, what's best?

AIM

To practise discussion techniques using comparatives and superlatives

EXAM LINK

Speaking: Part 3

ACTIVITY TYPE

A card-prompt speaking activity

CLASSROOM DYNAMICS

Pairwork

TIME TAKEN

10 minutes

WHEN TO USE

After Grammar: Exercise 5, page 60

PREPARATION

You will need one copy of the cut-up activity cards per pair

PROCEDURE

1 Divide the students into pairs and give each pair a set of cards face down in two piles: one pile of white cards (the topics) and one pile of grey cards (the adjectives).
2 Elicit the structure of Speaking Part 3, where they will need to talk about something together for two minutes.
3 Tell students to choose a card from each pile. They will have two minutes to discuss the topics using the adjective on the card in a comparative or superlative form. Allow students ten seconds before the discussion to think of the word they need to include. Set a time of two minutes for each discussion. Allocate one student per pair to keep time for the activity. Once the first discussion has finished, students repeat the steps for the next cards, until all the cards have finished.
5 At the end of the task, get feedback from the class. What interesting comparisons did students make? Did students' opinions vary?

ADAPTATION AND EXTENSION

- This activity can be adapted for Speaking Part 2, where students speak on their own for one minute. In pairs, Student A chooses a card and must speak about that topic for one minute, while Student B keeps time. The roles are then reversed.
- For stronger students, two adjective cards can be chosen per topic to increase the difficulty of the task.

5B Pen friend

AIM

To practise using adjectives to describe appearance

To practise writing skills related to Writing Part 1

EXAM LINK

Writing: Part 1

ACTIVITY TYPE

Students invent a character and complete a gap-fill email to a pen friend

CLASSROOM DYNAMICS

Small groups

TIME TAKEN

10 minutes

WHEN TO USE

After Vocabulary: Exercise 6, page 61

PREPARATION

You will need one copy of the activity per student

PROCEDURE

1 Divide the students into small groups of four or five students and seat them in a circle, facing inwards. Distribute a copy of the activity sheet to each student.
2 Tell students they are going to invent a person and complete an email to a pen friend. Explain 'pen friend' to students if necessary. Explain that they need to complete the sentence in the first part of their activity sheet and then fold it over to keep the information they wrote a secret. When all of the students in the group have finished, tell students to pass their piece of paper to the student to their left. The next student completes the next sentence using the adjectives of appearance about height and folds the piece of paper. Once complete, the students then pass the paper to the left. The next student completes the sentence about hair. The process continues until every part of the letter has been completed.
3 Once the task is over, ask students to read their emails aloud to their group. Tell students that this is their new pen friend.

ADAPTATION AND EXTENSION

- To extend the task, or for homework, students write a reply to their pen friend, describing themselves.
- For fast finishers, this can be done as a worksheet activity where students complete the sentences with adjectives of appearance from the unit.

5C Whispers relay

AIM

To practise listening and reading skills using vocabulary from the unit

EXAM LINK

Reading: Part 4 (gapped text)

ACTIVITY TYPE

A competitive relay activity where students listen for correct sentences and place them into a reading text

CLASSROOM DYNAMICS

Large groups

TIME TAKEN

12–15 minutes

WHEN TO USE

After Reading: Exercise 4, page 58

PREPARATION

You will need one copy of the cut-up activity per group

PROCEDURE

1 Divide the students into two large groups. Tell students to stand in two lines, one behind the other, facing the board.
2 Tell students this will be a *relay race*. Explain the term if necessary. Give the student at the front of each group a board pen, and sentence 1 to the student at the back. Explain that the student at the back will have 30 seconds to read and remember the sentence. After this time, the sentence will be taken away. The back student then whispers the sentence to the student in front of them, who then whispers the sentence to the student in front of them, and so on, until it reaches the student at the front. The student at the front writes the sentence they hear on the board. Do not correct any errors at this point. Once completed, they must pass the pen to the student behind them and run to the back to become the student at the back. That student will hear the next sentence.
3 The above steps are repeated for the next three sentences. Once all of the sentences are written on the board, the group must then come together and decide where the sentences fit in the text.
4 The first team to get all of the sentences correctly written and in the correct spaces the fastest is the winner. Feedback after the task to correct any errors in the sentences.

ADAPTATION AND EXTENSION

- This activity can be done outside of a classroom, in a larger space or outdoors. If no white board is available, students can write the sentences on a piece of paper at the front of each group.
- For fast finishers, this can be done as a worksheet activity where students read the text and decide where each sentence fits.
- To increase difficulty, play music while students are relaying the sentence.

ANSWER KEY

Box 1-3 Box 2-4 Box 3-2 Box 4-1

6A Trip to the national park

AIM

To practise modal verbs for rules

ACTIVITY TYPE

Creating a set of rules for different situations and presenting them to the class

CLASSROOM DYNAMICS

Small groups of four or five students

TIME TAKEN

20 minutes

WHEN TO USE

After Grammar: Exercise 3, page 72

PREPARATION

You will need one copy of the worksheet per group

PROCEDURE

1 Tell students that they are helping adult supervisors from school to take a group of younger children on a five-day camping trip to a large national park. Discuss what a national park is and the kind of things you might find there.

2 Divide the class into small groups of four or five students and give them a copy of the worksheet. Together students create a set of camp rules under the headings provided. There are some ideas in the boxes to help them and a modal verbs box at the top to remind them of the different modals we use to create rules. You could elicit one example for each category from the whole class before starting if you think this is necessary for your class.

3 Give students around ten minutes to do this in their groups. They should have at least two or three rules per category. Monitor closely and aid where necessary.

4 When all the groups have completed their set of rules, tell them to present the rules to the class and vote on which is the best.

5 Give some content and language feedback at the end of the activity.

EXTENSION TASK

- Divide the small groups into two (i.e. an original group of four would become two pairs) and give them one of the headings from the worksheet, e.g. *General Rules* or *What you need to bring*. Ask students to make a camp rules poster.

6B Our world

AIM

To practise using descriptive language (adjectives/verbs); to practise animal vocabulary and vocabulary to describe places; to practise using *there is/are*

ACTIVITY TYPE

Writing and giving clues to describe places and animals – and guessing

CLASSROOM DYNAMICS

Pairwork and groups of four

TIME TAKEN

20 minutes

WHEN TO USE

After Writing: Exercise 9, page 77

PREPARATION

You will need one copy of the worksheet per pair

PROCEDURE

1 On the board, write these sentence stems and elicit from the students the kind of language which can be used to complete them (see below). Encourage students to remember the vocabulary covered in the coursebook. Some examples you could elicit are:

It looks/feels/seems … bright, calm, clear, loud, scary, soft, friendly, etc.

It has … fur/wings/many parks/a museum, etc.

It's so … wild/ colourful/ empty/ cute, etc.

There is/are … a large park/ famous squares, etc.

2 Divide the class into pairs and give them a worksheet. Tell them to look at Part A and together, fill in the 'Our World' boxes with the answers to one of the places/animals at the top of the worksheet.

3 Write the example, *bull,* on the board and ask students to help you write three clues using the language elicited at the beginning of the lesson to help them. E.g. *It looks scary; it's big and black; it has horns.*

4 Now ask students to look at Part B of the handout. Give students around ten minutes to write three clues per category in their pairs. They shouldn't write the clues in the corresponding numbered boxes, but rather at random. Monitor and help where necessary.

5 Once completed, ask the pairs to swap their sheets with another pair. Give the students five minutes to look at the clues and the 'Our World' answers and try to match them.

6 Put the two pairs back together and let them confirm if their guesses are correct/incorrect.

EXTENSION TASK

- Put students into groups of four and give them some blank cards (up to ten). Ask the students to write the name of an animal or a place on each card. Each group then swaps cards with another group and places their new set of cards face down on the table in front of them. Taking turns, one student picks up a card and invents clues orally. The other members of the group need to guess what it is written on the card. The winner is the student with the most cards at the end of the game.

6C Holiday park

AIM
To practise using language of suggestion, agreement and disagreement in a group discussion

EXAM LINK
Speaking: Part 2 (discussion)

ACTIVITY TYPE
Thinking of ideas and discussing which is the best

CLASSROOM DYNAMICS
Small groups of four / pairwork

TIME TAKEN
20 minutes

WHEN TO USE
After Speaking: Exercise 5, page 75

PREPARATION
You will need one copy of the worksheet per group, cut into Part A and B as indicated. Part B should be cut into cards.

PROCEDURE
1 Divide the class into groups of four and give them a copy of Part A of the worksheet. Tell students that they are in charge of planning a fun day trip to a large local park as part of a holiday camp. Give students around five minutes in their groups to think of some things they could do at the park and write them in the spaces provided. One example has been added for them.
2 Now hand out the Part B cards and ask students to divide them up equally. Tell students that they should now discuss the ideas from Part A and decide which idea/s is/are the best. They are now ready to start the activity.
3 As a group of four with their cards in their hands, the students discuss the different ideas. While discussing, they should try to use the language on the cards in the conversation as naturally as possible.
4 When they have used a card, they should place it face up on the table in front of them. Once a card is face up on the table, other students in the group can also use it and, therefore, 'steal' the card. If they do this, they should pick up the card and place it face up in front of them.
5 Let the conversation go on for around five minutes. When you say 'stop', the group member with the most cards in front of them is the winner.
6 Students present the idea they have chosen to the class before having a whole-class vote on which is the best idea.

EXTENSION TASK
- Alone, ask students to write a short email to the students on the holiday camp to explain about their fun day in the park (about 100 words).

7A Find my opinions

AIM
To practise relative clauses with *who* and *which*

ACTIVITY TYPE
An individual activity where students form sentences with relative clauses

CLASSROOM DYNAMICS
Individual

TIME TAKEN
10–12 minutes

WHEN TO USE
After Grammar: Exercise 4. page 84

PREPARATION
You will need one copy of the activity per student, cut up into Worksheet A and B

PROCEDURE
1 Distribute a copy of Worksheet A to each student.
2 Explain that students complete the activity sheet with their own ideas. For example, students write what they love, like and dislike in the food column: *I love chocolate because it makes me happy, I like marshmallows because they are nice, I dislike eggs because they smell.* Allow students four or five minutes to write their answers. Monitor to correct any errors where necessary.
3 Once completed, ask the students to stand up and face outward. No student should be facing another. Ask the students to scrunch up their piece of paper into a ball. Tell students you will count to three, and the students must throw their piece of paper as high as they can, behind them. Once all of the pieces of paper have been thrown, ask students to collect one from the floor – making sure they don't pick up their own.
4 Students open the piece of paper and write sentences on Worksheet B including *who* and *which*, about the information on their sheets. Tell students they have to guess who wrote the information, e.g.: *I think Mary is the person who loves chocolate (because it makes her happy) London is the place which she loves.* Allow five minutes for this stage. Monitor to check students sentences and use of the relative clauses.
5 Once completed, ask students to read one or two of their sentences aloud, to see if they guessed the student correctly.

ADAPTATION AND EXTENSION
- To extend the activity, add a mingle stage to the beginning. Allow students two or three minutes to find a person for each like and dislike statement for each column on Worksheet A. Students write down the information but keep the name of the student a secret. Once completed, ask students to throw the paper as above. This time, the students must decide who said what and write a sentence for each, including a relative clause.

7B How's my food?

AIM
To practise adjectives to describe food

ACTIVITY TYPE
A competitive activity where students must race to find the word that fits the description

CLASSROOM DYNAMICS
Small groups

TIME TAKEN
10 minutes

WHEN TO USE
After Vocabulary: Exercise 3, page 85

PREPARATION
One copy of Worksheet A per pair. You will need the same amount of copies of Worksheet B as there are groups.

PROCEDURE
1 Before the class begins, stick the cut-up Worksheet B cards around the classroom. You will need to copy this activity so that each group can collect each word.
2 Divide the students into small groups of three or four. Distribute Worksheet A to each group.
3 Explain that this is a competitive activity where students will need to read the description of a food experience on their worksheet and one student from each group must race to to take the adjective which they think fits the description from the wall. They will need to walk around the classroom reading each word and choose the one they think fits best. Tell students only one group member at a time can go to find a word. Once they think they have found a suitable adjective, they must bring it back for the team members to write on the worksheet. Tell students there are surplus words scattered around the room.
4 Once all the groups have collected their words, feed back the answers as a whole class and correct any errors. Give points for each correct answer and a point for the team that finished fastest.

ADAPTATION AND EXTENSION
- To extend the task, students choose three adjectives from the task and write a short paragraph about their own food experience in the past.
- For stronger groups, repeat the steps as above, without giving out Worksheet A. One student from each group collects an adjective from around the room and brings it back to the group. The group must then write a grammatically correct sentence including their chosen adjective onto the board. Points are awarded for correct sentences. The winning team is the team who produces the most correct sentences

ANSWER KEY
salty; hard; sweet; sour; burned; dry; spicy; soft
Not used: hot, cold, juicy, crispy

7C What am I?

AIM
To practise speaking skills

ACTIVITY TYPE
A competitive team game where students guess the correct object described

CLASSROOM DYNAMICS
Two large groups

TIME TAKEN
15 minutes

WHEN TO USE
After Speaking: Exercise 4, page 87

PREPARATION
You will need one copy of the activity, cut up into cards

PROCEDURE
1 Divide the class into two large groups. Give Team A the grey cut-up activity sheet and give the white sheet to Team B.
2 Explain to the teams that this is a competitive activity where students will describe the words on their cards to the other team to guess. However, they only have two chances to guess each word.
3 Give both teams four or five minutes to look through the words and to prepare a written description for them. For example, if the word is *Delicious*, students could say *It is a word used to describe when something tastes nice or good.* Monitor during the sentence preparation to correct written descriptions.
4 Once students have finished preparing, Team A reads one of their descriptions to Team B. If they guess correctly, they receive one point. Repeat this step for Team B, and so on, until all of the words have been described. Ensure a different student is speaking each time, where possible. The winning team is the group that has correctly guessed the most words.
5 Feedback to the whole class at the end of the activity, focusing on any common errors.

ADAPTATION AND EXTENSION
- This activity can be extended so the teams write two or three of their own words to describe to the other group.
- For stronger groups, descriptions can be spoken rather than written, to shorten the activity length.

8A How well do you know me?

AIM
To practise using the present perfect simple

EXAM LINK
Speaking: Part 1 (interview)

ACTIVITY TYPE
Completing sentences for a partner and discussing

CLASSROOM DYNAMICS
Pairwork

TIME TAKEN
15 minutes

WHEN TO USE
After Grammar: Exercise 6, page 96

PREPARATION
You will need one copy of the worksheet per student

PROCEDURE
1 Ask students if they think they know a lot about you and the other members of the group. Write this sentence on the board and ask students to guess the information for you. *I have taught English for/since* … Confirm if they are correct or not.
2 Divide the class into pairs and hand out a copy of the worksheet to each student.
3 Explain they are going to complete the sentences for their partner individually first, using the words in italics to help them. They should not consult their partner at this point nor talk about the sentences. Monitor closely and aid where necessary.
4 Student A starts by reading the first sentence aloud to Student B, who confirms if the answer is correct or not. Student A puts a tick or a cross next to the sentence and then asks two extra questions. *E.g. You have studied English for five years. Do you enjoy studying English?* Student B then reads their first sentence aloud and the same process is repeated. This continues until the students have discussed all the sentences.
5 At the end, tell students to count up the number of ticks (correct answers) and read the verdict at the bottom of the handout. Get some class feedback to see which pair knows each other the best.

EXTENSION TASK
- This activity could be repeated with another member of the group.

8B Transport dominoes

AIM
To practise recognising collocations related to transport

ACTIVITY TYPE
Dominoes

CLASSROOM DYNAMICS
Small groups of three students

TIME TAKEN
10 minutes

WHEN TO USE
After Vocabulary: Exercise 5, page 97

PREPARATION
You will need one copy of the worksheet per group, cut up into dominoes

PROCEDURE
1 Divide the class into groups of three students and give them a copy of the dominoes cut up into cards. Ask students to place these, face up, on the desk in front of them.
2 Tell students to find the domino that says: 'Start here'. This is the first card in the domino cycle and will also be the last. Explain that all the dominoes have half sentences which they must match. The first half of the sentence is always on the grey shaded part. They should ignore the letters; these are only for checking answers.
3 Give students around ten minutes to put the dominoes together to make a complete circle. The first group to complete this is the winner.
4 Go through the answers with the whole class and bring the students' attention to the collocations.

EXTENSION TASK
- Get students to create their own version of the domino cards by creating new sentences using the verb collocations. Students could then pass these to another group to complete.

ANSWER KEY
C E H F K A J L B I G D

8C EduCamps

AIM
To practise multiple matching

EXAM LINK
Reading: Part 2 (matching)

ACTIVITY TYPE
Expressing your wishes for an educational camp and matching these to special trips

CLASSROOM DYNAMICS
Individual, pairwork and whole class

TIME TAKEN
20 minutes

WHEN TO USE
After Reading: Exercise 7, page 94

PREPARATION
You will need one copy of Part A (*Student* and *Camp Cards)* per group (of 12 students) and a copy of the Part B (*Note Card)* per student.

PROCEDURE

1 Tell students that half the class are going to be camp organisers and the others are students looking for a special educational camp.

2 Divide the class into two groups of six students (Group A and B). Give the students in Group A a *Student Card* each, and Group B a *Camp Card*. Allow students a few minutes to read through the information and clarify any unknown vocabulary on a one-to-one basis.

3 Now hand out a copy of the *Note Card* to each student. Tell the class that all of the students must talk to all of the organisers. The students should make notes on the *Note Card* about what the organisers tell them about the camps, and the organisers should make notes about what the students tell them about their dream camp.

4 Seat the organisers around the room and ask the students to mingle and speak to all of them (one at a time). The students should explain what camp they want to visit and the organisers should try to 'sell' their camp by giving information. Both organisers and students make notes.

5 Let this continue for around ten minutes. Now ask the class to look at their notes individually in order to find their perfect match (students try to pick the best camp, and the organisers try to choose the ideal student).

6 Get feedback from the class before going through the answers with everyone.

ADAPTION AND EXTENSION

- If you have fewer than 12 students in the class, you do not have to use all of the *Student Cards*, but some of the organisers will need to have two *Camp Cards*.
- If you wanted to do the activity in smaller groups of four students (or even pairs), you could give all the *Organiser Cards* to one student or pair of students, and all the *Student Cards* to the other. They could then work together to try to match the students to the perfect camp.
- This activity can be repeated by swapping roles.

ANSWER KEY

A 5; B 1; C 6; D 2; E 4; F 3

9A Through the grid

AIM

To practise forming the zero and first conditional

ACTIVITY TYPE

A speaking activity where students form opinion sentences in the zero and first conditional

CLASSROOM DYNAMICS

Pairwork

TIME TAKEN

10–12 minutes

WHEN TO USE

After Grammar: Exercise 3, page 108

PREPARATION

One copy of the worksheet per pair, cut up into Student A/ Student B worksheets

PROCEDURE

1 Divide the class into pairs and distribute the activity sheet to Student A and Student B.

2 Tell students that the aim of the activity is to pass through the grid by forming zero and first conditional sentences. Explain that this can only be done by moving vertically or horizontally to complete the squares.

3 Student A reads aloud the words in the 'start' square, and Student B must create the sentence and add their own ending. If Student A accepts the sentence, the square is coloured in. Student B then repeats the steps for Student A. If a sentence is not accepted, tell students to put an *X* and to choose another square.The winner is the student who reaches the finish box first. Set a time of ten minutes.

4 As a whole class, check the correct form of the conditionals and, if time allows, ask for feedback on interesting answers that students added to the sentences.

ADAPTATION AND EXTENSION

- As an alternative and for larger group work, divide students into two large groups and distribute the activity sheet. Team A reads the 'start' box to Team B, and Team B must work as a group to form conditional sentences with their own endings. The steps are repeated when it is Team A's turn to create a sentence. The first group to reach the finish box is the winner.
- For fast finishers, this can be done as a written activity. Cut up each row of the worksheet into strips, with four boxes per strip. Ask students to write the sentences with their own endings in a zero or first conditional sentence.

9B Collocation collector

AIM

To practise creating sentences with words that go together

ACTIVITY TYPE

A card-matching activity where students try to match the word pairs correctly and form sentences

CLASSROOM DYNAMICS

Pairwork or groups of three

TIME TAKEN

10 minutes

WHEN TO USE

After Vocabulary: Exercise 3, page 109

PREPARATION

One copy of the cut-up activity in two separate piles – white and grey

PROCEDURE

1 Divide students into pairs or groups of three and place the two piles of cards face down for each pair or group.

2 Tell students they are going to play a game. One pile contains verbs and the other nouns. Explain that students take it in turns to choose one card from each pile, and to decide if the words fit together or not. If they do, that student should try to make a sentence including the two words. If the partner or rest of the group accepts that the sentence is correct, then the student should keep the cards. If the team think the sentence is incorrect or the words do not fit together, the cards are returned to the bottom of the pile. Shuffle at least one pile of cards to ensure the same combination doesn't appear again.

3 Monitor during the task to ensure students are forming sentences and using the language correctly. Students continue until all of the cards have been used up. At the end of the game, the student with the most cards is the winner.

ADAPTATION AND EXTENSION

- To focus more closely on the language, ask students to write the sentences so you can correct the language as you monitor.
- This can be adapted to a memory-style game, where students only choose a noun card and try to remember which verb it fits with.
- This activity can be adapted to a miming game, where students pick up a verb and noun card and must act it to their partner, who guesses what the two words may be.

POSSIBLE ANSWERS

1 **Download** – An app, music, a film, a podcast
2 **Have** – A good time, dinner
3 **Watch** – A film
4 **Do** – A quiz
5 **Play** – Music, piano
6 **Forget** – A password, an answer
7 **Search for** – An answer, music
8 **Make** – A cake, music
9 **Delete** – An answer, music, an app
10 **Listen to** – Music, a podcast
11 **Go to** – The cinema
12 **Eat** – A cake

9C Pairs and preferences

AIM

- To practise expressing opinions using the phrases from the unit
- To practise discussion skills related to Speaking Part 3

EXAM LINK

Speaking: Part 3

ACTIVITY TYPE

A mingling activity where students find the person with a similar phrase to theirs and then decide with their partner which is better and explain why.

CLASSROOM DYNAMICS

Individual for the mingling activity and pair work for the discussion

TIME TAKEN

10 minutes

WHEN TO USE

After Speaking: Exercise 6, page 111

PREPARATION

You will need one or two copies of the activity, depending on the size of the class, cut up into cards

PROCEDURE

1 Hand out a card from Worksheet A to each student but tell them to keep the phrase on the card a secret

2 Explain to students that they walk around to find the person in the room with a similar phrase to theirs and they should partner up with the first person they find with a similar phrase. Example phrases: *reading a newspaper*, so another student may have *reading the news online* – or, *swimming at the beach* and *swimming in a pool*.

3 Once students have found their partner, they have two minutes to discuss and agree on the phrase they prefer and be able to say why. Monitor the activity to ensure it is correctly time limited, and that the students are using phrases and vocabulary to help them with Speaking Part 3.

4 Once the pairs have finished, hand out a card from Worksheet B to each student. Students should find another partner who has a similar phrase to them, as in the steps above. Students have two minutes to discuss and agree on the phrase they prefer and be able to give a reason. Set a time limit.

5 After completion, go through some examples together and see what the students preferred and why, correcting any errors where necessary.

ADAPTATION AND EXTENSION

- For a quieter activity, students can be put into pairs and can be given both word cards to discuss.
- To practise Speaking Part 2, this can be done as a long turn task where students are given the word cards and speak for one minute each about their given topics.